MW01116488

COMMAND THE MORNING 365: DAILY PRAYER DEVOTIONAL VOLUME 1 (HOPE EDITION)

by John Miller

Copyright © 2018 John Miller

Published by One Life Books

Printed in the United States of America

COMMAND THE MORNING 365 (HOPE EDITION)

DAILY PRAYER DEVOTIONAL COVERING ALL 365 DAYS OF THE YEAR

VOLUME 1: DAY 1 — 90

John Miller

Published by One Life Books
Copyright © 2018 John Miller

VISIT JOHN'S WEBSITE AT:
www.johnmillerbooks.com

LIKE JOHN'S FACEBOOK PAGE AT:
facebook.com/johnmillerauthor

This Daily Prayer Devotional is dedicated to you if you want to learn about and apply deep truths from the word of God so that you can make impact in your generation and bring glory to the name of the Lord.

MILLER'S BOOK CATALOG

Before moving on to the content of this book, please take a moment to browse through our current book catalog. All our books are available for sale on Amazon.com. Please also visit this page to find an up-to-date list of our books:
https://www.amazon.com/John-Miller/e/B00NMDON9G

CATEGORY: NIGHTLY PRAYER BOOKS

— Nights of Bliss 365 Nightly Prayer Devotional Volume 1 — Night 1 to 90
— Command the Night: Daily Prayer Manual

CATEGORY: DAILY PRAYER BOOKS

——HOPE EDITION OF COMMAND THE MORNING 365

— Command the Morning 365: Daily Prayer Devotional (Hope Edition) —
Volume 1 — Day 1 to 90 [Dateless, topic-based edition]

——GRACE EDITION OF COMMAND THE MORNING 365 (FULL DEVOTIONALS COVERING ALL 365 DAYS OF THE YEAR)

— Command the Morning 365: Daily Prayer Devotional (Grace Edition) —
Volume 1 — January / February / March
— Command the Morning 365: Daily Prayer Devotional (Grace Edition) —
Volume 2 — 2nd Quarter — April / May / June
— Command the Morning 365: Daily Prayer Devotional (Grace Edition) —
Volume 3 — 3rd Quarter — July / August / September
— Command the Morning 365: Daily Prayer Devotional (Grace Edition) —
Volume 4 — 4th Quarter — October / November / December

——SUB-CATEGORY: DAILY PRAYER MANUALS (MANUALS FOR QUICK & POWERFUL DAILY PRAYERS)

— Command the Morning: Daily Prayer Manual for Business owners
— Command the Morning: Daily Prayer Manual for Working People
— Command the Morning: Daily Prayer Manual for Wives & Mothers
— Command the Morning: Daily Prayer Manual for Husbands & Fathers
— Command the Morning: Daily Prayer Manual for Single Women
— Command the Morning: Daily Prayer Manual for Single Men
— Command the Morning: Daily Prayer Manual for Students

— Command the Morning: Daily Prayer Manual for the Family

CATEGORY: SALVATION BOOKS

— The Last Week of Jesus Christ
— Jesus Christ the Healer
— Jesus Christ the Deliverer
— Jesus Christ the Miracle Worker
— Jesus Christ the Storyteller

CATEGORY: PURE FASTING AND PRAYER BOOKS

— 70 DAYS FASTING AND PRAYER PROGRAM (VOLUME 1)
— 70 DAYS FASTING AND PRAYER PROGRAM (VOLUME 2)

CATEGORY: CAREER / BUSINESS / LIFE / BREAKTHROUGH

——*OPEN HEAVENS*

— Open Heavens Prayers for Gainful Employment
— Open Heavens Prayers for Fertility & Pregnancy

——*PRAYER RAIN SERIES*

— Powerful Prayers For Business Breakthrough
— Breakthrough Prayers For Startups & Entrepreneurs
— Breakthrough Prayers For Family-Sponsored Immigration
— Breakthrough Prayers For Employment-Based Permanent Residency
— Breakthrough Prayers For Investment-Based Immigration

——*BREAKTHROUGH BOOKS*

— Pray Your Way Into Breakthroughs - Turnaround Edition - Powerful Prayers That Bring A Turnaround & Unleash Breakthroughs Into Your Life

CATEGORY: DELIVERANCE BOOKS

— Prayers that Remove the Consequences of Ancestral Evils & Sins from Your Life

— Prayers that Nullify the Consequences of Negative Words & Deeds on Your Birth

— Prayers that Prevent the Replication of Ancestral Problems

— Prayers that Reverse Already-Replicated Ancestral Problems

— Prayers that Transfer Ancestral Blessings Into Your Life

— Prayers that Materialize the Benefits of Ancestral Actions In Your Life

— Prayers that Nullify Negative Genetic Traits from Your Life

— Prayers that Materialize Positive Ancestral Traits in Your Life

— Birthday Deliverance Series Box Set (Book 1 - 8): Deliverance that Removes Your Inherited Problems & Provokes the Release Of Your Ancestral Blessings

CATEGORY: ANNUAL PRAYER BOOKS

— Pray Your Way Into Breakthroughs

— Pray Your Way Into Breakthroughs for Wives & Mothers

— Pray Your Way Into Breakthroughs for Husbands & Fathers

— Pray Your Way Into Breakthroughs for Single Women

— Pray Your Way Into Breakthroughs for Single Men

— Pray Your Way Into Breakthroughs for Business Owners

— Pray Your Way Into Breakthroughs for Working People

— Pray Your Way Into Breakthroughs for Students

CATEGORY: PRAYER BOOKS ON DREAMS

——LITERAL DREAMS SERIES

— Prayers To Prevent The Manifestation Of Dreams Of Death

— Prayers To Prevent The Manifestation Of Dreams Of Rape

— Prayers To Prevent The Manifestation Of Dreams Of Sicknesses & Diseases

— Prayers To Prevent The Manifestation Of Dreams Of Separation & Divorce

CONTENTS

INTRODUCTION

God has loaded His word with incredible wisdom meant for the salvation, protection and prosperity of His children. Volume 1 of Command the Morning 365: Daily Prayer Devotional (Hope Edition) is the first of four devotional volumes designed to prayerfully guide you through God's word throughout the year. If you want to live a life that pleases God and at the same time gain access to divine information that can help you be all you should be, this is the book that you need. You will get the remarkable opportunity of learning about uncommon truths from the word of God. This book also provides you with guidance on how to apply these truths in your life as well as powerful prayers that will cause the benefits of these truths to manifest themselves in your life.

This Hope edition of CTM 365 is topic-based and dateless. This means that instead of relying on calendar dates, the devotional has a list of days as well as topics attached to each day. This allows you to either read the devotional from day to day or by topic. Unlike the calendar-based system, you can pick up this volume [and the three other volumes] at anytime and complete the 90 days of devotionals without worrying about lapsed dates.

CTM 365 DPD is a true daily prayer devotional. It is called 365 because it includes teachings, scriptures and powerful prayers for all 365 days of the year. All the teachings and scriptures are highly inspiring and will fire you up and keep you that way each day of the year. The devotionals are applicable to your daily life and so provide lessons that you can put into action immediately, enabling you to live in accordance with God's will. Each day also includes powerful prayers that have been inspired by the teachings. These prayers have only one purpose—to bring the scriptures to life in your own life. They are completely result-oriented and intended to ensure that the promises of God's word thoroughly manifest in your life everyday of the year.

Your time, especially in the mornings, has been put into consideration. Therefore, the devotionals have been designed to be brief BUT power-packed. As you go through each day of this devotional, you will see that your relationship with God will become closer, tighter and more functional. This book will also help you secure divine guidance and protection so that you can go out and come in everyday with the total awareness and confidence that God is with you. It contains teachings that explore multiple dimensions of God's word which will bring you wisdom, discretion, deliverance, peace of mind, multiple promotions, financial breakthrough, prosperity and other benefits essential for your time on the earth. This book will also give you an assurance—through God's Spirit—of an eternity with the Almighty and His saints. Get this powerful devotional and have yourself a wonderful year!

God bless you.

Your brother-in-Christ,
John

CONNECTING WITH THE ANSWERER OF PRAYERS

"If you declare with your mouth, 'Jesus is Lord,' and believe in your heart that God raised Him from the dead, you will be saved. For it is with your heart that you believe and are justified, and it is with your mouth that you profess your faith and are saved." — Romans 10:9-10 (NIV)

The first step in getting your prayers answered is connecting with the person who will answer them. In Christianity, this "connecting" is referred to as "giving your life to Jesus". It involves the complete surrender of your thoughts, your deeds, spirit, soul and body to Jesus for Him to govern. In return, you get all the benefits of God's kingdom — He will take up responsibility for your daily life, your protection and the protection of your possessions. He will fill your mind with wisdom and understanding, become responsible for your health and if you desire it, make you prosper. Most importantly per this book, He will give you a listening ear and answer your prayers. This section gives you the opportunity to give your life to Jesus Christ so you can start enjoying all the associated benefits.

PRAYERS

If you are ready to accept Jesus as your Lord and Savior, read these words both in your heart first and then out loud with your mouth:

1. Lord Jesus, I believe that You are the Son of God, who created the universe.

2. I believe in my heart that God gave You up and sent You to this earth to die for my sins.

3. I believe that after you died, God the Father raised You from the grave and brought You back to life.

4. I declare that You are the Lord! And so today, I hand my life over to You for You to become the Lord of it.

5. All my thoughts, words and deeds, I lay plainly before You to be totally responsible for.

6. You have said in Your word that if I open the door of my life to You, You will come in. Therefore, I open my heart to You today.

7. I invite you in to come and become the Lord of my life.

8. Come Lord Jesus and take total control of my life.

9. Come Jesus and become my personal Lord and Savior.

10. Thank You for accepting me and giving me the assurance of eternal life.

With these words spoken in your heart and confessed with your mouth, you have given your life to Jesus Christ. You are now what is known as a born-again christian with full rights to the benefits of the kingdom of God including getting your prayers answered.

"Let the morning bring me word of Your unfailing love, for I have put my trust in You. Show me the way I should go, for to You I entrust my life."(Psalm 143:8 NIV)

"In the morning, LORD, you hear my voice; in the morning I lay my requests before you and wait expectantly."
(Psalm 5:3 NIV)

DAILY PRAYER DEVOTIONALS THAT BRING RESULTS

THANK YOU FOR GETTING THIS BOOK. BY GOD'S GRACE, MORE BOOKS ARE ON THE WAY THAT WILL LIKELY COVER MORE AREAS OR THEMES OR TOPICS OF INTEREST TO YOU. THE BEST WAY TO KNOW WHICH BOOKS ARE BEING RELEASED IS BY GETTING AN ALERT OR A NOTIFICATION FROM US. IF YOU WANT TO GET ACCESS TO THE LATEST UPDATES ON NEW BOOKS AS WELL AS OTHER ESSENTIAL INFORMATION FROM BROTHER MILLER, PLEASE JOIN OUR READERS' MAILING LIST (FOR EMAIL UPDATES), LIKE OUR FACEBOOK PAGE (FOR FACEBOOK UPDATES) AND FOLLOW US ON TWITTER. GOD BLESS YOU.

VISIT THE PAGE BELOW TO JOIN NOW

http://johnmillerbooks.com/signup/

LIKE JOHN'S FACEBOOK PAGE AT:

facebook.com/johnmillerauthor

FOLLOW JOHN ON TWITTER AT:

twitter.com/johnmillerbooks

RECOMMENDED PRE-READING. WE RECOMMEND THAT YOU USE <u>ANY VERSION</u> OF OUR COMMAND THE MORNING DAILY PRAYER MANUAL BEFORE USING CTM 365.

HERE ARE THE VERSIONS OF COMMAND THE MORNING DAILY PRAYER MANUAL AVAILABLE

COMMAND THE MORNING DAILY PRAYER MANUAL **(GENERAL EDITION)**

COMMAND THE MORNING DAILY PRAYER MANUAL **FOR WORKING PEOPLE**

COMMAND THE MORNING DAILY PRAYER MANUAL **FOR BUSINESS OWNERS**

COMMAND THE MORNING DAILY PRAYER MANUAL **FOR STUDENTS**

COMMAND THE MORNING DAILY PRAYER MANUAL

FOR SINGLE MEN

COMMAND THE MORNING DAILY PRAYER MANUAL
FOR SINGLE WOMEN

COMMAND THE MORNING DAILY PRAYER MANUAL
FOR HUSBANDS AND FATHERS

COMMAND THE MORNING DAILY PRAYER MANUAL
FOR WIVES AND MOTHERS

COMMAND THE MORNING DAILY PRAYER MANUAL
FOR THE FAMILY

DAY 1 TO 30

DAY 1

HOW TO HANDLE YOUR NEW BEGINNINGS

"And now, O Lord my God, thou hast made thy servant king instead of David my father: and I am but a little child: I know not how to go out or come in... Give therefore thy servant an understanding heart to judge thy people, that I may discern between good and bad: for who is able to judge this thy so great a people? And the speech pleased the Lord, that Solomon had asked this thing."
— 1 Kings 3:7,9-10 (KJV)

DAILY EXHORTATION

Every new period such as the beginning of a new year [or week or month], the days following the celebration of a birthday, the day after your wedding, the day after any kind of anniversary, the day you begin a new job or take up a new workplace position, etc. can be likened to ascension to a new throne. Despite your experiences in life, you have never been in these particular places or times or seasons or situations before. For instance, you have never been in today before today. Therefore, today is new for you. To that extent, it will do you a world of good to ask for help so that you can prosper in your new place, position, role, season or situation.

But, from whom should you ask this help? Who is the person who knows how you will fare in the situation you are currently in and can show you the way?

Our opening scripture provides the answer. To get help, you have to do as Solomon did. First, you should acknowledge that it was God that brought you to this new situation or period in which you find yourself. Next, humble yourself before God and admit that you do not know what the future holds. Let God know that you take Him as the Omnipresent, Omniscient and Omnipotent God. That is, let God know that you consider Him to be the only one who is everywhere, the only one who knows all things and the only one who has all power to do all things.

After this, just as Solomon did, ask Him directly to give you a heart of wisdom and of understanding so that you can receive divine insight with which to do and surpass all that is expected of you in the place, time, season, situation or period in which you have found yourself. If you do this, as it was for Solomon, the Almighty will be pleased with you. What does God being pleased with you translate to in reality? Let's find out very quickly from scripture:

1 Kings 3:10-12 (NET) "*The Lord was pleased that Solomon made this request. God said to him, 'Because you asked for the ability to make wise judicial decisions, and not for long life, or riches, or vengeance on your enemies, I grant your request, and give you a wise and discerning mind superior to that of anyone who has preceded or will succeed you.'*"

1 Kings 3:13 (NET) "*Furthermore, I am giving you what you did not request—riches and honor so that you will be the greatest king of your generation.*"

1 Kings 3:14 (NET) "*If you follow my instructions by obeying my rules and regulations, just as your father David did, then I will grant you long life.*"

As you can see, if because of your humility and your good sense to ask God for wisdom and understanding, He becomes pleased with you, He will grant you your request. As a result, you will always bask in the atmosphere of divine insight which will make you a person of unassailable excellence. Not only that; God will go beyond what you have asked of Him and give you other things which He knows you will need for success in your role, time, season, situation or circumstance.

Further, by reason of your humble request, the optional human benefit of long life will become enabled in your life and you will get it as long as you obey the word of God all the days of your life. Do you want these benefits in your life? Are you willing to humble yourself and ask God for wisdom and understanding? If yes, get yourself ready!

TODAY'S PRAYERS

1. Mighty God, I am at the beginning of _____ (period, situation, role in which you find yourself). I acknowledge and confess that I need your help. Come to my aid, in the name of Jesus.

2. Righteous Father, I am only a little child and I have no experience in this phase of my life. Therefore, I come before You today and I ask You to give me a heart of wisdom and of understanding so that I can have access to the

divine insight that will help me excel in this phase of my life, in the name of Jesus.

3. My God, let this wisdom and understanding be unleashed in my life so that I can dwell permanently in an atmosphere of discernment. In this atmosphere, let me make correct decisions, deal wisely with people, deliver powerful results and properly execute anything that is committed into my hands, in the name of Jesus.

4. Lord, by reason of Your gift of wisdom, understanding and discernment, let me become a success as a _____ (area of life where you need it e.g. as a husband, wife, parent, student, professional, christian leader, political leader, etc.), in the name of Jesus. [Repeat prayer for every area of your life that you want God's wisdom to work for you]

5. Now Lord, as it was for Solomon, let it be that by reason of my humility and my request to You, the windows of heaven will be opened unto me and all other things which You know that I need to live a fulfilled life, will be poured into my life in abundance, in the name of Jesus.

6. O Lord, holy and true, I am ready to live in absolute obedience to Your word. Therefore,

let long life be my lot on this earth. And do not let me just live long, let me also live a life that is useful to You and to my fellow human beings to Your glory, in the name of Jesus.

7. Thank You O God for answering my prayers, in Jesus' mighty name, amen.

If you have the need and the time, please feel free to add more prayers at this point.

Blessing: As you humble yourself to make the right request to the Almighty, not only will He answer you, He will also surprise you above and beyond your expectations, in the name of Jesus.

DAY 2

DIVINE RESCUE FROM OBSCURITY

"And the king said, Is there not yet any of the house of Saul, that I may shew the kindness of God unto him? And Ziba said unto the king, Jonathan hath yet a son, which is lame on his feet. And the king said unto him, Where is he? And Ziba said unto the king, Behold, he is in the house of Machir, the son of Ammiel, in Lodebar."
— 2 Samuel 9:3-4 (KJV)

DAILY EXHORTATION

Before his best friend—Jonathan—died, David promised him that he would show kindness to his family when he became established. Therefore, when he became king of Israel, David began looking for members of Saul's / Jonathan's family but he couldn't find any of them. Why? Because the only surviving descendant of Jonathan was not in Jerusalem, the capital, but in a place called Lodebar. This Lodebar, quite clearly, can be considered a place of obscurity. It represents any situation that hides you from prosperity or breakthrough. It is a place (physical or circumstantial) that hides you from your helpers, who may be actively looking for you. It is a place of ignorance about one's divine blessings. It is a place you are domiciled at while benefits you are eligible for go to waste or go to someone else.

But what are the kinds of benefits or blessings you will miss out on if you decide to remain in or cannot get out of Lodebar? Let's take a quick look at scriptures:

2 Samuel 9:7 (KJV)**, 9-11** (NET) *"And David said unto him, Fear not: for **I will surely shew thee kindness** for Jonathan thy father's sake, **and will restore thee all the land of Saul thy father; and thou shalt eat bread at my table continually**... Then the king summoned Ziba, Saul's attendant, and said to him, '**Everything that belonged to Saul and to his entire house I hereby give to your master's grandson**. You will cultivate **the land** for him—you and your sons and your servants. You will bring **its produce and it will be food** for your master's grandson to eat. But Mephibosheth, your master's grandson, will be **a regular guest at my table**.' (Now Ziba had fifteen sons and twenty servants.) Ziba said to the king, 'Your* *servant will do everything that my lord the king has instructed his servant to do.' So Mephibosheth was a regular guest at David's table, just as though he were one of the king's sons."*

If you remain in Lodebar, you will not have access to unprecedented kindness from high places. Remaining in Lodebar means lack of access to generational benefits and blessings. It means no possibility of divine restoration for whatever you have lost. It means remaining in the "house of Machir" as an object of pity. It means an inability to access business success as well as assets such as land, workers, etc. It means lack of access to the high and mighty of society or royalty all the days of your life.

Clearly, this is an undesirable place or situation to be in. On the other hand, if you relocate to Jerusalem, God will inspire the high and mighty to show you kindness. In Jerusalem, generational blessings will come to you, you will enjoy divine restoration, you will no longer be an object of sympathy or pity, you will experience business success and your coffers will be filled with assets including of things and of people and you will rub shoulders with the high and mighty of the land. Hopefully, you should be thinking to yourself *"How do I come out of Lodebar if I am already there? And how do I move to Jerusalem in order to access my blessings*"

In 2 Samuel 9:5 (KJV), the Bible says "***Then king David sent, and fetched him [Mephibosheth] out of the house of Machir, the son of Ammiel, from Lodebar.***"

First, you need to call upon the Lord to inspire your helpers to remember you just as David remembered his promise to Jonathan. Next, you need to ask God to inspire men and women to speak in your favor whenever the issue of your blessings are being deliberated on, just as Ziba spoke out for Mephibosheth.

Next, just as it was for Mephibosheth, you need to ask God for your helpers to summon you or send for you and to bring you out of the house of Machir in your Lodebar to your Jerusalem, so that you can come in direct contact with your helpers.

Finally, you need to ask the Lord to inspire your helpers to release benefits to you that will change the current trajectory of your life from whatever it is now to God's best for you. Are you ready to leave the house of Machir? Are you ready to leave Lodebar behind and enter into your Jerusalem? Are you ready for life-changing blessings? If yes, get yourself ready!

TODAY'S PRAYERS

1. My Father, I am tired of staying in obscurity in the house of Machir at Lodebar. I call upon you this morning: By Your mighty and powerful hand, come and deliver me from Lodebar now, in the name of Jesus.

2. Adonai, just as David remembered the house of Saul, inspire men and women to remember me and to begin to look for me in order to become instruments of blessings for my destiny, in the name of Jesus.

3. El Shaddai, just as Ziba spoke up for Mephibosheth, anywhere and anytime the matter of my blessings is being discussed by people, let men and women speak up in my favor so that I can become a living target of Your blessings, in the name of Jesus.

4. Abba Father, make my helpers send for me so that I can depart from the house of Machir at Lodebar and relocate permanently to the Jerusalem of my destiny, in the name of Jesus.

5. Jehovah, in Jerusalem, let the benefits and the blessings that have been set aside for me be released into my hands, in the name of Jesus.

6. O Lord, through these benefits and blessings,

let me know what it means to find favor in Your sight and enjoy Your best for my life. Let me enjoy generational and ancestral blessings. Let me experience divine restoration so that everything that I have lost can return to me multiple-fold. Let me find career and business success and let my tangible and intangible assets multiply all to Your glory, in the name of Jesus.

7. Thank You Mighty God for answering my prayers this morning, in Jesus' mighty name, amen.

If you have the need and the time, please feel free to add more prayers at this point.

Blessing: May you be summoned out of Lodebar and into the Jerusalem of destiny so that you can access the blessings that have been apportioned to you, in the name of Jesus.

DAY 3

HOW TO DO THE GREATEST THING

"If I speak in the tongues of men and of angels, but I do not have love, I am a noisy gong or a clanging cymbal. And if I have prophecy, and know all mysteries and all knowledge, and if I have all faith so that I can remove mountains, but do not have love, I am nothing. If I give away everything I own, and if I give over my body in order to boast, but do not have love, I receive no benefit."
— 1 Corinthians 13:1-3 (NET)

DAILY EXHORTATION

Our opening scripture says that even if you have all the knowledge, gifts and all the power in the world to do anything you wish BUT you have no love in your life, you are a noisy gong, a clanging cymbal and you are nothing! It even says that if you die for other people for any reason other than genuine love in your heart, you will not be blessed and you will have no benefit whatsoever. In Mark 12:31 (NET), the Bible says "*'... Love your neighbor as yourself.' There is no other commandment greater than these.*" God takes the issue of love very seriously and this is why He made it a commandment. If you do not want to be a clanging cymbal, a noisy gong or nothing before the Lord, you must find a way to fulfill this divine commandment of love to the letter. But how do you do this? What exactly does love entail? Is there some sort of guide from the word of God that reveals what exactly one needs to do in order to comply with this commandment? Yes, there is. Let's take a look at God's guide to love from scriptures:

1 Corinthians 13:4-7 (NET) "*Love is patient, love is kind, it is not envious. Love does not brag, it is not puffed up. It is not rude, it is not self-serving, it is not easily angered or resentful. It is not glad about injustice, but rejoices in the truth. It bears all things, believes all things, hopes all things, endures all things.*"

Loving, God's way is very different from the love of the world or of unbelievers. To love God's way, you must learn to become patient with other people. To love means to always show others kindness and consideration. It means to eschew envy and to become genuinely happy for others when good things happen to them. It means losing the ability to boast about your natural endowments, gifts, talents, skills or achievements. It means having the ability to remain your humble self regardless of what you achieve in life.

Love means being polite to everyone regardless of their class or status in life. It means gaining the ability to control yourself and not easily give in to provocation. It means casting out the evil trait of hatred and bitterness from your life entirely. Love means always standing for truth, fairness and justice and being resolutely against injustice. It means becoming a person of perseverance and one who hopes for good in the lives of others.

If you can become someone who embodies all of these qualities, it means you have become a man or woman of love and therefore a person who loves his or her neighbor. This means that you will become 'somebody' as well as a person of substance and worth before God Almighty. All people of worth in the eyes of the Lord benefit from His matchless benefits and blessings.

So, considering all the above, are your ready to love? Do you want to fulfill God's great commandment? Are you ready to become someone who calls on the Lord and grabs His attention by virtue of your worth or value before Him? If the answer to all these is yes, get yourself ready!

TODAY'S PRAYERS

1. Rock of Ages, I want to fulfill the commandment of love. Be merciful unto me. Give ear to my prayers this morning and answer them, in the name of Jesus.

2. Elohim, I do not want to be a noisy gong, a clanging cymbal or a worthless person before You. I also do not want my deeds for others to go to waste. Therefore, I ask: Come to my aid this morning, in the name of Jesus.

3. Father, this morning I have been reminded that love is the greatest trait that you desire from all human beings. Therefore, I ask: Make me a person of love. Give me the divine enablement and force of character to love my neighbors as myself, in the name of Jesus.

4. Holy Spirit of God, my life is available to You. From this morning, cause me to become patient, kind, to rejoice in the truth, to bear all things, to believe all things, to hope all things and to endure all things, in the name of Jesus.

5. My Lord and my God, come into my life this morning to do Your great work. Lay hold of

any spirit of envy, bragging, being puffed up, rudeness, self-serving behavior, anger, resentment and injustice that may be in my life. Cast out and banish all these foul spirits and negative traits from my life now and forever, in the name of Jesus.

6. By reason of the love that is now in my heart and in my life, Father, let me be able to stand before You as a person of worth and of value. Therefore, whenever I call upon You, hear me and let me receive Your tangible and intangible divine benefits and blessings, in the name of Jesus.

7. Thank You Father God for answering my prayers, in Jesus' mighty name, amen.

If you have the need and the time, please feel free to add more prayers at this point.

Blessing: As you become a person of love, may all the blessings of love find their way into your life, in the name of Jesus.

DAY 4

THE WORTH OF 10,000 MIGHTY MEN

"...The king told his troops, 'I am going out with you.' But his men objected strongly. 'You must not go,' they urged. 'If we have to turn and run—and even if half of us die—it will make no difference to Absalom's troops; they will be looking only for you. You are worth 10,000 of us, and it is better that you stay here in the town and send help if we need it.'"
— 2 Samuel 18:2b-3 (NLT)

DAILY EXHORTATION

Even though Absalom had usurped his father's (David's) throne and driven him into exile, he still was not satisfied. Absalom wanted David dead. Therefore, he decided to locate him in exile and move against him with the army of Israel. Son or no son, David and the men he escaped with also got ready to defend themselves against the assault of Absalom. Despite David's advanced age, he was still a fighting machine and wanted to go with his troops to face the army of Israel. Our opening scripture says that his men objected saying "**You are worth 10,000 of us**". Powerful words! And these words carry even more weight when you look at the nature of the men who uttered them:

2 Samuel 17:7-8 (NKJV) "*So Hushai said to Absalom: 'The advice that Ahithophel has given is not good at this time. For,' said Hushai, '**you know your father and his men, that they are mighty men, and they are enraged in their minds, like a bear robbed of her cubs in the field**...'*"

The Bible says that the men who made this declaration concerning David were "mighty" and they were fierce. This means that they were the best of the best fighters Israel had to offer and yet these men declared that David alone was worth 10,000 of them! Can you imagine that? As a believer, you can tap into this kind of anointing that was on the life of David. That is, the anointing of exceptionalism, high value and heavy worth. Even though this declaration was made concerning David in the context of warfare, for you, it can be in any context.

God can make you worth more than 10,000

men or women in your workplace and therefore make you their head. In your business, God can make you worth more than 10,000 men and make you the undisputed industry leader. If you are a student, perhaps in competition with thousands of others for some sort of prize or scholarship, God can make you worth 10,000 other students in the eyes of the awarders and in so doing cause you to win the prize or scholarship. If you find yourself in any kind of setting where other people are involved, for whatever purpose, God can make you worth more than 10,000 of them and therefore first amongst equals.

But, what is it that makes a person so valuable that he or she would be worth 10,000 mighty men in the eyes of other people. Let's take a quick look at scriptures:

1 Samuel 16:12-13 (KJV) "...*And the Lord said, Arise,* **anoint him***: for this is he.* **Then Samuel took the horn of oil, and anointed him in the midst of his brethren: and the Spirit of the Lord came upon David from that day forward...**"

What made David exceptional and highly valuable was the anointing of God and the Spirit of God that it unleashed into his life. With the help of this Spirit, David was able to kill Goliath and do many other great exploits. By reason of these, his influence and worth before the people of Israel skyrocketed. This is the only reason why those mighty men considered him to be worth 10,000 of them. In the same vein, if you want to be exceptional and highly valuable in the midst of a crowd, you too will need the anointing of the Almighty and His Holy Spirit. If you desire this in your life, get yourself ready!

TODAY'S PRAYERS

1.   El Shaddai, I want to live an exceptional life that will bring glory to Your holy name. Help me today, in the name of Jesus.

2.   My Father and my God, my life is available for You this morning. As it was for David, let the oil of anointing that can make one exceptional fall upon my life now, in the name of Jesus.

3.   Holy Spirit of God, by reason of the anointing, invade my life this morning and fill me to the brim with divine power, in the name of Jesus.

4.   O Lord, just as it was for David, by reason of the presence of Your divine power in my life,

let me do great exploits that will bring glory and honor to You, in the name of Jesus.

5. My God, use the exploits that I will do as a basis for my worth and value in the eyes of people to surge high, to Your glory, in the name of Jesus.

6. Messiah, just as it was for David, let me become equal to or worth more than 10,000 mighty men put together even in my generation. And just as this designation preserved the life of David, let me also enjoy the benefits of this designation all the days of my life, in the name of Jesus.

7. Thank You Almighty God for answering my prayers, in Jesus' mighty name, amen.

If you have the need and the time, please feel free to add more prayers at this point.

Blessing: May the anointing of God upon your life bring honor to your life for good, in the name of Jesus.

DAY 5

HOW TO BECOME A LAMP AND A BEACON

"But Abishai son of Zeruiah came to David's rescue; he struck the Philistine down and killed him. Then David's men swore to him, saying, 'Never again will you go out with us to battle, so that the lamp of Israel will not be extinguished.'"
— 2 Samuel 21:17 (NIV)

DAILY EXHORTATION

One day the Israelites went to war against the Philistines. David, at this point, had achieved a lot and had gotten much older. As the fight raged on, perhaps by reason of his age, David became exhausted. Yet, there was a Philistine on the battlefield who had vowed to kill him. As this man approached David, an Israeli soldier named Abishai came to David's aid and struck down the Philistine. It is at this point that we arrive at our opening scripture.

Just as we saw yesterday, David's men again took a decision to preserve his life and told him not to go out to battle with them any longer. The reason we saw yesterday was because David alone was worth the lives of 10,000 men. This time, the reason given was because David was the **"Lamp of Israel"** and therefore, they could not afford to see him extinguished. Other versions of the Bible refer to David as the "light of Israel", "beacon of Israel" and "hope of Israel". Powerful words to describe a man!

But what is a lamp? A lamp is a device or tool that produces light and in some cases, heat. This means that the Israelites considered David as a light leading their national path and guiding them toward their national destiny. They also saw him as a source of warmth against the harsh cold of their enemies. Lamps usually require a source of energy such as some kind of oil, battery, solar or electrical energy. Without this source of energy, a lamp would not work.

So, what was the source of David's energy? Well, it's the same as we saw yesterday:

1 Samuel 16:12-13 (KJV) "...*And the Lord said, Arise, anoint him: for this is he.* ***Then Samuel took the horn of oil, and anointed him in the midst of his brethren: and the Spirit of***

the Lord came upon David from that day forward..."

What made it possible for David to be a lamp unto his people was the anointing of God upon his life and the Spirit of God that was released for his sake by reason of the anointing. Do you know that you can also become a lamp unto your people and in fact, the world?

Matthew 5:14-16 (NET) "*You are the light of the world. A city located on a hill cannot be hidden. People do not light a lamp and put it under a basket but on a lampstand, and it gives light to all in the house. In the same way, let your light shine before people, so that they can see your good deeds and give honor to your Father in heaven.*"

Through the anointing of God upon your life and the presence of His Holy Spirit in your life, just like David, you too can become a guide, leading others unto God and showing them the right way to go in different areas of their lives. With divine empowerment, you can also receive the wherewithal to provide warmth [financial, emotional, spiritual, etc.] to people around you who have been afflicted by the harsh cold of life. Is this something that you desire? Do you also want to become a lamp like David was? If yes, get yourself ready!

TODAY'S PRAYERS

1. Yahweh, let the anointing that can make me fulfill my destiny in my own generation fall upon me this morning, in the name of Jesus.

2. Messiah, by reason of the anointing, release Your Holy Spirit into my life so that I can receive divine power to do great deeds to Your glory, in the name of Jesus.

3. My Lord and my God, I ask: As it was for David, make me a lamp in my own generation, in the name of Jesus.

4. Father, by reason of the anointing, let me become a light to my people and to the world. Through my words and deeds, let me guide people to You and provide them effective counsel in any area of life that they need it, in the name of Jesus.

5. Lord, by reason of the anointing, let me become a source of warmth to people. Give me the supernatural wherewithal to provide people with warmth from their spiritual, financial, emotional or any other kind of winter that they might be going through, in the name of Jesus.

6. Now Lord I ask: As it was for David, do not

let my lamp be extinguished by my enemies and do not let me die before my time, in the name of Jesus.

7. Thank You everlasting Father for answering my prayers, in Jesus' mighty name, amen.

If you have the need and the time, please feel free to add more prayers at this point.

Blessing: May God make you a lamp providing light and warmth to all who need it to His glory, in the name of Jesus.

DAY 6

SPIRITUAL TEMPERATURE

"To the angel of the church in Laodicea write the following: 'This is the solemn pronouncement of the Amen, the faithful and true witness, the originator of God's creation: 'I know your deeds, that you are neither cold nor hot. I wish you were either cold or hot! So because you are lukewarm, and neither hot nor cold, I am going to vomit you out of my mouth!'"
— Revelation 3:14-16 (NET)

DAILY EXHORTATION

The word "lukewarm" is an interesting word. For instance, one antonym of lukewarm is "cold". But another antonym of lukewarm is "hot". It has two antonyms on two opposing extremes. Nobody likes drinking lukewarm water (at least by choice) because it doesn't provide the desired satisfaction. Depending on the situation, most people would rather drink something hot or something cold and be satisfied. When it comes to our spiritual lives, heaven also prefers that we are either hot or cold and not lukewarm.

A lukewarm person is neither here nor there. Our opening scripture reveals a number of things which are important for you to be aware of as a believer.

First, it is by your deeds that the Lord determines whether or not you are hot, cold or lukewarm with regard to your spiritual life. Also, whenever God finds out that a person is spiritually lukewarm, He will sooner or later spit out or vomit that person from His mouth. What does this mean? It means God will reject such a person. From that person, He will withdraw His divine protection, divine peace, divine favor and all other benefits of being His child. The person is then exposed to the wiles and attacks of the devil which can only bring regret, pain, sorrow and ultimately, death.

As a true believer, you should be curious to now what exactly can negatively influence a person's deeds and make them become lukewarm. Let's find out what this is from the Bible:

Revelation 3:16-17 (NET) "*So because you are lukewarm, and neither hot nor cold, I am going to vomit you out of my mouth! Because you say, 'I am rich and have acquired great wealth, and need nothing,' but do not realize* *that you are wretched, pitiful, poor, blind, and naked..."*

The Laodicean church said "*I am rich and have acquired great wealth, and need nothing*" and God identified this as the source of their spiritual lukewarmness. Therefore, whenever you become completely dependent on something for your well-being to the extent that you feel you have little need for God, you have become a lukewarm Christian. Being "rich" and "having great wealth" does not apply to money alone. It could also mean being dependent on your beauty or handsomeness, your intelligence, your oratorical skills or some other thing. Once you feel that thing alone can provide you with everything else, you have become lukewarm. The scripture we just read also reveals to us more consequences of being vomited by God including becoming wretched, pitiful, poor, blind and naked.

From these scriptures, it is easy to recognize who a hot believer is. He or she is completely dependent on God for everything. A hot believer is one who understands that whatever he or she has is from God Almighty and would always desire to maintain that connection with Him. You are hot when you consciously set aside time to read the word of God, to pray, to worship and to fellowship with other believers on a regular basis. You are a hot Christian when every word you say and every behavior you exhibit is in line with the word and the will of the Almighty. A hot Christian is a permanent resident in the mouth of the Lord. He will never spit you out. This means that all the days of your life, you will have access to His divine favor, protection, peace, etc. It also means, as we've just read, you will never become spiritually or physically wretched, pitiful, poor, blind or naked. Rather, you will benefit from spiritual and physical wealth, become a helper of destinies and receive spiritual insight and protection.

So, if you are already lukewarm or you feel your spiritual temperature is gradually nearing lukewarmness, what do you do? Let's find out from scripture:

Revelation 3:18-20 (NET) "...*take my advice and buy gold from me refined by fire so you can become rich! Buy from me white clothing so you can be clothed and your shameful nakedness will not be exposed, and buy eye salve to put on your eyes so you can see! All those I love, I rebuke and discipline. So be earnest and repent! Listen! I am standing at the door and knocking! If anyone hears my voice and opens the door I will come into his home and share a meal with him, and he with me...*"

Revelation 3:21-22 (NET) "*I will grant the one who conquers permission to sit with me on my throne, just* *as I too conquered and sat down with my Father on His throne. The one who has an ear had better hear what the Spirit says to the churches."*

As you can see, in order to come out of a state of spiritual lukewarmness, you need to go shopping in the mall of heaven. First, you need to buy gold from God. This gold is what will give you true wealth. Second, you need to buy white clothing from God. This white clothing will clothe you and protect you from exposure and shame. Finally, you need to buy and apply eye salve on your eyes so that they can be opened to see spiritual realities and truths.

In addition to these, becoming spiritually hot means accepting God's rebuke and discipline. It means becoming zealous for the Almighty and turning away from your sins permanently. It means listening carefully to hear Christ knocking at the door of your heart so that you can let Him in.

If you do all of these and you succeed in becoming and staying spiritually hot, not only will you be an overcomer on this earth, the Lord Jesus Christ also promises that you will sit with Him on His throne in eternity.

So, what's it going to be? Would you like to increase your spiritual temperature? Do you want to become a fiery hot believer? If yes, get ready!

TODAY'S PRAYERS

1. O Righteous Father, I want to increase my spiritual temperature so that I can become spiritually hot. Come to my aid this morning, in the name of Jesus.

2. My Lord and my God, forgive me for every time I have said to myself, consciously or unconsciously, that "I am rich, I am wealthy, I need nothing, I need nobody". Forgive me for every time I have been self-conceited and lukewarm and forgive me for every time my deeds have changed for the worse because of my ignorance, in the name of Jesus.

3. Now Lord, I declare to You that I am open to Your rebuke and Your discipline. Therefore, I ask: Do not vomit me out of Your mouth. Do not reject me. Do not cut me off from Your divine protection, divine peace, divine favor and all other benefits of being Your child. Save me from spiritual wretchedness, poverty, blindness and nakedness, in the name of Jesus.

4. Jehovah, this morning I have arrived at the Mall of Heaven in order to shop. According to Your word, sell me gold so that I can be rich indeed and have true wealth. Sell me

white clothing so that I can be clothed in righteousness and protected from the cold of spiritual shame. Father, sell me eye salve so that my spiritual eyes can be opened to see spiritual realities. Fill my cart with the true treasures of heaven so that I can become spiritually hot, in the name of Jesus.

5. Lord, I declare unto You this morning that Yes, I see You standing at the door of my life. Yes, I hear You knocking. I have opened the door of my heart to You. King of kings, come in and come and dine with me forever. My Lord and my Savior, come and rule over my life forever, in the name of Jesus.

6. Messiah, let it be that by reason of my resolve and my determination, when that day comes and I enter into eternity, according to Your word, I will sit with You on Your throne in heaven forevermore, in the name of Jesus.

7. Thank You O God for answering my prayers, in Jesus' mighty name, amen.

If you have the need and the time, please feel free to add more prayers at this point.

Blessing: May you receive what you desire. May your spiritual temperature be increased and may you become spiritually hot, in the name of Jesus.

DAY 7

CURB THAT FEELING

"And when the woman saw that the tree was good for food, and that it was pleasant to the eyes, and a tree to be desired to make one wise, she took of the fruit thereof, and did eat, and gave also unto her husband with her; and he did eat." — Genesis 3:6 (KJV)

DAILY EXHORTATION

The same devil who facilitated the fall of the first family, by causing them to lust after fruit, is still at work causing the downfall of millions of people all over the world every single day. How does he succeed in doing this? Let's take a look at scriptures:

John 8:44 (NET) *"You people are from your father the devil, and you want to do what your father desires. He was a murderer from the beginning,* **and does not uphold the truth, because there is no truth in him. Whenever he lies, he speaks**

***according to his own nature, because he is a liar and the father of lies.**"*

Genesis 3:2-4 (NET) "*The woman said to the serpent, 'We may eat of the fruit from the trees of the orchard; but concerning the fruit of the tree that is in the middle of the orchard God said, 'You must not eat from it, and you must not touch it, or else you will die.'* **The serpent said to the woman, 'Surely you will not die'...**"

James 1:14-15 (NET) "*But each one is tempted when he is lured and enticed by his own desires. Then when desire conceives, it gives birth to sin, and when sin is full grown, it gives birth to death.*"

Here's how the devil causes human downfall: The devil comes to people—just as he went to Eve—and he lies to them by projecting false thoughts into their hearts. He can do this because lying is his nature. He'll suggest to people to fornicate, to commit adultery, to cheat, to become fraudulent, to steal, to defame, to harass, to assault, to rape, to maim, to kill, etc. And he'll tell them that they'll feel great when they do it or they won't get caught or they'll experience great peace after the fact or some other thing. Then, as we see from the third scripture above, whenever these lies gel with the evil desires or fantasies of a person's heart, sin is produced. This sin comes with several consequences including that person's downfall and physical or spiritual death.

The world is filled with stories of men and women whose once-bright stars suddenly fell and crashed because of a moment or several moments of fulfilling the lusts and dark desires of their hearts. Their careers, marriage, family, wealth, etc. all gone in a single moment. Many have moved from their glorious mansions in neighborhoods of the rich and famous to dark, smelly prison cells. Many have died all because of their inability to curb that lust, that desire or that feeling.

If you do not want to experience this kind of downfall, what do you do?

1 Peter 2:11 (NET) "*Dear friends, I urge you as foreigners and exiles to keep away from fleshly desires that do battle against the soul...*"

2 Timothy 2:22 (NLT) "*Run from anything that stimulates youthful lusts. Instead, pursue righteous living, faithfulness, love, and peace. Enjoy the companionship of those who call on the Lord with pure hearts.*"

Titus 2:11-12 (NET) "*For the grace of God has appeared, bringing salvation to all people. It trains us to reject godless ways and worldly desires and to live self-*

controlled, upright, and godly lives in the present age..."

Galatians 5:22-23 (NET) *"But the fruit of the Spirit is love, joy, peace, patience, kindness, goodness, faithfulness, gentleness, and self-control. Against such things there is no law."*

The first thing to do to save yourself from spiritual or physical downfall is to recognize that, as a believer, you are supposed to be a foreigner or a pilgrim on earth. This is because your eternal home is in heaven. Therefore, it is incumbent upon you to realize that you've got to do everything you can to ensure that you return to your native home when the time comes.

The second thing you have to do is to identify those things that very easily stimulate lusts and evil desires in your heart. This is necessary so that when you see them, you can recognize them and run far away from them. But it doesn't end there. You should replace those evil lusts and desires with divine alternatives such as a deep interest in living a righteous life, faithfulness, love, peace and associating with true believers.

The third thing you should do is to ask God to cause His divine grace to enter into your life. According to the scripture above, you need this grace because it will train you to reject godless ways and worldly desires and to live a self-controlled, upright, and godly life.

Finally, you need to ask God to cause your life to begin to bear the fruit of His Holy Spirit. Amongst other benefits, the fruit of the Spirit will equip you with self control so that you can resist the lusts and evil desires that can bring you down.

Do you want to save yourself from downfall, spiritual / physical death? Do you want to curb that negative feeling and banish it from your life? Do you want to be above lusts and evil desires so that your destiny can perpetuate and manifest? If yes, get yourself ready!

TODAY'S PRAYERS

1. Heavenly God, I do not want to suffer a downfall neither do I want to experience spiritual death. Therefore Lord, Arise for my sake and let any voice of the enemy that may be speaking lies and evil suggestions to me regarding any area of my life, be silenced forever, in the name of Jesus.

2. This morning I recognize and I acknowledge that I am a foreigner and a pilgrim traveling through this earth. Father, by reason of this, I ask that You give me the spiritual fortitude to continue and to finish my journey on the earth so that I can make it back to my eternal home, in the name of Jesus.

3. My Lord and my God, do not let me deceive myself. Help me to identify anything that easily stimulates lusts and evil desires in my life. From today, whenever I encounter these things, I shall run away from them and in so doing free myself from their hold upon my life, in the name of Jesus.

4. My God, from today, instead of succumbing to lusts and evil desires, I want to begin pursuing righteous living, faithfulness, love and peace. I also want to know what it means to find enjoyment in the companionship of true believers. Help me Lord to make all these a reality in my life, in the name of Jesus.

5. Great and Mighty God, release Your grace and the fruit of Your Holy Spirit into my life. According to Your word, let Your grace train me to reject godless ways and worldly desires. And by reason of Your grace and the fruit of the Spirit in my life, let self-control come alive in me so that I can live an upright and godly life in my generation, in the name of Jesus.

6. Adonai, use the new leaf that I have turned today to preserve me from a downfall and to help me in fulfilling my destiny. As I go out

today, let every step I take, every word I speak and everything I do move me closer to the fulfillment of my divine assignment on the earth, in the name of Jesus.

7.   Thank You El Shaddai for answering my prayers, in Jesus' mighty name, amen.

If you have the need and the time, please feel free to add more prayers at this point.

Blessing: May you obtain victory over lusts and evil desires to the glory of God, in the name of Jesus.

DAY 8

SECURING THE PLACE OF ALL PLACES

"In my Father's house are many mansions: if it were not so, I would have told you. I go to prepare a place for you. And if I go and prepare a place for you, I will come again, and receive you unto myself; that where I am, there ye may be also." — John 14:2-3 (KJV)

DAILY EXHORTATION

Our opening scripture contains words spoken by Jesus 2,000 years ago. 2,000 years ago!!! This means that Jesus Christ has been preparing this place He talked about for over 2,000 years! God Almighty created the whole earth in just 7 days. There are some places you can visit on earth which are so beautiful that words cannot properly describe them. You'll have to visit those places to see for yourself how wonderful those places look. If it took only 7 days to create such amazing beauty, please try to imagine what the place Jesus has been preparing for over 2,000 years will look like! Please, please, please do not miss heaven for any reason. There is nothing or nobody here on earth that is worth going to hell for. As a believer, Jesus has already assured you that He has gone to prepare this place and He will return to take you there. Never ever let go off this assurance. Keep it front and center in your life's journey.

So, you might want to know what to you could do in order to secure your place in heaven. Let's find out what that is from scripture:

John 14:1-3 (NET) *"Do not let your hearts be distressed. You believe in God; believe also in me."*

John 14:23 (NET) *"Jesus replied, 'If anyone loves me, he will obey my word, and my Father will love him, and we will come to him and take up residence with him.'"*

To secure your place in the greatest piece of real estate in the universe, you only have to believe in God and in His Son, Jesus Christ. Also, you have to become familiar with the teachings of Jesus Christ and obey them to the letter. If you can do these, you will secure your mansion and your eternal place in heaven.

Do you want to avoid hell fire? Do you want to live in an unimaginably beautiful new world which human words cannot describe? Do you want to spend your eternity in amazing bliss? Do you want to secure your own place in the kingdom of God? If yes, get yourself ready!

TODAY'S PRAYERS

1. I believe that Jesus Christ is right now in heaven preparing a place for me and for other believers. Today, I lay claim to my own place in God's kingdom, in the name of Jesus.

2. I believe that right now, mansions are being constructed in heaven for all of God's children. Today, I lay claim to my own mansion, in the name of Jesus.

3. I believe that Jesus will soon return in order to receive all of God's children into heaven. Today, I lay claim to my own place on that glorious trip, in the name of Jesus.

4. O Lord, as I begin to consciously study Your word, help me so that I can understand the truth that it has to offer me, in the name of Jesus.

5. Father, as Your word enters into my mind, my soul and my spirit, give me the grace to obey Your word and live it out in my closet and also in front of the whole world, in the

name of Jesus.

6. Merciful God, I do not want to go to hell fire. Instead, I want to spend my eternity in the new world that You are creating for Your children. Seal up my destiny and bind it with You for good and forever, in the name of Jesus.

7. Thank You precious God for answering my prayers, in Jesus' mighty name, amen.

If you have the need and the time, please feel free to add more prayers at this point.

Blessing: May you secure your place in God's kingdom through your belief and your obedience, in the name of Jesus.

DAY 9

EYES THAT NEVER LEAVE THE PRIZE

"When they had crossed over, Elijah said to Elisha, 'Ask what I shall do for you before I am taken from you.' And Elisha said, 'Please, let a double portion of your spirit be upon me.' He said, 'You have asked a hard thing. Nevertheless, if you see me when I am taken from you, it shall be so for you; but if not, it shall not be so.'" — 2 Kings 2:9-10 (NASB)

DAILY EXHORTATION

Elijah's time on the earth had come to an end. However, before he was taken away, he asked his protégé, Elisha, what he wanted as a parting gift. Our opening scripture reveals that Elisha requested for a double portion of his master's anointing. In response, his master told him that it could be done but only if Elisha could meet a particular condition. You see, some Christians believe that every good thing in the Bible will come to them simply because they have given their lives to Christ. Certainly, as a believer, if you remain in Jesus, you will receive certain benefits and make heaven. BUT there are certain things that you may never access except you fulfill or meet certain conditions. You may pray, you may fast, you may do this and do that but until you meet that condition, the benefit you are interested in may never come to you. Let's see an example in the Bible:

Psalm 37:4 (ESV) *"Delight yourself in the LORD, and He will give you the desires of your heart."*

The above scripture promises that God will give you the desires of your heart [a car, a spouse, a job, a promotion, some kind of spiritual benefit, etc]. However, this will only happen if you fulfill the preceding condition, which is to "Delight yourself in the Lord." If you fulfill that condition, you will get what you want and if you do not, you will get nothing. It doesn't matter if you have been a Christian for 30 years or if your father is/was a pastor or your mom is/was a deaconess. Condition not met, promise not fulfilled. Condition met, promise fulfilled.

This was the same situation Elisha found himself in on this day. According to Elijah, all he had to do was to "keep his eyes on the prize". He said "*If you see me when I am taken from you, it shall be so for you; but if not, it shall not be so.*" Elisha wanted more than anything to make an impact in his own generation. Therefore, he fixed his eyes on Elijah and those eyes never left him throughout the day. The Bible says that after Elijah dropped his condition, both of them began talking and walking along the way. Yet, Elisha's eyes were fixed on Elijah. He was not carried away by the talking or the walking. Therefore, it was no surprise that when the moment of destiny came, Elisha was fully ready. Let's see what happened in the Bible:

2 Kings 2:11-12 (KJV) "*And it came to pass, as they still went on, and talked, that, behold, there appeared a chariot of fire, and horses of fire, and parted them both asunder; and Elijah went up by a whirlwind into heaven.* **And Elisha saw it, and he cried, My father, my father, the chariot of Israel, and the horsemen thereof.** *And he saw him no more...*"

The Bible confirms that Elisha saw the fiery rapture of his master, Elijah. To confirm that he saw it, Elisha called out to his master while the rapture was taking place and he described what he was seeing in detail. He mentioned the chariot that he saw as well as the heavenly horsemen that rode the chariot. Therefore, by keeping his eyes fixed on the prize, Elisha was able to fulfill the condition of what was promised to him.

Now, did heaven do its own part? Let's find out from scripture:

2 Kings 2:13-14 (NET) *"He picked up Elijah's cloak, which had fallen off him, and went back and stood on the shore of the Jordan. He took the cloak that had fallen off Elijah, hit the water with it, and said, 'Where is the Lord, the God of Elijah?' When he hit the water, it divided and Elisha crossed over."*

Since the condition had been met, heaven had no choice but to fulfill Elisha's request for double-portion power. Therefore, when Elisha hit the water with the cloak, it had no choice but to divide for the man of power to cross over.

The most important thing that you have to learn in today's devotional is that there is power in God to do anything. But not everything is available to just anyone. Some wonderful benefits have conditions attached. If you want those kinds of benefits, like Elisha, you have to keep your eyes wide open so that you can fulfill or meet any condition attached to whatever it is that you want. This is why some Christians are wealthy and some are poor. This is why some Christians live in good health and some are constantly sick. The difference is that some go all out to meet the conditions attached to divine benefits while some do not.

This morning, what will it be for you? Do you have a desire? Are you willing to keep your eyes on the prize until you get it? Do you want to enjoy the complete ramifications of Christianity? If yes, today is your day, get yourself ready!

TODAY'S PRAYERS

1. O Lord my God, my heart is filled with all kinds of dreams, desires, plans and goals which I know You can make come to pass. Come to my aid today, in the name of Jesus.

2. Father, I thank You for making me realize that certain benefits of the kingdom are locked behind conditions. Accept my thanks and my praises, in the name of Jesus.

3. Heavenly Father, whenever something I need in life requires the fulfillment of a condition, by Your grace and mercy, give me the strength and complete wherewithal to meet or fulfill the conditions for the release of that thing, in the name of Jesus.

4. My God, as it was with Elisha, in the journey of my life, do not let me be sidetracked. Do not let me be carried away by the vicissitudes

of life. Give me extraordinary focus. Let my eyes always be fixed on the prize so that I can fulfill whatever condition is placed before me and get what I need, in the name of Jesus.

5.   Lord, as it was for Elisha, after I have met heaven's conditions for the release of any divine benefit I desire, let heaven release that benefit into my hands of destiny, in the name of Jesus.

6.   Messiah, let every benefit that is released into my life by reason of the fulfillment of divine conditions help me to fulfill my destiny and make impact for You in this world, in the name of Jesus.

7.   Thank You Father for answering my prayers, in Jesus' mighty name, amen.

If you have the need and the time, please feel free to add more prayers at this point.

Blessing: Since you have determined in your heart to meet divine conditions tied to divine benefits, may you experience uncommon blessings and may you be lifted high amongst your peers in your generation to the glory of God, in the name of Jesus.

DAY 10

UNCONVENTIONAL MEDICINE

"A merry heart doeth good like a medicine: but a broken spirit drieth the bones." — Proverbs 17:22 (KJV)

DAILY EXHORTATION

Another version of our opening scripture says *"Being cheerful keeps you healthy. It is slow death to be gloomy all the time."* (Proverbs 17:22, GNT). There are people who take certain kinds of medicines in order to keep themselves from getting sick. And many more people take medicines to treat one health condition or the other that they have. Our opening scripture is very clear: It is saying that if you want to keep disease away from your life or if you need healing from a particular ailment, you need to develop a merry heart and become cheerful. If this is true [and it is], it means that you have to become pragmatic in order for it to work in your life. So, as you intentionally program yourself and your time to study the word of God and to pray, you also have to intentionally program yourself to take this unconventional medicine.

How does one develop a merry heart? A cheap way to do this is to set aside time to remember the funny and / or happy moments you have had in times past and replay them in your mind. Another way is to acquire books, magazines, audio and video products meant to elicit laughter and happiness. There are a lot of products out there that are funny because they are vulgar and nasty. Please avoid these. Instead, get products that are funny without the vulgarity or the nastiness. A good search should turn up very many Christian and decent secular comedic products.

Once you have acquired these products, create a timetable and in that timetable, plug-in time slots for you to consume these comedic products. For instance, on your commute to work, you can listen to clean, funny audio programs in your car. Or, you can set aside certain evenings of your work week and anytime during your weekends to watch movies and other video programs that will cause you to laugh or feel good. When the time comes for you to enjoy these products, let yourself go and have yourself a good time. In addition, create time to be in the company of your loved ones, friends, relatives, fellow believers and other people with whom you can relax and have a good time. If you do this in addition to whatever it is you are doing to keep healthy [such as good nutrition, exercise, etc], you will certainly live a long, healthy life. This is the word of the Lord and it is guaranteed to come to pass in your life if you apply it.

So, do you want to keep sickness away? Do you need mental as well as physical healing? Are you ready to try this unconventional medicine? If yes, get yourself ready!

TODAY'S PRAYERS

1. Almighty God, I thank You for the wisdom that is in Your word. As I apply it, let the transformative power that is in it bring powerful changes for good into my life, in the name of Jesus.

2. Father, from today, let me see developing a merry heart and being cheerful as equal to eating right and doing physical exercise in the maintenance of my health and well-being, in the name of Jesus.

3. Holy Spirit of God, give me wisdom to design a timetable for my life in which I can slot in time for consuming products designed to

elicit laughter and happiness, in the name of Jesus.

4. My God, help me to craft my life such that I can spend time with my loved ones, relatives, friends and other people with whom I can have and share happy moments, in the name of Jesus.

5. Lord, as I read, listen to or watch comedic products, let me always remember that I am obeying Your instruction. Let me always let myself go so that the medicine of a merry heart that I am consuming can do its work in my life. Likewise, whenever I am in the company of good people with whom I am having a great time, let me always remember that I am using Your prescription and Your unconventional medicine, in the name of Jesus.

6. My Father and my God, as I have decided today to incorporate merry times and moments of cheer into my life, let me reap the rewards that have been promised me in Your word. Let my merry heart work like medicine in my life to keep disease away and to bring me healing whenever I need it, in the name of Jesus.

7. Thank You Mighty Father for answering my

prayers, in Jesus' mighty name, amen.

If you have the need and the time, please feel free to add more prayers at this point.

Blessing: May the medicine of a merry heart and of good cheer work in your favor, in the name of Jesus.

DAY 11

LIFTED

"The LORD lifteth up the meek: He casteth the wicked down to the ground."
— Psalm 147:6 (KJV)

DAILY EXHORTATION

God had blessed Abraham immensely. He had vast numbers of livestock and great wealth in gold and silver. Some of that blessing had also rubbed off on his relative, Lot. While staying with Abraham, Lot too had accumulated livestock, a large staff and some wealth. As time went on, quarrels and squabbles began to emerge between Abraham's staff and Lot's staff. The following passage described how Abraham handled the situation:

Genesis 13:8-11 (NET) *"Abram said to Lot, 'Let there be no quarreling between me and you, and between my herdsmen and your herdsmen, for we are close relatives. Is not the whole land before you? Separate yourself now from me. If you go to the left, then I'll go to the right, but if* *you go to the right, then I'll go to the left.' Lot looked up and saw the whole region of the Jordan. He noticed that all of it was well-watered (before the Lord obliterated Sodom and Gomorrah) like the garden of the Lord, like the land of Egypt, all the way to Zoar. Lot chose for himself the whole region of the Jordan and traveled toward the east. So the relatives separated from each other."*

What you have just read is an example of what it means to be meek. There are many definitions for meekness but a few of them are *"being patient"*, *"being slow to anger"* and *"not inclined to resentment"*. Abraham could have driven Lot away but because of the meekness in his life, he instead chose to resolve the matter amicably. Now, our opening scripture says that "the Lord lifts up the meek". With regard to Abraham's display of meekness in the example we just saw, in what way did God subsequently lift him up? Let's find out from scripture:

Genesis 13:14-17 (NET) *"After Lot had departed, the Lord said to Abram, 'Look from the place where you stand to the north, south, east, and west. I will give all the land that you see to you and your descendants forever. And I will make your descendants like the dust of the earth, so that if anyone is able to count the dust of the earth, then your descendants also can be counted. Get up and walk throughout the land, for I will give it to you.'"*

What a lifting! The Almighty rewarded Abraham with an intergenerational blessing. As you know and as you read this, the descendants of Abraham—the nation of Israel—are occupying the very land that was promised to their ancestor, Abraham. So, you can see very clearly that the word of the Lord is true. Meekness can work wonders for you. It is a behavior or a pattern of life that has a promise attached. It can attract unimaginable blessings into your life. If you choose to become meek today, the Almighty will see to it that you are lifted. Do you need a lifting? Are you ready to be meek? If yes, get yourself ready!

TODAY'S PRAYERS

1. Everlasting Father, for every time that I have been impatient, quick to anger or resentful, I ask that You forgive me, in the name of Jesus.

2. Mighty God, I connect to this morning's word. Therefore, I ask: Through Your Holy Spirit, Father, teach me to be meek, in the name of Jesus.

3. Lord, as it was for Abraham, whenever conflicts arise or whenever episodes of unfairness arise, let the engine of meekness

start up within me. Instead of me reacting on a basic human level, let me respond with wisdom and calmness in the same manner Abraham did, in the name of Jesus.

4. Father, as it was for Abraham, any time I apply meekness to any tense situation in my life, let that situation always receive resolution, in the name of Jesus.

5. My God, I want to walk in the way that You want me to walk. I want to live the way that You want me to live. Therefore, I ask You to be my constant guide in the journey of my life, in the name of Jesus.

6. Now Lord, I ask: In the same manner Abraham received an unimaginable lifting, let me also receive great liftings by reason of the spirit of meekness in my life, in the name of Jesus.

7. Thank You Father for answering my prayers, in Jesus' mighty name, amen.

If you have the need and the time, please feel free to add more prayers at this point.

Blessing: As you carry the banner of meekness, may God lift you up and may you never fall, in the name of Jesus.

DAY 12

SHOW ME MERCY

"Blessed are the merciful, for they will be shown mercy." — Matthew 5:7 (NET)

DAILY EXHORTATION

God promised the children of Israel the land of Canaan. But between the time the promise was made to Abraham and the emergence of the generation of Israelites who would actually possess the land, towns, cities and kingdoms had already occupied the land. They could not just walk in and settle. They had to fight their way to their breakthrough. They had to defeat every single occupant on the land before they could possess their possession.

The first city that stood on their path was Jericho. Before they attacked the city, Joshua sent spies to check it out. Unfortunately, word got to the king that 2 spies had entered into Jericho and that in fact, they were in the house of a woman called Rahab.

So, the king of Jericho sent an urgent

message to Rahab. Let's see what happened in scripture:

Joshua 2:3-7, 15-16 (NET) "*So the king of Jericho sent this order to Rahab:* **'Turn over the men who came to you**—*the ones who came to your house—for they have come to spy on the whole land!'* **But the woman hid the two men** *and replied, 'Yes, these men were clients of mine, but I didn't know where they came from. When it was time to shut the city gate for the night, the men left. I don't know where they were heading. Chase after them quickly, for you have time to catch them!'* **(Now she had taken them up to the roof and had hidden them in the stalks of flax she had spread out on the roof.)** *Meanwhile the king's men tried to find them on the road to the Jordan River near the fords. The city gate was shut as soon as they set out in pursuit of them... Then Rahab let them [the 2 spies] down by a rope through the window. (Her house was built as part of the city wall; she lived in the wall.) She told them, 'Head to the hill country, so the ones chasing you don't find you. Hide from them there for three days, long enough for those chasing you to return. Then you can be on your way.'*"

Rahab hid the 2 spies and also lied to protect them. If she had not done this, they would have been arrested and executed. But because of her courage and her actions, their lives were preserved. Plus, because of the information she provided to the spies, the Israelites got a feel for the atmosphere within Jericho and this in turn emboldened them to attack the city. And attack it they did with great fury!

What Rahab did was that she showed mercy to the spies. In other words, she was merciful to them. Our opening scripture says that the merciful are blessed because they will also be shown mercy. Since Rahab was merciful to these spies, was she in turn shown mercy? Let's find out from scripture:

Joshua 6:25 (KJV) "*And Joshua saved Rahab the harlot alive, and her father's household, and all that she had; and she dwelleth in Israel even unto this day; because she hid the messengers, which Joshua sent to spy out Jericho.*"

Rahab showed the spies mercy and as a result, she was also shown mercy. This proves that our opening scripture is sure and certain to manifest in the life of anyone who applies it. In Proverbs 21:21 (KJV), the Bible says "*He that followeth after righteousness and mercy findeth life, righteousness, and honour.*" This is saying that if you want the rewards of mercy such as life, righteousness and honor, you have to "pursue" mercy. This means that you must train yourself to the point that "mercy" becomes second nature to you or a character trait in your life. To pursue mercy means that whenever you can, like Rahab, you will help people as much as you can. If you do this, according to the word of the Lord, you too will be shown mercy.

In addition, you will enjoy life, righteousness and honor all the days of your life. Is this something you want in your life? If yes, please get yourself ready for this morning's prayers!

TODAY'S PRAYERS

1. My Lord and my God, all the days of my life, let Your mercy speak for me, in the name of Jesus.

2. O Lord my God, through the power of Your Holy Spirit, let the spirit of mercy be unleashed into my life now and forever, in the name of Jesus.

3. Father, by reason of the spirit of mercy and as it was for Rahab, whenever I see people in need or in danger and I have the means to help, let me become an agent of mercy to these people, in the name of Jesus.

4. O Lord I pray, as it was for Rahab, through the acts of mercy that I will show people, let

the problem in their lives or the danger that they face come to an end, in the name of Jesus.

5. Messiah, according to Your word, as I show others mercy, let me be blessed. Let me also be shown mercy at any point in my life that I need it, in the name of Jesus.

6. Everlasting God, according to Your word, as I pursue righteousness and mercy everyday of my life, let me find life, let me find righteousness and let me find honor, in the name of Jesus.

7. Thank You Merciful God for answering my prayers, in Jesus' mighty name, amen.

If you have the need and the time, please feel free to add more prayers at this point.

Blessing: May the spirit of mercy come and rest in your life so that you too can benefit from mercy, in the name of Jesus.

DAY 13

CONFIDENCE THAT BRINGS RESULTS

"The Lord said to Moses, 'Why do you cry out to me? Tell the Israelites to move on. And as for you, lift up your staff and extend your hand toward the sea and divide it, so that the Israelites may go through the middle of the sea on dry ground.'" — Exodus 14:15-16 (NET)

DAILY EXHORTATION

Our opening scripture is one of the most profound passages in the Bible. Think about a beach you've seen or visited and just imagine for a second, the sea of that beach parting into two all the way to the other beach or shore on the other side and dry land appearing in the middle. This was the great miracle that God surprised His children with when they were being pursued by their erstwhile slave masters, the Egyptians. This episode has a great lesson for you to learn and to inculcate into your life. But first, let's take a look at the scriptures that will open our understanding regarding this morning's devotional:

Exodus 14:10-12 (NET) "*When Pharaoh got closer, the Israelites looked up, and there were the Egyptians marching after them, and they were terrified. The Israelites cried out to the Lord, and they said to Moses, 'Is it because there are no graves in Egypt that you have taken us away to die in the desert? What in the world have you done to us by bringing us out of Egypt? Isn't this what we told you in Egypt, 'Leave us alone so that we can serve the Egyptians, because it is better for us to serve the Egyptians than to die in the desert!*'"

Exodus 14:13-14 (NET) "*Moses said to the people, 'Do not fear! Stand firm and see the salvation of the Lord that He will provide for you today; for the Egyptians that you see today you will never, ever see again. The Lord will fight for you, and you can be still.*'"

Even though the Israelites were a covenant people, at the time, they were not deeply spiritual people. They were not as spiritual as Moses and his brother, Aaron, were. Therefore, when immense pressure came knocking on their door in the form of the army of Pharaoh behind them and the Red Sea in front of them, they had no option but to murmur.

But Moses had a deeper relationship with

God. It was he that God appeared to through the burning bush on Mount Horeb. It was he that God used to perform the miracles of the plagues in the land of Egypt. It was he that God called to lead His people out of Egypt and into the promised land. Thus, his own thinking was different. To him, the God that called him and had used him to do wonders will not now abandon His children to be re-enslaved or massacred on the shores of the Red Sea.

Therefore, in response to the cries of the Israelites, he was confident enough to say *'Do not fear! Stand firm and see the salvation of the Lord that he will provide for you today; for the Egyptians that you see today you will never, ever see again. The Lord will fight for you, and you can be still.'* BUT do you know that Moses did not know exactly what God was going to do? He did not know the processes or elements of nature or divine techniques God would employ to deliver His people. This was why he was standing there. All he had was great faith that neither he nor his people would die in that place on that day. And according to our opening scripture, boy, was his faith rewarded.

Imagine again that you were Moses on that day—that as you stretched out that staff toward the Red Sea, it began to separate and dry land showed up. You would be surprised and shocked! But, you would also feel that your faith in God had been over-rewarded. This is the great lesson for you today: Sometimes, you know what you want God to do and how you want Him to do it BUT at other times, you do not. No one had ever seen a sea parting before, so no one expected it. When you encounter a situation or circumstance in which you cannot see a solution but unless a solution shows up, you may suffer damage, Moses has shown you what to do!

Like him, fortify your faith in God. According to the words of Moses, do away with the fear in your heart. Stand firm and powerfully anticipate the salvation that the Lord will provide for you. Expect forcefully that your problems [a.k.a your Egyptians] will disappear forever. Then stand still as you wait for the Lord your God to fight for you in the way that He chooses. Are you ready to use your faith in the manner just described to solve your challenges? If yes, today is your day. Get yourself ready!

TODAY'S PRAYERS

1. My Father and my God, this morning I ask You to make me more like Moses, in the name of Jesus.

2. O Lord my God, whenever pressure comes knocking on my door in the form of problems

behind me and challenges ahead of me, let me always remember who I am. Let me remember that it was because of me that You sent Your son to die on the Cross of Calvary. Let me remember the episodes from my past when You came through for me. Let me remember that I am Your child and that You have given me a destiny to fulfill. And in that moment, let my faith and my confidence in You be renewed, in the name of Jesus.

3. Eternal King, whenever pressure comes knocking at my door, as it was for Moses, let the faith in my heart drive out fear from my life, in the name of Jesus.

4. Merciful God, whenever pressure comes knocking on my door, let me stand firm and wait to see the salvation that You shall provide for me, in the name of Jesus.

5. Great and Mighty God, whenever pressure comes knocking on my door, from today, I will stand still and let You fight for me, in the name of Jesus.

6. I decree that by reason of my actions of faith and as it was for Moses and the children of Israel, my Red sea will part and dry ground will appear through it. And while I walk on the dry ground and cross over to the other

side for my good, the Egyptians pursuing me will disappear and I will never see them again forever and ever, in the name of Jesus.

7. Thank You miracle-working God for answering my prayers, in Jesus' mighty name, amen.

If you have the need and the time, please feel free to add more prayers at this point.

Blessing: May your strong confidence in the Almighty be over-rewarded in your favor, in the name of Jesus.

DAY 14

THE POWER OF DIVINE CONFUSION

"But the Lord came down to see the city and the tower that the people had started building. And the Lord said, 'If as one people all sharing a common language they have begun to do this, then nothing they plan to do will be beyond them. Come, let's go down and confuse their language so they won't be able to understand each other.'"
— Genesis 11:5-7 (NET)

DAILY EXHORTATION

When you first read our opening scripture, you may think to yourself *"Why did God confuse the language of the early humans at Babel? Why did He make it so that they couldn't understand each other?"* Well, the first answer to that comes from the scripture that precedes this one. Let's take a quick look at it:

Genesis 11:1-4 (NET) *"At one time all the people of*

the world spoke the same language and used the same words. As the people migrated to the east, they found a plain in the land of Babylonia and settled there. They began saying to each other, 'Let's make bricks and harden them with fire.' (In this region bricks were used instead of stone, and tar was used for mortar.) Then they said, 'Come, let's build a great city for ourselves with a tower that reaches into the sky. This will make us famous and keep us from being scattered all over the world.'"

So, you might think "*They wanted to build a tower and become famous in order to prevent themselves from being scattered all over the world... what's wrong with that?*" Here's what's wrong with that:

Genesis 1:27-28 (GNT) "*So God created human beings, making them to be like himself. He created them male and female, blessed them, and said, '**Have many children, so that your descendants will live all over the earth and bring it under their control**. I am putting you in charge of the fish, the birds, and all the wild animals.'"*

God created man in order to multiply and fill up the whole earth and live all over the world. BUT, these our ancestors came up with this silly scheme to build a great city and stay in one spot! These people were disobedient and their purpose was contrary to the purpose of God for mankind.

Now, whether they were disobedient or not, God made a very important comment in our opening scripture. He said "*If as one people all sharing a common language they have begun to do this, then nothing they plan to do will be beyond them.*" He knew that these people by reason of their common language and their common purpose, if left alone, would have succeeded in bringing to pass their erroneous desire. Therefore, the Almighty came down and confused their language. From one language, very many languages emerged.

In Genesis 11:8-9 (NET), the Bible says "*So the Lord scattered them from there across the face of the entire earth,* **and they stopped building the city**. *That is why its name was called Babel—because there the Lord confused the language of the entire world,* **and from there the Lord scattered them across the face of the entire earth**." With a single act of divine confusion, God achieved His two goals. He stopped the vain, misguided project of our ancestors and caused them to scatter all over the word, language by language, in order to fulfill His original plan for mankind.

There are many lessons to learn from this morning's devotional but let's focus on one. If you know you are a full believer, living according to the word and will of God and you find yourself in a situation where people united by a common, vain or evil purpose gang up against you, you now have a single, powerful weapon to use against them. They have gathered against you because they speak a common language of evil and they have a common purpose BUT with the weapon of divine confusion, God can confuse their language. And in the same manner He scattered the early humans and stopped them from building their city, He will scatter your enemies and terminate their evil agenda against your life. So, are you currently experiencing opposition from a group of people? Do you want it stopped? If yes, get yourself ready!

TODAY'S PRAYERS

1. Heavenly Father, I believe that I am living according to Your will and Your word. Be with me and protect me, in the name of Jesus.

2. If there be any group of people with a common language and a common evil purpose to do evil against me, as You did in Babel, come down and come to my rescue, in the name of Jesus.

3. My Lord and my God, let the common language of the modern-day Babylonians gathered against me be confused, in the name of Jesus.

4. Father, let Your divine language confusion cause members of any evil group gathered against me to scatter asunder, in the name of Jesus.

5. Everlasting God, let the scattering of my enemies cause their evil purpose and agenda against me to be abandoned and to come to a sudden end forever and ever, in the name of Jesus.

6. Alpha and Omega, from now and throughout the days of my life, let me live out the purpose that You have assigned for my life to Your glory. Let me also have children and descendants that will dominate the world and fill the earth with the goodness of Your will and Your word, in the name of Jesus.

7. Thank You Father God for answering my prayers, in Jesus' mighty name, amen.

If you have the need and the time, please feel free to add more prayers at this point.

Blessing: May any gang up against you scatter and may the plot of your enemies come to nothing, in the name of Jesus.

DAY 15

FOR WHOM DO I TOIL?

"Then I returned, and I saw vanity under the sun: There is one alone, without companion: He has neither son nor brother. Yet there is no end to all his labors, Nor is his eye satisfied with riches. But he never asks, 'For whom do I toil and deprive myself of good?' This also is vanity and a grave misfortune."
— Ecclesiastes 4:7-8 (NKJV)

DAILY EXHORTATION

If you are solely career- or business-minded and you have no time for anyone or anything else, this morning's devotional is asking you to re-examine the path you are taking in life before it is too late. Now, it is understandable when you're young that you have a need to make your mark in life. At this stage of life, you need time to concentrate and focus in order to make a name for yourself and establish the foundations of your financial security. This focus may cause you to sacrifice relationships, your social life, etc. because it is supposed to be temporary. However, if you've already built a good career or business and you are still laser-focused on making money to the exclusion of all other things, something is wrong somewhere.

Our opening scripture says that if after securing yourself financially, you still are without a spouse, without children and you have cut yourself off from your siblings, you are living a life of vanity and of misfortune. It is not success to be in this kind of state. It is misfortune. But, as a child of God, your focus should be on how to take corrective steps to rearrange your life in line with God's will.

If you are interested in doing this, your first task is to change your attitude toward money. A person with a stable career or business needs to learn contentment. That is, being satisfied with what you have—especially the money that you have. Contentment does not equal complacency. No one is saying do not make money. But, at every stage of your life, you should look at what you have and be happy with what God has blessed you with. Consider that people with far less have families and satisfying relationships. So, what is the laser-focus on money all about? Once this is done, intentionally create time to expand your interaction with people. If your relationship with your family [parents and siblings] is strained, give them a call and begin to rebuild the bridge between you and them.

Next, if you are a grown man, it is time to look for a lovely woman to marry and if you are a woman, it is time to look for a godly man to marry. And hopefully when you do, your marriage will be blessed with children whose dynamic lives will add color to your life. If you take these steps, you will find that advancing your career / business will become even sweeter. When next the question "*for whom do I toil?*" comes up, you will be able to answer powerfully — "*I am toiling for myself, for my spouse, for my kids, for my descendants, for my parents, for my siblings, the people that I love and the work of God*". That sounds and feels a lot better than saying "*I am toiling only for myself*".

If you follow the steps we have discussed this morning, you will be delivered from punishing labor without satisfaction, a vain life and the spirit of misfortune. If this is something you'd like to do, get yourself ready!

TODAY'S PRAYERS

1. O Lord of hosts, deliver me from the spirit of vanity, in the name of Jesus.

2. Great Deliverer, according to Your word, have mercy on me and cast out any spirit of misfortune that may be in my life, in the name of Jesus.

3. My Father, through the power of Your Holy Spirit, teach me contentment until it becomes a trait in my life, in the name of Jesus.

4. My God, let the bridge that has been burned between me and _____ (name of relative / friend), be rebuilt so I can cross over it and make amends. Also bless me with new relationships that will bring real joy to my life, in the name of Jesus.

5. O Lord my God, by Your grace and mercy, bless me with a spouse after Your own heart. Also bless me with children that will add color to my life for the rest of my days, in the name of Jesus.

6. Rock of Ages, redesign my perspective on life for good. Let me see clearly who I am toiling for and usher me into a life of deep meaning, significance and substance, in the name of Jesus.

7. Thank You Heavenly Father for answering my prayers, in Jesus' mighty name, amen.

If you have the need and the time, please feel free to add more prayers at this point.

Blessing: May your life be renewed and may it be filled with godly purpose, in the name of Jesus.

DAY 16

WAIT A MINUTE!

**"Now when Judas, who had betrayed
Him, saw that Jesus had been condemned,
he regretted what he had done and
returned the thirty silver coins to the chief
priests and the elders"
— Matthew 27:3 (NET)**

DAILY EXHORTATION

The story of Judas is one that we all need to be
mindful of and learn from. In John 12:6, the Bible
identifies Judas as a thief. This was the kind of
person he was. He was essentially, actively living
in sin. Therefore, when he betrayed Jesus and
was paid 30 pieces of silver, he initially saw the
whole thing as just another one of his schemes.
However, our opening scripture reveals to us that
this time was different.

Once Judas realized that Jesus had been
condemned and would soon be killed, he
immediately regretted his action and wanted to
return the money they paid him. Ultimately,

here's what the Bible says about what happened:

Matthew 27:5 (NET) "*So Judas threw the silver coins into the temple and left. Then he went out and hanged himself.*"

Judas committed suicide. Now, the question is: In that moment, which our opening scripture reveals, when he went to speak with the chief priests and the elders, what pushed Judas to do something as drastic as going to hang himself. The answer lies in the following passage which precedes the one above:

Matthew 27:3-4 (GNT) "*When Judas, the traitor, learned that Jesus had been condemned, he repented and took back the thirty silver coins to the chief priests and the elders.* **'I have sinned by betraying an innocent man to death!***" he said.* **'What do we care about that?' they answered. 'That is your business!'**"

Judas was filled with guilt. He entertained the idea that by returning the money he collected, he could "undo" what he had done. He hoped that he would be told everything would be ok and everything would return to normal. He thought the chief priests and elders were religious leaders who believed in fairness and justice and things like that. He thought that by returning the money, he could get salvation, get penitence and atonement. BUT, he was met with the harsh feedback **"*WHAT DO WE CARE ABOUT THAT, THAT IS YOUR BUSINESS!*"**. On hearing this, he ran off and hanged himself. He did not stop to think about the words of Jesus. He did not stop to remember that God sent this same Jesus to die for the sins of everyone on earth including this his sin of betrayal. Judas did not stop to think of hell fire. He did not wait to think about the eternal consequences of what he was about to do. If Judas had thought about all these, he would have calmed down, looked for Jesus and begged Him for forgiveness. And his history would have been very different from what it is today.

The lesson you should learn from this morning's devotional is that if you have done something wrong, something disgraceful, wait a minute! Don't do anything drastic! No matter what you have done or what has been done to you, 10 seconds in the unbelievable heat of hell fire will show you that nothing on earth is worth going to hell for. If like Judas, you are seeking comfort in human beings, you may be disappointed. In the same manner they told Judas "What do we care about that? That is YOUR BUSINESS!", it is likely that this is what you will hear from many people, if you do something wrong.

Therefore, it is incumbent upon you to craft your own words of hope, your own words of consolation, your own phrases of penitence and redemption based upon the word of God.

For example:

"For all have sinned and come short of the glory of God. Therefore, I know that I am not the only sinner in the world".

"The Bible says You shall not kill. Therefore, I will neither kill myself nor any other person."

"Jesus Christ said 'those the Father has given me will come to me, and I will never reject them.' I am one of these people and I know that Jesus will never reject me"

"The word of God says 'Come now, let us reason together, says the LORD: though your sins are like scarlet, they shall be as white as snow; though they are red like crimson, they shall become like wool.' By reason of this word, I believe that as I confess my sins to the Lord, my life will become as white as snow and as pure as wool."

Instead of going to the chief priests and elders who were envious of Christ and had been seeking for ways to kill Him for years, if Judas had reminded himself of these scriptures and many more like them, he could have caught himself. In the same manner, if you find yourself in the heat of the moment, WAIT A MINUTE! Instead of seeking solace in people who may make matters worse for you, remind yourself of these scriptures and others like them, personalize them and repeat them to yourself over and over until they begin to take effect in your life.

So, do you want a much more resilient personality? Do you want to live above the harsh / cold words of mankind? Do you want to preserve your life? Do you want to move on with your life after you have made a mistake or an error? If yes, get yourself ready!

TODAY'S PRAYERS

1. Lord Jesus, I believe in the power of Your blood to save to the uttermost. Come to my aid this morning.

2. My God, whenever I make a mistake or an error, let me always catch myself and bring Your word into the moment so that I do not do anything drastic, in the name of Jesus.

3. Father, I ask: Let the cold / harsh words of human beings lose their power to push me to make rash decisions that I will regret forever, in the name of Jesus.

4. My God, whenever I find myself in a tense moment, let me always command myself to

'wait a minute' while I stream into my mind Your word on the forgiveness of my sins, Your word on Your love for me and Your promises of redemption and new beginnings, in the name of Jesus.

5. King of kings, with the entrance of Your word into my tense moments, let every balloon of tension, fatal stress and irrationality in my life be deflated and let me pull myself back into Your safe arms, in the name of Jesus.

6. I receive a new kind of mind. I receive a resilient heart. I receive the power to move on from my errors and not linger in them. I receive the power of a sound mind, I receive the gift of preservation of life, in the name of Jesus.

7. Thank You Mighty God for answering my prayers, in Jesus' mighty name, amen.

If you have the need and the time, please feel free to add more prayers at this point.

Blessing: May you never destroy yourself by reason of the thoughtless words of other people or by reason of your own deeds, in the name of Jesus.

DAY 17

THE WIND AND
THE SPIRIT

"The wind blows wherever it will, and you hear the sound it makes, but do not know where it comes from and where it is going. So it is with everyone who is born of the Spirit." — John 3:8 (NET)

DAILY EXHORTATION

During the nighttime visit of Nicodemus, the Pharisee, to Jesus, the following conversation took place:

Jesus: "...*Verily, verily, I say unto thee, Except a man be born again, he cannot see the kingdom of God.*" (John 3:3, KJV)

Nicodemus: "*How can a man be born when he is old? can he enter the second time into his mother's womb, and be born?*" (John 3:4, KJV)

This was the first time anyone had spoken

about a concept such as this. Born Again? What does that mean? Nicodemus could not comprehend what Jesus was saying. Therefore, Jesus explained further:

Jesus: *"I tell you the solemn truth, unless a person is born of water and spirit, he cannot enter the kingdom of God. What is born of the flesh is flesh, and what is born of the Spirit is spirit."* (John 3:5-6, NET)

Still, Nicodemus could not understand. And it was at this point that Jesus made the comment in our opening verse:

Jesus: *"Do not be amazed that I said to you, 'You must all be born from above.'* ***The wind blows wherever it will, and you hear the sound it makes, but do not know where it comes from and where it is going. So it is with everyone who is born of the Spirit."*** (John 3:7-8, NET)

You see, when the wind blows, you can see its effects. For instance, you can hear the sound that it makes. You can see it causing waves on the sea or blowing something down the road or swaying the branches and leaves of a tree. BUT, you cannot see it. You cannot see what it looks like. You cannot determine its origin or its destination. You just see it at work. And this is exactly how it is with someone who is born again and born of the Spirit. Nicodemus was trying to understand how a person's life could be so transformed to the extent that he or she would then become qualified to enter into heaven.

The simple answer is that just as the details of the true nature of the wind are unknown to man, you cannot understand the spiritual details of how the Spirit does its work in a man. So, you would see that someone who was once a fornicator would all of a sudden abandon his sin and never return to it. A thief, who has become born of the Spirit, would suddenly stop stealing... and so on. We can only see the impact and the power, we cannot say how it is that the Spirit does His mighty work in our lives.

The lesson for you this morning is that if you believe in God and you have given your life to Him, you should not worry about the details. He will cause the divine changes you desire to manifest in your life. Also, if you are waiting on God for a miracle, it is not for you to worry about what steps God would take in order to cause that miracle to happen in your life. Only believe and the Spirit of God will get it done for you.

So, do you want to experience the power of God in your life? Are you ready to feel the impact of God's spirit in the areas of your life that need it? Do you want to make heaven? If yes, get yourself ready!

TODAY'S PRAYERS

1. This morning, O Lord, I rededicate my life to You, in the name of Jesus.

2. This morning, O Lord, I ask that You fill me afresh with Your precious Holy Spirit, in the name of Jesus.

3. O my God, from today, I accept that what You want me to know is what I will know and what You do not wish for me to know, I do not want to know, in the name of Jesus.

4. My God, in the same manner that the wind blows and I can feel it on my body, hear its sound and see its impact on my environment, let Your precious Holy Spirit invade my life and change me from whatever I am now to whatever You want me to be. Let these changes carry sufficient power to see me to the successful end of my race on this earth, in the name of Jesus.

5. My Lord and my God, I want to make heaven. Therefore, according to Your word, since I am born again and since I am born of

water and of the Spirit, let Your Holy Spirit within me always witness unto me about my eternal place in Your kingdom so that my heart can be at peace, in the name of Jesus.

6.   O Lord my God, this is my need at this point in time: _____ (mention your need). By any means necessary, let Your Holy Spirit cause this need to be met in my life, in the name of Jesus.

7.   Thank You Most High God for answering my prayers, in Jesus' mighty name, amen.

If you have the need and the time, please feel free to add more prayers at this point.

Blessing: May the mysteries of the Christian faith work to produce great results in your life, in the name of Jesus.

DAY 18

BE GOOD,
LEAVE SOMETHING

"A good man leaveth an inheritance to his children's children: and the wealth of the sinner is laid up for the just."
— Proverbs 13:22 (KJV)

DAILY EXHORTATION

Another version of our opening scripture says *"If you obey God, you will have something to leave your grandchildren. If you don't obey God, those who live right will get what you leave."* Profound stuff! Whether you are holy or not, you will leave something behind but who gets to keep what you leave behind, depends on the quality of your spiritual life. It is true that the descendants of many evil people actually inherit things from their wicked parents or ancestors but sooner or later, as history as shown over and over again, they usually lose that inheritance to the just. The world is a tough place. These days, in many countries of the world, it is tough to get good jobs. Some of those who have good jobs have to put up with all kinds of injustices and irrational demands just to keep those jobs. And many other people make heavy, personal sacrifices for the sake of their jobs which they are likely to regret at some point in their lives. For some though, they have good careers and have managed to achieve work-life balance.

That said, one of the greatest ways to protect your children and descendants from the vicissitudes of life is to live a clean, righteous life and to leave them a functional inheritance for them. An inheritance means that your children do not have to suffer what you suffered. It means they do not have to endure what you endured. It means they do not have to start from zero like you probably did. It means that they can get the best education possible for the attainment of their dreams. It means they can get to work on their dreams earlier in life so that they have sufficient time to achieve them. It means they can have their own families earlier in life because they have no financial fear. It means that they do not have to compromise their faith for a job, a promotion or a contract. They can say "No" to irrational demands and care less about the consequences.

An inheritance means your descendants will have the foundation required to propagate your good name and legacy from generation to generation to the glory of God. An inheritance from a righteous father or mother is a blessing.

Do you want to leave an inheritance for your children? Do you want to ensure that what you have worked for stays in your family line? If yes, get yourself ready!

TODAY'S PRAYERS

1. Heavenly Father, I want to leave an inheritance for my children and my descendants. Help me, in the name of Jesus.

2. El Shaddai, I do not want everything that I am working for in life to go to strangers but to my own offspring. Therefore, I confess to You all my sins and my bad habits and I ask You to forgive me. Give me the grace to forsake these sins and to never return to them, in the name of Jesus.

3. Messiah, through the presence of Your Holy Spirit in my life, give me the grace that will work with my will so that I can live a righteous life and always be in good standing before You, in the name of Jesus.

4. My Father, bless the work of my hand. By Your grace and mercy, let the returns and the profit on my labor be multiplied so that I can accumulate wealth in this life, in the

name of Jesus.

5. Lord, keep me on the straight and narrow path so that I can also accumulate wealth of character and of a good name which I can pass on to my children, in the name of Jesus.

6. Merciful God, when my time comes and I pass on my good name, my good character, the chronicles of my faith and my earthly wealth to my children, let them use them in every way to fulfill the destiny that You have given them to Your glory, in the name of Jesus.

7. Thank You Everlasting Father for answering my prayers, in Jesus' mighty name, amen.

If you have the need and the time, please feel free to add more prayers at this point.

Blessing: May you live a righteous and a wealthy life so that you can leave a goodly inheritance for your descendants, in the name of Jesus.

DAY 19

BEHAVE YOURSELF, CHANGE YOUR DESTINY

"But Sarah noticed the son of Hagar the Egyptian—the son whom Hagar had borne to Abraham—mocking. So she said to Abraham, Banish that slave woman and her son, for the son of that slave woman will not be an heir along with my son Isaac!'" — Genesis 21:9-10 (NET)

DAILY EXHORTATION

At a point in her life, because of her advanced age, Sarah felt that having her own son was out of the question. So, she arranged for Abraham, her husband, to become a father through her servant, Hagar. All agreed and Hagar became pregnant. However, as soon as Hagar became pregnant, she began to lose her respect for her employer, Sarah. As a result, Sarah unleashed terror on her and she ran away. But, while she was roaming about in the desert, an angel appeared to her and essentially told her to return to her master but to become humble and submissive. The angel also said the following about the child she was pregnant with:

Genesis 16:11-12 (NLT) *"You are now pregnant and will give birth to a son. You are to name him Ishmael (which means 'God hears'), for the Lord has heard your cry of distress. This son of yours will be a wild man, as untamed as a wild donkey! He will raise his fist against everyone, and everyone will be against him. Yes, he will live in open hostility against all his relatives."*

Please understand that this prophecy was not just about the baby itself but about the fate of all of his descendants. In any case, Hagar returned to Sarah and became submissive as the angel told her. In time, she gave birth to her baby and called him, Ishmael. Many years later, through Jehovah's miraculous intervention, a very old Sarah also gave birth to her own son, Isaac.

Then, the first evidence of the angel's prophecy began to manifest. According to our opening scripture, Ishmael began to "mock" Isaac. And Sarah noticed it. The word "mock" here essentially means "bully". Ishmael was bullying the child of destiny. He was bullying what was essentially a miracle. He was bullying

God's promised child. Ishmael's negative destiny had started to manifest for evil. Therefore, he and his mother were banished! Here's what happened after Abraham died:

Genesis 25:5-6 (NET) "***Everything he owned Abraham left to his son Isaac.*** *But while he was still alive, Abraham gave gifts to the sons of his concubines and sent them off to the east, away from his son Isaac.*"

And here is what became of Ishmael and his own descendants:

Genesis 25:17-18 (NET) "*Ishmael lived for 137 years. Then he breathed his last and joined his ancestors in death. Ishmael's descendants occupied the region from Havilah to Shur, which is east of Egypt in the direction of Asshur.* **There they lived in open hostility toward all their relatives.**"

Here are the lessons to learn from today's devotional:

1. Always Behave Yourself: The same kind of negative behavior that that ushered Ishmael's mother out of his father's house was what he too began to exhibit. You have to know who you are and understand the circumstance in which you have found yourself. There are ways to behave that will cause you to achieve breakthrough. There's something called "stooping to conquer". That is, using strategic humility to get what you want. But it appears Ishmael knew nothing about that. How can you be bullying a miracle? How can you bully a child that was born to a woman who was almost 100 years old? Many people who are at the top of their game today in academics, ministry, politics, the world of business, etc. had to go through a period of strategic humility so that they could get whatever they wanted. Again, Ishmael was unaware of this and so he got himself and his mother banished. And when his father died, he got no inheritance but only a handful of gifts. Too bad.

2. A Negative Destiny Can Be Changed: The Bible tells us about the story of Jabez whose life was going nowhere he liked. He cried out to the Lord to bless him and enlarge his coast and the Lord did so. The Bible also tells us about the story of king Hezekiah, who was sick and had been told to put his house in order as he would certainly die in a few days. However, he cried out to God. God heard his cry and his life was extended by 15 years. These examples [there are more in the Bible] show that you should not accept whatever negativity has been placed before you. "*You will become a wild man, like an* *untamed donkey, will fight everyone, be hostile to everyone, etc.*" Both Hagar and Ishmael could have said "*O God, we do not desire this kind of life. Change our story!*" But they did not and until this very day, the descendants of Ishmael are the most hostile people in the whole world. In your case, like Hezekiah and Jabez, you can ask God to change your story.

Are you ready this morning to imbibe strategic humility into your life? Have you been told that you will not end up well or something along those lines? Do you want to alter the trajectory of your life from negativity to glory? Do you want to fulfill a glorious destiny and lay a solid foundation for your descendants? If yes, get yourself ready!

TODAY'S PRAYERS

1. Holy One of Israel, I have only one life to live. Help me so that I do not mess it up, in the name of Jesus.

2. Father, unleash Your Holy Spirit into my life today. Let Him fill up my spirit, soul and body. Let Him invade my mind and have access to my thoughts, emotions and behavior, in the name of Jesus.

3. Heavenly Father, let any ignorance that I have about the circumstances of my life fade away. Let me become fully aware of the nuances of my life so that I can prepare myself to always do the right thing, in the name of Jesus.

4. This morning, O Lord, I ask for the gift of strategic humility. Give me the grace to learn how to stoop to conquer in order to achieve the breakthrough that I need, in the name of Jesus.

5. Messiah, if anything evil has been prophesied concerning my life and if anyone has spoken negativity concerning my future, have mercy on me Lord and let the evil prophecies and the negativity be nullified and come to nothing, in the name of Jesus.

6. My God, let the exact opposite of any evil prophecy spoken against me come to pass in my life. Let me live a long, healthy life filled with positivity and breakthroughs, which I will enjoy and also pass on to my descendants to Your glory, in the name of Jesus.

7. Thank You Rock of Ages for answering my prayers, in Jesus' mighty name, amen.

If you have the need and the time, please feel free to add more prayers at this point.

Blessing: As you begin to implement strategic humility in your life and as you seek to please God all your days, you will be amazed at the great and mighty blessings of spirit, soul and body that He will release into your life, in the name of Jesus.

DAY 20

BETTER THAN PERFUME

"A good reputation is better than precious perfume; likewise, the day of one's death is better than the day of one's birth."
— Ecclesiastes 7:1 (NET)

DAILY EXHORTATION

Precious perfume and the day of one's birth have one thing in common—which is that you most likely played no part in their existence. When you need perfume, you simply go to a shop and purchase it. Then, when you wear it, people praise you for how nice you smell. BUT, you did not invent the perfume, you simply bought it and used it. Ditto your birthday. Your parents, either planned or unplanned, met together and then you were born. All the credit for that goes to them and not to you.

On the other hand, a good reputation and what you are on the day that you die are all about **YOU**. It takes a lot of effort to craft a good reputation for oneself. Your reputation is about what people know about you from what they see about you. What you show to the world usually comes from your upbringing and your own personal grooming. For example, in Proverbs 22:6 (KJV), the Bible says "*Train up a child in the way he should go: and when he is old, he will not depart from it.*" This means that your good reputation reflects the work of your parents and also your personal ability to receive and stick to the training they have given to you. The Bible also says in Philippians 4:8 (NET) "*Finally, brothers and sisters, whatever is true, whatever is worthy of respect, whatever is just, whatever is pure, whatever is lovely, whatever is commendable, if something is excellent or praiseworthy, think about these things.*" Therefore, if people see that you are a truthful person, a person worthy of respect, a just person, someone who is pure in speech and conduct, a lovely person, someone who does commendable things, an excellent and a praiseworthy person, it is because you personally decided to follow the word of God. You personally decided to think as the Bible says to think which then manifests in your behavior, which they can see.

Regarding the day of your death, unlike your birthday when you played no part and had no memory of anything, as a believer, it should be a powerful day of walking down the divine memory lane. It should be a day when you would say "*I have fought a good fight, I have finished my course, I have kept the faith*" (2 Timothy 4:7, KJV). It should be a day of celebrating the fact that you gave your life to Jesus, you served in His vineyard, you are filled with His Holy Spirit, you followed peace with all men as much as you could, a day to look back at the lives that you touched and helped build up, a day to look back at the spouse and the children or other descendants you are leaving behind whom you have filled to the brim with God's word and way, a day to remember how you lived according to the word and the will of God, a day to reach the peak of destiny fulfillment and a day to fully expect to wake up within the pearly gates of heaven on high.

These are some of the reasons why our opening scripture says that a good reputation and the day of one's death are better than precious perfume or one's birthday. Are you ready to begin working on or to fortify your reputation? Are you ready to ensure that the day of your death is a day of joy for you? If yes, get yourself ready!

TODAY'S PRAYERS

1. Almighty God, I desire a good reputation. Come to my aid, in the name of Jesus.

2. Most High God, I want the day of my death to be better than the day of my birth. Help me, in the name of Jesus.

3. O God, let the good life training that I received from my parents or indeed from any other person, which was based on Your word, begin now to guide my thoughts, my words and my deeds, in the name of Jesus.

4. My Father, take my thoughts, my words and my behavior from whatever they are now and make them true, make them worthy of respect, make them just, make them pure, make them lovely, make them commendable, make them excellent and make them praiseworthy. Let people see the manifestation of all these in my life so that my reputation can become good and solid to Your glory, in the name of Jesus.

5. Rock of Ages, let me read Your word and let me do it. Let my life and whatever emanates from it be pleasing unto You. Let my relationships with my family and with other people be pleasing to You. Let my thoughts and my words be pleasing to You. Let the works of my hands be pleasing to You. Let everything concerning me be pleasing to You so that on the day of my death, I too can say

"I have fought a good fight, I have finished my course, I have kept the faith", in the name of Jesus.

6. Messiah, by Your grace and mercy, give me a good reputation on this earth and let the day of my death be indeed better than the day of my birth, in the name of Jesus.

7. Thank You Father God for answering my prayers, in Jesus' mighty name, amen.

If you have the need and the time, please feel free to add more prayers at this point.

Blessing: As you listen to and do the will of God, may He give you a good name and cause the day of your death to be better than the day that you were born, in the name of Jesus.

DAY 21

THE CAMEL
AND THE NEEDLE

"Again I say, it is easier for a camel to go through the eye of a needle than for a rich person to enter into the kingdom of God."
— Matthew 19:24 (NET)

DAILY EXHORTATION

As you know, most of the people who top the charts of the richest people in the world are either atheists or people who believe in strange religions. Even king Solomon, who was so wise, so rich and so powerful, because of his involvement in idol worship through his many wives, has a questionable eternal residence. This is why our opening scripture says that "*it is easier for a camel to go through the eye of a needle than for a rich person to enter into the kingdom of God.*"

However, David, Solomon's father, who was also rich and powerful, is very certainly in heaven right now. Further, our Lord Jesus Christ, who spoke the words in our opening scripture did not live in a palace BUT he never lacked for anything. Jesus had everything He wanted. How do we know this? Because the Bible provides us with a glimpse into how His ministry was funded. Let's take a quick look at this in scripture:

Luke 8:3 (NLT) "*Soon afterward Jesus began a tour of the nearby towns and villages, preaching and announcing the Good News about the Kingdom of God. He took his twelve disciples with him, along with some women who had been cured of evil spirits and diseases. **Among them were Mary Magdalene, from whom he had cast out seven demons; Joanna, the wife of Chuza, Herod's business manager; Susanna; and many others who were contributing from their own resources to support Jesus and his disciples.***"

Joanna was the wife of Chuza. Chuza was king Herod's business manager. Think about the nations of the world that have kings and queens. Consider how wealthy these people are and then consider how wealthy any single individual managing their wealth would be. The wife of such a wealthy man [who would be a multimillionaire in today's terms] was a sponsor of Christ's earthly ministry.

Jesus also had other wealthy disciples such as Joseph of Arimathea. In addition, Jesus could by

Himself create money out of nothing as He demonstrated in Matthew 17:24–27. Further, the devil offered to give Jesus the whole world and all of its kingdoms but Jesus turned it down. In Luke 9:3, He sent out His disciples and told them specifically not to take anything with them—no walking stick, no bag, no bread, no money, no extra clothing. Then in Luke 22:35, He asked them "*When I sent you without purse, bag or sandals, did you lack anything?*" They all answered "Nothing". Why? Because provision was made for them by a God who owns and has everything!

From the examples of David and of Jesus [and there many others in the Bible], you will see that what separates rich men who go to heaven from those that do not is an unwavering adherence to the word of God and a willingness to always use your resources to do good. The Bible refers to money as a defense. So, we all need it. But before it comes and while it is with you, you must always subdue yourself under the will of God. You must command yourself to remember that everything belongs to God and that all flesh will someday give account of their lives to Him.

Also, the Bible is filled with all kinds of calls to give to all kinds of people such as orphans, strangers, the poor, ministers of God, etc. You must research these kinds of people and purposes and commit yourself to giving of your resources to them on a regular basis. This way you will be like David, rich and powerful, yet holy until the end.

Do you want to be rich but escape the lot of Solomon and others like him? Do you want to be like David—rich, powerful and holy? If yes, today is your day. Get yourself ready!

TODAY'S PRAYERS

1. O Lord my God, I want to be wealthy and yet enter into Your Kingdom. Come to my aid, in the name of Jesus.

2. Great Redeemer, I want to be like David who was rich, powerful and yet remained humble and committed to You until the end of his days. Help me, in the name of Jesus.

3. My Lord and my God, from today, let me develop an unwavering adherence to Your word, in the name of Jesus.

4. Father, cause me to subdue myself under Your will so that I will always see You as the beginning and the end of everything, in the name of Jesus.

5. Eternal King, let me develop a thirst to give

my wealth purpose. Let me study Your word in order to find out the purposes of wealth and let me use the wealth you have given and will give me to fulfill those purposes for the benefit of others and to Your glory, in the name of Jesus.

6. Alpha and Omega, let me never forget that I will one day give an account of how I am living my life. By reason of this, regardless of how much money I accumulate in my life, let me never leave the narrow and straight path of righteousness so that, at the end of the day, I can enter into Your eternal Kingdom, in the name of Jesus.

7. Thank You Most High God for answering my prayers, in Jesus' mighty name, amen.

If you have the need and the time, please feel free to add more prayers at this point.

Blessing: May you never miss your way in life because of riches. May your eyes be stayed on heaven and on God, in the name of Jesus.

DAY 22

WHAT YOUR NEIGHBOR LOST THAT YOU FOUND

"When you see your neighbor's ox or sheep going astray, do not ignore it; you must return it without fail to your neighbor... You shall do the same to his donkey, his clothes, or anything else your neighbor has lost and you have found; you must not refuse to get involved."
— Deuteronomy 22:1,3 (NET)

DAILY EXHORTATION

When it comes to neighbors, if you want to live in peace, it's always best to mind your own business. BUT, the Bible says *"Love your neighbor as yourself."* (Mark 12:31). Many believers wonder how exactly one should love one's neighbor as oneself. Our opening scripture for today provides us with a powerful way to do that. Essentially, it says that if you see your neighbor's ox or sheep going astray, you should do your best to return the ox or the sheep to him or her. The passage goes beyond things which have gone astray to also include things which have gotten lost. Thus, if you happen to find your neighbor's lost donkey or lost clothes, you should return them to him or her. Then, it adds that "*if you find anything else your neighbor has lost and you have found*" you should also return it to him or her.

If you are a Christian eager to love your neighbor as yourself, the word "anything" there should excite you. Now, there are a number of things you have to consider:

1. This passage refers to things belonging to your neighbor that went astray or got lost and that you saw going astray or you found. This places a limit on how far you should go in this regard. This means that you cannot be yoked with responsibilities for things that you did not see or that you did not find. Neither should you go looking for things which belong to your neighbor that did not go astray or are not missing.

2. These days, neighbors do not usually have things that go astray like Oxen, sheep or donkeys. Some neighbors have pets like dogs and cats. So, in this case, by all means, if you find a pet that has gone astray, you can return them to your neighbors. However, since our opening scripture

says you should return "*anything else*", you should consider that one thing neighbors usually have and which could go astray or get lost is a family member such as a spouse, a son or a daughter.

There are two dimensions to this. In the ordinary dimension, your neighbor's little son or daughter could get lost. If you find such a child, you can do your part and return him or her to your neighbor. BUT, there is also the spiritual dimension. In this case, your neighbor's spouse or child has spiritually gone astray or is lost. It could be that you saw your neighbor's spouse [who was previously a good Christian] drinking themselves to stupor or in an extramarital affair. Or you saw your neighbor's son in a gang or using hard drugs at some corner somewhere and their daughter prostituting herself. What you have seen is your neighbors "thing" gone astray or gone missing. In this case, how do you play your part in returning your neighbor's thing home? It depends on whether or not your neighbor knows and whether or not he or she is a believer.

If your neighbor does not know about his / her spouse's or child's situation, you can return that spouse or that child through prayer in your own closet. This means that despite the issues of your own life, you will make out time to pray to the Lord to bring that spouse, boy or girl back to his or her senses. This is line with the word of

God in 1 Timothy 2:1 (NET) which says "... *I urge that requests, prayers, intercessions, and thanks be offered on behalf of all people*".

If your neighbor knows about the situation of his / her spouse or child and is also a believer, you can offer to pray together regarding the situation. This is line with the word of God in Matthew 18:19 (NET) which says "*Again, I tell you the truth, if two of you on earth agree about whatever you ask, my Father in heaven will do it for you.*" This is a powerful way to return anything that belongs to your neighbor which went astray or was lost but you saw or found.

So, with what you have learned today, are you ready to play your part as a neighbor? Are you ready to practically love your neighbor as yourself? If yes, get yourself ready!

TODAY'S PRAYERS

1. Jehovah, I want to live in accordance with Your word. I want to love my neighbor as myself. Help me, in the name of Jesus.

2. Holy Father, make me come alive to my responsibilities as a neighbor and teach me all the ways through which I can demonstrate love to my neighbor and in so doing, fulfill your divine commandment, in the name of

Jesus.

3. From today, Father, let me become conscious of the fact that if anything belonging to my neighbor goes astray or gets missing and I see that thing or find it, it is my responsibility to return it to my neighbor or call his or her notice to it, in the name of Jesus.

4. My God, even though I want to show love to my neighbor, let me always respect myself. Do not let me go about looking for things which belong to my neighbor but which have not gone astray and are not missing, in the name of Jesus.

5. My God, if ever the spouse, child or relative of my neighbor goes astray or becomes lost to the world but they do not know about it and I find out, let the consciousness be in me to enter into my closet to pray for the redemption of that person. Whenever I do this, O Lord, have mercy on my neighbor and answer my prayer of intercession for him or her, in the name of Jesus.

6. Merciful God, if ever the spouse, child or relative of my neighbor goes astray or is lost to the world and they know about it, touch that neighbor's heart so that we can both come to You in prayer concerning their loved

one. Whenever this happens, O Lord, give ear to our prayers and let the prodigal loved one return home and forsake their erroneous ways, in the name of Jesus.

7. Thank You Everlasting Father for answering my prayers, in Jesus' mighty name, amen.

If you have the need and the time, please feel free to add more prayers at this point.

Blessing: As you have consciously decided to obey God and show practical love to your neighbor, may God reward you in ways you can never imagine, in the name of Jesus.

DAY 23

PROTECTION FROM MISFORTUNE

"Surely, no one knows his appointed time! Like fish that are caught in a deadly net, and like birds that are caught in a snare— just like them, all people are ensnared at an unfortunate time that falls upon them suddenly." — Ecclesiastes 9:12 (NET)

DAILY EXHORTATION

Misfortune is a real thing. It is an ill wind blowing about with no target. Anyone could be its victim. This is why you will see someone who just left his home 10 minutes ago, killed in a car crash. Or someone you saw just yesterday but overnight was shot by armed robbers and is now paralyzed. Or someone who went for a jog but was maimed by a terrorist 30 minutes later.

Misfortune is out there everyday and it will always find people to visit. As a full believer in Christ, you should know that your case is different. If you know the child of whom you are and the fact that God has given you a divine assignment on the earth, you will understand that He has also made special provisions for your safety and well-being.

Insofar as you have faith in God, even if the the rest of the world are caught in the deadly net or snare of misfortune, you will be preserved.

Before we pray, let's examine a number of scriptures dedicated to your protection against misfortune and the agents of misfortune:

Romans 8:31 (KJV) "*What shall we then say to these things? If God be for us, who can be against us?*"

Philippians 4:6-7 (NET) "*Do not be anxious about anything. Instead, in every situation, through prayer and petition with thanksgiving, tell your requests to God. And the peace of God that surpasses all understanding will guard your hearts and minds in Christ Jesus.*"

2 Timothy 1:7 (KJV) "*For God hath not given us the spirit of fear; but of power, and of love, and of a sound mind.*"

Numbers 23:23 (NET) "*For there is no spell against Jacob, nor is there any divination against Israel. At this time it must be said of Jacob and of Israel, 'Look at what God has done!'*"

Isaiah 54:17 (KJV) "*No weapon that is formed against thee shall prosper; and every tongue that shall rise against thee in judgment thou shalt condemn. This is the heritage of the servants of the LORD, and their righteousness is of me, saith the LORD.*"

Psalm 31:4 (GNT) "*Keep me safe from the trap that has been set for me; shelter me from danger.*"

Psalm 140:4 (NET) "*O LORD, shelter me from the power of the wicked! Protect me from violent men, who plan to knock me over.*"

Psalm 138:7 (NET) "*Even when I must walk in the midst of danger, you revive me. You oppose my angry enemies, and your right hand delivers me.*"

Isaiah 41:10 (NET) "*Don't be afraid, for I am with you! Don't be frightened, for I am your God! I strengthen you—yes, I help you—yes, I uphold you with my saving right hand!*"

As you can see, even though misfortune is real, there is provision for protection of believers from this negative phenomenon. As you pray this morning's prayers, as long as you believe in God and in His word, you will receive divine protection from any form of misfortune. By reason of this, where others may be living their lives in fear, you will be filled with divine confidence powered by the knowledge which you have that God has got your back. Get yourself ready!

TODAY'S PRAYERS

1. Since God is for me, no one or nothing can be against me. Therefore, I am not a candidate of misfortune, in the name of Jesus.

2. O Lord my God, according to Your word, every day of my life, uphold me with Your saving right hand so that I do not fall victim to calamity, in the name of Jesus.

3. According to the word of the Lord, no weapon formed against me shall prosper. Therefore, I command any deadly net assigned to catch me to burn to ashes, in the name of Jesus.

4. According to the word of the Lord, I have been sheltered from the power of the wicked. Therefore, any snare manufactured against my destiny shall be utterly destroyed, in the name of Jesus.

5. By the power in the Blood of Jesus, I come against any demonic spell or any divination

assigned against this day. I decree that I am not your candidate. Therefore, I command you to come to nothing and to have no effect upon my life, in the name of Jesus.

6.   I decree and declare that because I am a child of the Most High God, sudden destruction will never be my lot. I have no fear because God has given me a sound mind. No evil shall befall me and I will spend my days executing the divine agenda that the Almighty has crafted for me, in the name of Jesus.

7.   Thank You Father God for answering my prayers, in Jesus' mighty name, amen.

If you have the need and the time, please feel free to add more prayers at this point.

Blessing: May the hand of God never leave you so that evil will never befall you, in the name of Jesus.

DAY 24

UNBELIEVABLE POWER

"When I look up at the heavens, which your fingers made, and see the moon and the stars, which you set in place, Of what importance is the human race, that you should notice them? Of what importance is mankind, that you should pay attention to them, and make them a little less than the heavenly beings? You grant mankind honor and majesty; you appoint them to rule over your creation; you have placed everything under their authority, including all the sheep and cattle, as well as the wild animals, the birds in the sky, the fish in the sea and everything that moves through the currents of the seas. O Lord, our Lord, how magnificent is your reputation throughout the earth!"
— Psalm 8:3-9 (NET)

DAILY EXHORTATION

You are capable of doing much more than you are doing right now! But do you know that? Do you know that on your head right now is a crown of honor, glory and majesty? Are you using this crown? Do you know what it is for?

When God created you, He innately endowed you with power to rule over everything He created. He gave you the authority to control both everything that you see and do not see around you. Some people are afraid of most animals and keep away from them. But do you know that there are some people who have mastered the taming all kinds of animals? There are people who—with only natural skills—have tamed lions, tigers and all sorts of wild animals. That they are doing it confirms our opening scripture regarding the power of human beings over creation. There are also people who go to the heights and the depths of the earth to find plants and animals which they then take into laboratories in order to create all kinds of products for the benefit of mankind. All plants, animals and inanimate objects created by God have some kind of health benefit, industrial use or some other thing attached to them.

If you take time to think about the earth and your role in it, you too will find that nothing is out of your reach. It is possible that God has ordained you to discover something that will benefit mankind and in so doing become a source of breakthrough for you. But to do this, you have to participate. You have to acknowledge the divine power that God has placed in your life. You must embrace your role as a ruler and as a person of authority on this earth and then go ahead and use it to your own benefit.

If you do this, nature will respond because it is subservient to you and it reveal its secrets to you. Many have done this and they are the better for it. Hopefully, it will be your turn today.

TODAY'S PRAYERS

1. Almighty God, the Great I Am, I acknowledge the crown of honor, glory and majesty that You have placed on my head. I want to start using it from today. Help me, in the name of Jesus.

2. Mighty Father, according to Your word, I acknowledge that You have made me a ruler over everything that You have created on earth. From today, I want to start ruling. Come to my aid, in the name of Jesus.

3. King of kings, I acknowledge that You have

placed all the works of Your hand under my authority. I want to begin to use my authority. Therefore, I ask that You come to my aid, in the name of Jesus.

4. My Lord and my God, let my awareness be opened so that I can clearly see myself within the context of Your creation. From today, let me begin to see myself as Your representative on this earth. Let me begin to see very clearly that all of nature was created for my use in order for me to do what I want with them, in the name of Jesus.

5. Father, I know that other people have embraced their role as rulers on this earth. They have embraced animals, plants and other objects that You created and their lives have been made better by this. I also ask that You shall cause nature to reveal its secrets to me so that I can discover something of value for the benefit of mankind, in the name of Jesus.

6. By virtue of the authority that I have as a ruler on the earth, O Lord, let nature— animals, plants and other objects—become a source of breakthrough for me throughout my time in this world, in the name of Jesus.

7. Thank You Father for answering my prayers,

in Jesus' mighty name, amen.

If you have the need and the time, please feel free to add more prayers at this point.

Blessing: As you embrace your role as a ruler on the earth, may God bless you with the secrets nature has to offer, in the name of Jesus.

DAY 25
HELP SHOULD NOT EQUAL PARALYSIS

"Rebekah's nurse Deborah died and was buried under the oak tree outside Bethel. So Jacob called it the Tree of Crying."
— Genesis 35:8 (GWT)

DAILY EXHORTATION

When Rebekah left the house of her parents in order to move to the house of Isaac, her husband, she did not go alone. The Bible tells us the following about the people who went with her:

Genesis 24:59 (KJV) "*And they sent away Rebekah their sister, and her nurse, and Abraham's servant, and his men.*"

Genesis 24:61 (NET) "*Then Rebekah and her female servants mounted the camels and rode away with the man. So Abraham's servant took Rebekah and left.*"

Rebekah was accompanied by her nurse as

well as a number of female servants. Expectedly, their purpose was to help with her duties as a wife and perhaps help take care of her children whenever she began having them.

Now, even today, servants are still an important part of many homes all over the world. These servants go by all kinds of titles such as domestic, domestic worker, house help, maid, housekeeper, etc. They do all kinds of things. They clean, rearrange, go grocery shopping, cook, some take the kids to school and pick them up, etc. But do you know that in many homes where house helps are employed, many of the family members do not know how to do anything? They do not know how to cook, how to clean or how to do anything at all! This is what is called **help paralysis**. That is, when you become functionally paralyzed because someone else is doing everything for you. Further, many employers of domestics mistreat them to such an extent that many of them quit or run away after inflicting heavy damages on the house or stealing something valuable.

If you have a house help working for you or you plan to have one, today's devotional would be of help to you. You see, despite the presence of a nurse and many female servants, all the members of Isaac's household were very hands-on. It appears as if, even though they had help, the members of Isaac's household had determined to be independent and to be useful to themselves. Let's take a look at some scriptures which prove this:

Genesis 25:29-30,34 (NET) "***Now Jacob cooked some stew,*** *and when Esau came in from the open fields, he was famished. So Esau said to Jacob, 'Feed me some of the red stuff—yes, this red stuff—because I'm starving!' ...* ***Then Jacob gave Esau some bread and lentil stew****; Esau ate and drank …*"

Genesis 27:1-4 (NET) "*When Isaac was old and his eyes were so weak that he was almost blind, he called his older son Esau and said to him, 'My son!' 'Here I am!' Esau replied. Isaac said, 'Since I am so old, I could die at any time. Therefore, take your weapons—your quiver and your bow—and go out into the open fields and hunt down some wild game for me.* ***Then prepare for me some tasty food, the kind I love, and bring it to me. Then I will eat it so that I may bless you before I die.***'"

Genesis 27:6-9, (NET) "*Rebekah said to her son Jacob, 'Look, I overheard your father tell your brother Esau, 'Bring me some wild game and prepare for me some tasty food. Then I will eat it and bless you in the presence of the Lord before I die.' Now then, my son, do exactly* *what I tell you! Go to the flock and get me two of the best young goats.* **I'll prepare them in a tasty way for your father, just the way he loves them... So he went and got the goats and brought them to his mother. She prepared some tasty food, just the way his father loved it.**"

As you can see, even with the nurse and the domestic servants, the household of Isaac did not have help paralysis. Rebekah knew how to cook. Her sons—Esau and Jacob—despite their careers, also knew how to cook. In addition, the household of Isaac did not mistreat their workers and as a result, they stayed with them till the very end. You can find the evidence for this in the scripture below which also happens to be our opening scripture:

Genesis 35:8 (GWT) "*Rebekah's nurse Deborah died and was buried under the oak tree outside Bethel.* **So Jacob called it the Tree of Crying.**"

Remember the nurse that went with Rebekah to her new husband's house? This is that same nurse. Her name was Deborah. She spent so many years in the house of Isaac and was there until she died. In fact, when she died, the entire family was so moved that they named the tree under which they buried her "the Tree of Crying"! They were weeping and crying because their maid died! Can you imagine that?

The household of Isaac has today given you a template to follow when you have people working for you. Having people working for you should not lead to the functional paralysis of members of your family. Rather, it should provide you with an avenue to learn — how to cook, how to clean, how to do all kinds of things. Having workers should also be an opportunity for you to demonstrate the love of God to such an extent that those workers will never of their own volition seek to run away or leave you. Do you want something like this? Do you want to enjoy this wonderful thing that Isaac and his family had going? If yes, get yourself ready!

TODAY'S PRAYERS

1. Lord God Almighty, You have blessed me to the extent that I now have people working for me. I give you thanks and praises for this important milestone in my life, in the name of Jesus.

2. Holy One of Israel, I ask that You would let my relationship with my workers be like it was between Isaac's household and their own

workers, in the name of Jesus.

3.   My God, do not let me or any member of my family suffer from help paralysis, in the name of Jesus.

4.   Father, let the presence of workers in my home and in my place of business be an opportunity for me and my family to learn what we can for them even as they work for us, in the name of Jesus.

5.   As it was for the household of Isaac, as people work for us, let there be a transfer of essential life skills from them to us. Let the transfer of these skills make us more useful to ourselves and also to each other, in the name of Jesus.

6.   Almighty God, as it was for the household of Isaac, let the presence of workers in my house and in my place of business be an opportunity for me to show them the love of Christ. Let it be that as I show my workers practical, Biblical love, they will desire to stay with us for as long as possible in an atmosphere of godliness and love, in the name of Jesus.

7.   Thank You Father God for answering my prayers, in Jesus' mighty name, amen.

If you have the need and the time, please feel free to add more prayers at this point.

Blessing: May God let you see domestics, house helps and other kinds of workers as a blessing and as a unique opportunity to demonstrate the love of God, in the name of Jesus.

DAY 26

DON'T GET IT FROM HERE, GET IT FROM THERE

"Abraham said to his servant, the senior one in his household who was in charge of everything he had, 'Put your hand under my thigh so that I may make you solemnly promise by the Lord, the God of heaven and the God of the earth: You must not acquire a wife for my son from the daughters of the Canaanites, among whom I am living. You must go instead to my country and to my relatives to find a wife for my son Isaac.'"
— Genesis 24:2-4 (NET)

DAILY EXHORTATION

"*Make a solemn promise*" also means "*swear to me*". These are strong words. It was time for Isaac to marry. Abraham used these words to do two things — first, to express his displeasure for the citizens of Canaan, the country in which he lived and second, to express his favor toward the people of his native land. The issue here was not spirituality. Since, at the time, Abraham was the only person on earth who had a direct relationship with God, all other people regardless of location were not spiritually adequate. Most people in those days were idol worshipers. Abraham's insistence on finding a daughter-in-law from his own country (Harran or Paddan Aram) was because of the negative character of the people of Canaan.

It is true that spirituality influences behavior. As you know, the fruit of the Holy Spirit can influence us and make us loving, joyful, peaceful, patient, kind, good, faithful, gentle, and have self-control. But, some people from certain parts of the world are naturally wild or wicked whereas some other people are naturally gentle. However, as good as it may be, coming from a so-called gentle area or country without giving one's life to Christ has no benefits in the kingdom of God.

In any case, Abraham had done his character assessment of the Canaanites and he was certain that if Isaac married a native of the land, it could negatively affect the direction of his life especially with regard to the promise God had placed in their family line. So, he wanted him to swear, which the servant did. Thereafter, the servant went and he returned with Rebekah from Abraham's country whom Isaac eventually married. But, was Abraham correct in his character assessment of the Canaanites? Let's find out from scripture:

Genesis 26:34-35 (KJV) "*And Esau was forty years old when he took to wife Judith the daughter of Beeri the Hittite, and Bashemath the daughter of Elon the Hittite:* **Which were a grief of mind unto Isaac and to Rebekah.**"

Genesis 28:6-9 (NET) "*Esau saw that Isaac had blessed Jacob and sent him off to Paddan Aram to find a wife there. As he blessed him,* **Isaac commanded him, 'You must not marry a Canaanite woman.'** *Jacob obeyed his father and mother and left for Paddan Aram.* **Then Esau realized that the Canaanite women were displeasing to his father Isaac.** *So Esau went to Ishmael and married Mahalath, the sister of Nebaioth and daughter of Abraham's son Ishmael, along with the wives he already had.*"

You can see quite clearly that Abraham was right. Esau married Canaanite women and they became a source of grief and anxiety for his parents. By reason of this, when Jacob was ready to marry, Isaac repeated the words of Abraham, his father, and told Jacob his son to go their native land, Harran or Paddan Aram in order to find a wife.

The lesson for you to learn here is two-fold:

1. Your Character is the most important asset that you have. Your character will ultimately determine your reputation for better or for worse. Your character can also influence other members of your family and as such determine the reputation of your entire family just as it determined the reputation of Canaan and that of the citizens of Paddan Aram. If the son of a man as wealthy as Isaac had married a Canaanite, it would have been great for her family and her people. But that opportunity went elsewhere. In the same manner, good character can cause opportunities to come to you and the members of your household.

2. Whenever you want to do something major, before you do that thing, like Abraham did, include character assessment in your calculations. Abraham was super-aware of his environment. He was careful about the direction of his family line because of the promise that had been deposited in it by God. He knew Canaanites could corrupt their inheritance. So, he avoided marriage with them. He did business with them, he showed them love, he was a wonderful friend to them BUT he did not take the relationship as far as marriage to avoid trouble. You also have to learn from this. Whenever you want to do something like a marriage or an important business venture, do a thorough character assessment. And now that salvation is free to all mankind, you should also do a spiritual assessment. What is the history of this person? What is their behavior in good times or in bad? How do the people of this person behave? Are these people believers? etc. Esau did not do any of this. He married not one but two Canaanites and there was trouble. Do not be like Esau so that you will not live your days in regret, trying to correct your errors. Do the right thing from the beginning.

So, do you need God's grace to help you with all of this? If yes, get yourself ready!

TODAY'S PRAYERS

1. Holy Spirit of the living God, this morning, do Your work in my life. Cause my life to bear Your fruit. Let this fruit affect my character for good, in the name of Jesus.

2. My God, let my character, which has been affected by Your Holy Spirit, receive enough power to broadcast Your values to my family

members and any other person around me. Let this divine broadcast affect their lives and change their character for good, in the name of Jesus.

3. O Lord, let my good character and the good character of the people around me create a positive reputation for us all. And let this reputation become a divine agent which will attract human favor to each and everyone of us, in the name of Jesus.

4. Everlasting God, anytime I am about to do anything major in life, let me hear the wise words of Abraham. Let me also hear the wise words of Isaac speaking to me. "*Do not choose from Canaan*", in the name of Jesus.

5. Abba Father, let me always carry out a thorough character assessment of anyone or persons that I want to do anything major with so that I do not live the rest of my life in regret or trying to correct my errors, in the name of Jesus.

6. Finally Lord, I ask, let Your Holy Spirit guide me in all my decisions. Through His divine insight, let me always make the right decision so I can have positive outcomes concerning the matters of my life, in the name of Jesus.

7.   Thank You Father for answering my prayers, in Jesus' mighty name, amen.

If you have the need and the time, please feel free to add more prayers at this point.

Blessing: May you never choose from Canaan. May God guide you at all times to make the right decisions for your life, in the name of Jesus.

DAY 27

WILL YOU DO THE RIGHT THING FOR THEM?

"I have chosen him so that he may command his children and his household after him to keep the way of the LORD by doing what is right and just. Then the LORD will give to Abraham what he promised him." — Genesis 18:19 (NET)

DAILY EXHORTATION

Our opening scripture for today looks simple but is actually quite nuanced and very powerful. Abraham had just finished attending to the angels who came to tell him that he and his wife would, in some months time, have the child they had waited for all their lives.

But that was the bright part of the visit of these angels to the earth. They had a second and much more darker mission. They were on their way to judge and to destroy the perverted cities of

Sodom and Gomorrah. But as they were about to leave, here's what happened:

Genesis 18:16-19 (NET) "*When the men got up to leave, they looked out over Sodom. (Now Abraham was walking with them to see them on their way.) Then the Lord said, 'Should I hide from Abraham what I am about to do?* **After all, Abraham will surely become a great and powerful nation, and all the nations on the earth will pronounce blessings on one another using his name. I have chosen him so that he may command his children and his household after him to keep the way of the Lord by doing what is right and just. Then the Lord will give to Abraham what he promised him.**'"

Here they were, messengers of God going to judge and to destroy these already-established cities or nations. But they were standing in the house of a man who was going to be a founder of a new nation. Isn't that something? On the day that God announced the birth of a child that would lead to the proliferation of a new nation, He destroyed an old, existing nation. It was important for Abraham to hear these words from these angels. They were going to destroy Sodom and Gomorrah because they were people who lived in all kinds of sin and sexual perversion. So,

God, through these angels, told Abraham that He chose him specifically because he would command his children and his household to keep the way of the Lord and do what was right and just.

The people of Sodom and Gomorrah did not have a person like Abraham. They did not have anyone to command them to do what was right and just and to keep the way of the Lord. Abraham already had the generational promise but since he was the founder of a new nation, God wanted him to see what could happen to nations that reject God, that reject the way of the Lord and that reject righteousness and justice.

And what did Abraham have to do to avoid the fate of these ungodly people? He was to command his children and his household after him in the way of the Lord by doing what was right and just. Only by doing this, would God make His promises to him manifest. Wow! Are you a husband or a wife? Are you a dad or a mom? Do you plan to be a husband, wife, dad or mom? If yes, there's work for you to do regarding your children and your household. Do you have dreams for your children? Do you want your kids to turn out right in life? Do you want to have peace of mind concerning your children? Do you want to spend your time receiving praises from people you know and also from strangers commending you for the work you've done on your children? Do you want to protect your children from spiritual attacks and divine judgment? Do you want your children to be all they can be in the Lord? Do you want your children to ultimately end up in heaven? If your answer to all of these is yes? There's something you have to do. According to the word of the Lord, you must learn to "command" your children and your household.

Very quickly, what does that mean? Another version of this text says "direct". Another says "encourage". And another says "teach". If you want your good expectations for your kids to come to pass, you must train them concerning the Lord. If you want the promises of God to manifest in your household, you must teach them and direct them to follow the way of the Lord. How do you do this? Morning devotionals, times set aside for singing hymns, attending church services together during the week and on Sundays, living a godly life as an example to them, praying thematically together, ensuring that they are observing and carrying out commandments as written in the word of God such as alms-giving, kindness, etc., letting them know the consequences of sin and the blessings of obedience to the word of God.

If you do this, just as it happened for

Abraham, the things that God has promised in His word will come to pass in your life. You and your household will never know wrath or judgment [like the people of Sodom and Gomorrah did] but only blessings and promotions.

Is this something you desire? If yes, this is your morning! Get yourself ready!

TODAY'S PRAYERS

1. My Father in heaven, I do not want myself or any member of my family to be the object of divine judgment, wrath or punishment. Therefore, I ask that you have mercy and help me, in the name of Jesus.

2. Holy One of Israel, what I want is for myself and my household to keep Your ways by doing what is right and just before You. Therefore Lord, I ask: Come to my aid, in the name of Jesus.

3. Now Lord, according to Your word, teach me how to command myself, my children and my entire household to do Your will, in the name of Jesus.

4. Messiah, make me an agent of spiritual encouragement, training and direction in my

family, in the name of Jesus.

5. Father, as I issue divine commands, as I provide encouragement, as I direct and as I make myself a living example to my children and my household, let their hearts be good soil. Let these seeds I am planting in their lives germinate and becoming trees of righteousness bearing the fruit of the Spirit, in the name of Jesus.

6. Elohim, just as it was for Abraham, by reason of our adherence to Your word and Your will in our household, let Your promises as written in Your word manifest in our lives. Let my good expectations for every member of my family come to fruition. Save us from judgment and wrath and let us only know Your blessings and promotions, in the name of Jesus.

7. Thank You Messiah for answering my prayers, in Jesus' mighty name, amen.

If you have the need and the time, please feel free to add more prayers at this point.

Blessing: May God make you a source of encouragement to the members of your household so that His promises for you can come to fruition, in the name of Jesus.

DAY 28

BEWARE OF DOEG IN THE TEMPLE

"It so happened that one of Saul's officers was there, worshiping the LORD that day. His name was Doeg the Edomite, and he was the strongest of Saul's shepherds."
— 1 Samuel 21:7 (CEV)

DAILY EXHORTATION

What day is our opening scripture referring to? It is referring to the day David, through Jonathan's help, escaped to a place called Nob, a town dedicated to priests.

When he got there, he met Ahimelek, the main priest. As far as Ahimelek was concerned, David was a national hero [for killing Goliath], the king's son's best friend, the king's son-in-law and a high-ranking officer in the Jewish army. But David was concerned that if he was plain to Ahimelek and told him the truth about his situation, he would not receive any help from the priest. So he told him lies. Let's take a look at this in scripture:

Ahimelek: "*Why are you by yourself with no one accompanying you?*" (1 Samuel 21:1, NET)

David: "*The king instructed me to do something, but he said to me, 'Don't let anyone know the reason I am sending you or the instructions I have given you.' I have told my soldiers to wait at a certain place.*" (1 Samuel 21:2, NET)

If you put yourself in the position of the priest, knowing who David was, you would have no reason to doubt whatever he was telling you. He thought David was telling him the truth. So, on the basis of these lies, Ahimelek met David's request for some temple bread and for a weapon [which happened to be the weapon he used to kill Goliath]. Thereafter, David left Nob and fled to a place called Gath.

Now, this whole incident would have been a non-issue and would have passed away into history without incident BUT our opening scripture reveals a problem. According to our opening scripture, while David was interacting with Ahimelek, one of Saul's officers, a man called Doeg, was there and he saw everything. Our opening scripture says Doeg was there "worshiping" the Lord. However, other versions of the Bible do not use the word "worship" but instead they say Doeg was "detained" before the Lord. This implies that he was in the presence of the Lord against his will. Or he resented the fact that he was there. But he saw everything that occurred between David and the priest. Therefore, when Saul eventually discovered that David had escaped, Doeg spoke up. Let's take a look at what he said in scripture:

1 Samuel 22:9-10 (NET) *"But Doeg the Edomite, who had stationed himself with the servants of Saul, replied [to Saul],* **'I saw this son of Jesse come to Ahimelek son of Ahitub at Nob. He inquired of the Lord for him and gave him provisions. He also gave him the sword of Goliath the Philistine.'"**

This was true but this was also a lie because it excluded the fact that David lied to Ahimelek. Therefore, Doeg made it seem as if the priest was complicit in the escape of David, which wasn't true. As a result of this [ultimately] false testimony, the very bitter king Saul killed Ahimelek and his entire family as well as 85 other priests at Nob. Not only that, he killed all of Nob's men and women, its children and infants, and its cattle, donkeys and sheep.

And this happened because of the malicious

and incomplete testimony of Doeg, who was said to have gone to Nob to "worship" God.

There are lessons for you in today's devotional. Not every "worshiper" you see in the house of God is actually a worshiper. Many people you see in church are only "detained" there. Many people go to church only because they have a problem and would not otherwise be there. Some go there because they are forced to. Some go there because they are looking for a social connection. Some are there because they are looking for a husband or a wife.

But amongst these detained people, is a "Doeg" — a backstabber. Therefore, you have to be wise about whom you reveal the issues of your life to. If David had called Ahimelek aside, that is, out of view of anyone else, perhaps Doeg would not have seen them and Ahimelek's life and his family would have been spared. But he did not know to do this and Doeg saw everything. Be wise, be prudent, be careful so that you do not fall victim to pretenders in the house of God.

You should love all persons and be kind and be respectful to everyone. You should go to church focusing on your God, hearing His word and true worship. But today's devotional is for the use of wisdom when it comes to divulging the details of your life. As you can see, this wisdom is necessary for the preservation of your life.

Do you want to become wary of fake worshipers in the house of God? Do you need wisdom for conducting yourself in the temple? Do you want self-control for your place of worship? Do you want to preserve your life by controlling how much information you give out about yourself? If yes, get yourself ready!

TODAY'S PRAYERS

1. O Lord my lamp, whenever I go to Your house, give me the grace to always show other people the love that You have deposited in my life, in the name of Jesus.

2. My God, whenever I am in the place of worship, let my life and my conduct be a shining example and a physical manifestation of Your word, in the name of Jesus.

3. By reason of today's devotional, from today, Father, let me become aware that there could be a Doeg in my church who could use information about me against me. Let this reality become clear to me, in the name of Jesus.

4. My Shepherd, whenever I am at church or indeed any public place, let a guard come over my mouth so that I will only speak with

wisdom, in the name of Jesus.

5. O Lord, let me never say anything or do anything that anyone will see or hear and use against me. Do not let any information obtained from me by any Doeg be used against me, any member of my family or anyone associated with me, in the name of Jesus.

6. Now Lord, I ask: If there be any Doeg that has been assigned against me in order to collect information about me and bring me down, let that Doeg be arrested and let that Doeg receive Your divine judgment so that I can be protected from any kind of loss, in the name of Jesus.

7. Thank You Father God for answering my prayers, in Jesus' mighty name, amen.

If you have the need and the time, please feel free to add more prayers at this point.

Blessing: May God give you wisdom and may He protect you from the Doegs of this world, in the name of Jesus.

DAY 29

ALONG CAME A PROPHET

"And, behold, there came a man of God out of Judah by the word of the LORD unto Bethel..." — 1 Kings 13:1 (KJV)

DAILY EXHORTATION

When Solomon died, his son, Rehoboam, became king in his stead. But Rehoboam was not a wise man and imposed heavy taxes on his people. This tax led to a rebellion and gave room for the rise to power of someone called Jeroboam, who eventually became king over Israel. His coming into power had divine backing but once there, Jeroboam began to misbehave. Not only did he turn away from God. He also turned the people of Israel away from God toward idolatry. He set up idols and altars and caused the people to sin against God.

Then one day, a young prophet came into town. This prophet went to an altar on which Jeroboam was trying to make an evil sacrifice. He prophesied concerning the rise of a holy king and at the same time, he prophesied against the altar and the destruction of its priests. In a rage, king Jeroboam pointed at the prophet and called for him to be arrested. But the power of God was present. In that instant, amongst other things, the hand Jeroboam stretched out became paralyzed. Jeroboam begged for mercy and asked for the prophet's prayer for the restoration of his hand. The prophet interceded for him and the king's hand was restored.

Then, Jeroboam invited him to his home to reward him with a meal and a gift. To that, the prophet responded as follows:

1 Kings 13:8-10 (NET) "*But the prophet said to the king, 'Even if you were to give me half your possessions, I could not go with you and eat and drink in this place. **For the Lord gave me strict orders, 'Do not eat or drink there and do not go home the way you came.'** So he started back on another road; he did not travel back on the same road he had taken to Bethel.*"

God spoke to the prophet, the prophet delivered his message, the prophet was even used to perform a miracle, the prophet refused the king's offer according to divine instructions and the prophet was on his way out of Bethel as he was instructed. Mission accomplished, right? Not exactly.

Yes, the prophet had delivered his message BUT there was a problem with making it out of Bethel. Here's what happened:

1 Kings 13:11-15 (NET) "*Now there was an old prophet living in Bethel. When his sons came home, they told their father everything the prophet had done in Bethel that day and all the words he had spoken to the king. Their father asked them, 'Which road did he take?' His sons showed him the road the prophet from Judah had taken. He then told his sons, 'Saddle the donkey for me.' When they had saddled the donkey for him, he mounted it and took off after the prophet, whom he found sitting under an oak tree. He asked him, 'Are you the prophet from Judah?' He answered, 'Yes, I am.' He then said to him, 'Come home with me and eat something.'*"

In response to the old prophet's offer, the young prophet provided him with the same answer he had earlier given the king. Essentially, he declined the offer. But the old prophet was eager to have such a powerful man in his home by all means. So, he did the following:

1 Kings 13:18-19 (NET) "*The old prophet then said, 'I too am a prophet like you. An angel told me with the Lord's authority, 'Bring him back* *with you to your house so he can eat and drink." But he was lying to him. So the prophet went back with him and ate and drank in his house."*

You see, whenever God says something to you whether in the Bible or through His Holy Spirit, you must not deviate from it. If any human being comes with an update to that word but that update is contrary to what is written in the Bible or to what you heard from God, you must reject that update. It doesn't matter how highly placed that person is or for how long you have known them, you must reject the word of any human being whenever it contradicts the word of God.

As you can see for yourself, even a great prophet can lie. This does not mean that he is a false prophet. No. It just means that prophets are also human beings and can lie. And if you carry out the lie, you will suffer the consequences. So, what was the consequence for this young prophet who believed the word of the old prophet over God's original instruction to him? Let's find out in scripture:

1 Kings 13:23-24 (NET) "*When the prophet from Judah finished his meal, the old prophet saddled his visitor's donkey for him. **As the prophet from Judah was traveling, a lion attacked him***

on the road and killed him. *His corpse was lying on the road, and the donkey and the lion just stood there beside it."*

And so it was that the assignment of the prophet—which had a colorful beginning—came to an abrupt end.

The lesson here is not to avoid the prophets of God. God's prophets are divine messengers who make His will known to all mankind. Prophecies have transformed lives. They have made zeros into heroes and changed the destinies of entire nations. But when you hear a prophecy, check the Bible to see that it is in line with God's word. If it is, fine. If it is not, it could be a lie. And if you follow a lie, there could be consequences.

Are you ready to sharpen your spiritual senses? Are you ready to carry out the original word of God? Do you want to silence the voice of deception waiting to divert your destiny for their own selfish gains? Do you want to avoid the consequences of disobeying God? If yes, get yourself ready!

TODAY'S PRAYERS

1. Heavenly Father, I believe in You and I believe that You have instituted prophets for the benefit of mankind. May Your blessings

go to Your prophets, in the name of Jesus.

2. My God, I do not want to disobey You and I do not want to suffer the consequences of disobedience. Come to my aid, in the name of Jesus.

3. My Father and my God, whenever I hear the word of a prophet directed at me, give me the fortitude to always check in Your word in order to ensure that, that word is in line with Your own word, in the name of Jesus.

4. Any saddle being prepared for me by any prophet who is intending to deceive me, I command you to catch fire and burn to ashes. Any spiritual donkey or any other kind of channel that a prophet wants to use to catch up with me in order to deceive me, I command you to be paralyzed, in the name of Jesus.

5. Whenever deception proceeds from the mouth of any man and is directed at me, I shall open my mouth and counter it with God's divine instructions. Thereafter, I shall depart from the place of temptation so that I am not consumed, in the name of Jesus.

6. Jehovah, if I have obeyed spiritual lies in the past contrary to Your word, I ask that You

have mercy on me and forgive me. From today, shield me from lying prophets and protect me from the consequences of obeying the voice of deception, in the name of Jesus.

7. Thank You Great and Mighty God for answering my prayers, in Jesus' mighty name, amen.

If you have the need and the time, please feel free to add more prayers at this point.

Blessing: May you never fall victim to spiritual deception. You shall receive God's direct instructions and carry them out and you will not fail, in the name of Jesus.

DAY 30

PROVOKING DIVINE VISITATION

"In Gibeon the LORD appeared to Solomon in a dream by night: and God said, Ask what I shall give thee."
— 1 Kings 3:5 (KJV)

DAILY EXHORTATION

We all know the story of how Solomon became the wisest man in the world. And we all know that it was when God visited him in a dream by night that Solomon was offered the opportunity to ask whatever he wanted... and he asked for wisdom.

But, for someone who desires a similar kind of divine visitation, it will be interesting to know what Solomon did to provoke God to visit him in the manner that He did. Yes, Solomon had succeeded his father and yes, he was the new king but did he do anything to cause God to visit him with this life-changing offer? Let's find out from scripture:

1 Kings 3:3-4 (NET) "*Solomon demonstrated his loyalty to the Lord by following the practices of his father David*, except that he offered sacrifices and burned incense on the high places. **The king went to Gibeon to offer sacrifices, for it had the most prominent of the high places. Solomon would offer up a thousand burnt sacrifices on the altar there.**"

After Solomon did this, God paid him a visit. You see, Solomon, at the beginning of his royal journey was loyal to God. He showed this loyalty by following the practices of David, his father, who God loved so much. Also, when he wanted to offer sacrifices to God, he went to the most important spot that was at the time set aside for sacrifices. He transported 1,000 animals to that high place in order to honor His God. Think about it... 1,000 animals! So, there you have it — a glimpse into how to provoke divine visitation.

You can cause God to visit you by becoming loyal to him. You can demonstrate your loyalty to Him by following, sticking to and never deviating from His word. Then, you should ascend the most important place of worship and from there offer sacrifices to Him. Sacrifice? Yes. Should you go and purchase animals and burn them as Solomon did? No. Here's how you can achieve the same thing Solomon did without using his methods:

Psalm 51:16-17 (NET) "*Certainly you do not want a sacrifice, or else I would offer it; you do not desire a burnt sacrifice.* **The sacrifices God desires are a humble spirit—O God, a humble and repentant heart you will not reject.**"

The era of animal sacrifices are over forever. Jesus has made sure of that. So, what David is telling us in the scripture above is that the way to offer a sacrifice to God is have a humble heart and to have a repentant mindset. This means living a life that is permanently submissive to the will of God and having a heart that knows no arrogance to anyone.

So, in summary, the way to provoke a divine visitation is to unwaveringly stick to the word of God and develop a humble and repentant heart. If you do this, God will accept your sacrifice and visit you in His own way. Do you want need divine visitation? If yes, get yourself ready!

TODAY'S PRAYERS

1. Adonai, I have things that I want to accomplish in life and I know that I cannot do them all without Your help. Therefore,

give ear to my prayers this morning and answer me, in the name of Jesus.

2. Great Redeemer, from today, I pledge my loyalty to You, in the name of Jesus.

3. My God, as it was for Solomon, at the beginning of his rule, I too want to demonstrate my loyalty to You. Give me the grace to demonstrate my loyalty to You by learning Your word, following it, sticking to it and never deviating from it all the days of my life, in the name of Jesus.

4. Abba Father, from today, I am determined to work on my heart and my life. From today, I am determined to live with a humble and repentant heart. I am determined to submit to You and to live without arrogance to anyone. Let this be my portion, in the name of Jesus.

5. O Lord my God, let my sacrifice of a humble heart and a repentant mindset be acceptable to You, in the name of Jesus.

6. My God and my Refuge, as it was for Solomon, by reason of my loyalty and my sacrifices unto You, I invite You to pay me a visit, in Your own way, that will change my life for good forever, in the name of Jesus.

7. Thank You Messiah for answering my prayers, in Jesus' mighty name, amen.

If you have the need and the time, please feel free to add more prayers at this point.

Blessing: May God accept your sacrifice and visit you to bless you, in the name of Jesus.

THANK YOU FOR GETTING THIS BOOK. BY GOD'S GRACE, MORE BOOKS ARE ON THE WAY THAT WILL LIKELY COVER MORE AREAS OR THEMES OR TOPICS OF INTEREST TO YOU. THE BEST WAY TO KNOW WHICH BOOKS ARE BEING RELEASED IS BY GETTING AN ALERT OR A NOTIFICATION FROM US. IF YOU WANT TO GET ACCESS TO THE LATEST UPDATES ON NEW BOOKS AS WELL AS OTHER ESSENTIAL INFORMATION FROM BROTHER MILLER, PLEASE JOIN OUR READERS' MAILING LIST (FOR EMAIL UPDATES), LIKE OUR FACEBOOK PAGE (FOR FACEBOOK UPDATES) AND FOLLOW US ON TWITTER. GOD BLESS YOU.

VISIT THE PAGE BELOW TO JOIN NOW

http://johnmillerbooks.com/signup/

LIKE JOHN'S FACEBOOK PAGE AT:

facebook.com/johnmillerauthor

FOLLOW JOHN ON TWITTER AT:

twitter.com/johnmillerbooks

DAY 31 TO 60

DAY 31
THE POWER OF OIL

"Thou preparest a table before me in the presence of mine enemies: thou anointest my head with oil; my cup runneth over."
— Psalm 23:5 (KJV)

DAILY EXHORTATION

Let's take a quick look at two scriptures:

1 Samuel 16:13 (KJV) "*Then **Samuel took the horn of oil, and anointed him** in the midst of his brethren: **and the Spirit of the LORD came upon David from that day forward**. So Samuel rose up, and went to Ramah.*"

James 5:14-15 (NET) "*Is anyone among you ill? He should summon the elders of the church, and **they should pray for him and anoint him with oil** in the name of the Lord. **And the prayer of faith will save the one who is sick and the Lord will raise him up**—and if he has committed sins, he will be forgiven.*"

As you can see, there is something common to both scriptures and this thing is "oil". When God wanted to replace king Saul with someone else, he marked out that person [David] by instructing the prophet Samuel to anoint his head with oil. Immediately Samuel did this, the Spirit of God came upon David. Even though he had to wait a while for the actual fruition of God's plan, from that moment though he was already the king of Israel. In the second verse above, the Bible says that when a person is sick and they are prayed for and anointed by an elder, he or she will recover.

These two scriptures show very clearly that in the hands of people who know what they are doing, oil can be a very powerful instrument for the transfer of divine power. The power of the Spirit of God that was in Samuel's oil transformed David from an ordinary shepherd into the king of a nation. And oil prayed over by spiritual people can bring healing.

This brings us to our opening scripture, which provides us with the final example of the power of oil for this morning. David said that God prepared a table for him in the presence of his enemies. Then, God anointed his head with oil. And as a result of this, his cup ran over. By reason of the oil of anointing, David's cup ran over! An empty cup represents a need. A half-filled cup represents hope. A full cup represents satisfaction that your needs have been met. A cup running over represents continuity. It means that you are living in abundance and you have no fear of want or lack.

What is your cup or your need this morning? Is your spiritual cup empty? Is your health cup empty? Is your relationships cup empty? Is your professional cup empty? Is your financial cup empty? Is your character cup empty? Is your mental cup empty? Know now that the oil of anointing, filled with the power of the living God, can cause your cup to not only fill up but to overflow abundantly. When your cup is overflowing or running over, whatever problem you have that, that cup represents, will vanish forever. Are you ready for this? Do you want the power of God upon oil to solve whatever problem you have? Do you have faith in the word of God? If yes, you are a good candidate for this morning's prayers. Therefore, get yourself ready!

TODAY'S PRAYERS

IMPORTANT: Do you have some clean oil around in your house? Do you have a small bottle (2 to 3 inches tall)? If yes, pour some oil into this bottle and get it ready for this morning's prayers.

1. O Righteous Father, I believe in Your word with all of my heart. As I have read this morning, I believe in the power of the oil of anointing. Let it work for me, in the name of Jesus.

2. My Lord and my God, Your word says that the oil of anointing took David and transformed him from a shepherd into a king. As it worked for David, let it work for me today, in the name of Jesus.

3. Father, Your word says that the prayer of faith combined with oil will save the sick. As it worked for the New Testament saints, let it also for work for me today, in the name of Jesus.

4. O God, Your word also says that Your oil upon the head of David caused his cup to overflow and run over. As it worked for David, let it also work for me today, in the name of Jesus.

5. [*Now take the 2 or 3 inch bottle and raise it up*] Everlasting God, You do not change. What works for one saint will work for another regardless of the time in history. Therefore, with complete faith in my heart in Your word and in Your power, I lift up this bottle of oil, let Your divine power enter into this oil right

now, in the name of Jesus.

6. Now Lord, I have cups that need to overflow and run over. Lord, my _____ [spiritual / health / relationships / etc.] cup is empty. As I anoint my head now with this oil, let my _____ cup overflow and run over. Through Your power in this oil, let my problems be solved and my needs met, in the name of Jesus. [*Repeat this prayer and this process for each and every empty "cup" that you have in your life. Also every morning going forward, you should repeat this entire step until the oil in your bottle finishes. If you do this in faith, it will surprise you what the Lord will do!*]

7. Thank You Mighty God for answering my prayers, in Jesus' mighty name, amen.

If you have the need and the time, please feel free to add more prayers at this point.

Blessing: As it has worked for others for thousands of years, the Lord will use the oil of anointing to meet your needs and solve your problems, in the name of Jesus.

DAY 32

WHAT'S THAT FOLLOWING YOU?

"Surely goodness and mercy shall follow me all the days of my life: and I will dwell in the house of the LORD for ever."
— Psalm 23:6 (KJV)

DAILY EXHORTATION

Other versions of the Bible substitute the word "follow" with "pursue". The word "pursue" means to "be with", "to chase after", "to accompany", "to relentlessly seek for" and "to follow in order to overtake".

So, our opening scripture is saying that goodness and mercy will be with you, chase after you, accompany you, relentlessly seek for you and follow you in order to overtake you. Essentially, this verse is saying that you will never be free from God's goodness and mercy.

But what are these things? What is goodness and what is mercy? Goodness means favor. Favor is what happens to you when someone [in this case, God] is biased toward you and showers you with irrational love that others do not get. Favor means special attention. It means having very easy access to things other people work so hard to get in their lives. Mercy means freedom from punishment when you do something that deserves punishment. Whereas other people get punished for whatever wrong they do, mercy means you will be spared. And this mercy is available to everyone who knows about it or wants it because this is what Jesus died for. Through the blood of Jesus, all human beings who believe in Him, can have access to divine mercy.

So, to conclude this morning, these two things will follow you for the rest of your life — God's favor and His mercy. When some people look behind them or to their sides, they may find death, depression, troubles, sorrows, woes, etc. following them BUT for you, there will be none of these. Instead, the favor and the mercy of the Creator of the universe will be your companions forever and ever.

Are you tired of nasty things following you about everyday of your life? Do you want favor and mercy as companions? Do you want God to dispatch them into your life this morning? If yes, get yourself ready!

TODAY'S PRAYERS

1. Holy Father, I believe that Favor and Mercy are divine entities that can accompany a person and by reason of their presence, transform a person's life. I want them in my life. Help me, in the name of Jesus.

2. This morning Lord, I make a special request to heaven: Send me favor and send me mercy so that they can become my eternal companions, in the name of Jesus.

3. Rock of Ages, let the arrival of favor and mercy into my life cause _____ (the problems following you such as sickness, depression, fear, etc.) to be evicted from my life, in the name of Jesus. [Repeat this prayer for every problem you want favor and mercy to evict or displace from your life]

4. Messiah, let the arrival of Your divine favor into my life as a companion cause me to experience Your special love and Your special attention. By reason of Your divine favor, Lord, let me get easy access to things that other people work so hard to get, in the name of Jesus.

5. Father God, let the arrival of Your mercy into my life as a companion cause me to be

spared punishment. Through the power in the blood of Jesus, do not let me suffer dire consequences whenever I make a mistake or an error, in the name of Jesus.

6. Now Lord, I ask, as Your divine favor and mercy have come into my life, do not ever let them leave me. Let them follow me, pursue me and accompany me all the days of my life even as I continue to dwell in Your house forever and ever, in the name of Jesus.

7. Thank You Almighty God for all these wonderful blessings and for answering my prayers, in Jesus' mighty name, amen.

If you have the need and the time, please feel free to add more prayers at this point.

Blessing: According to the word of the Lord, surely goodness and mercy shall follow you all the days of your life, in the name of Jesus.

DAY 33

THE FLY AND
THE PERFUME

**"As dead flies cause the perfumer's
ointment to stink, so also does a little
foolishness to one's reputation of wisdom
and honor." — Ecclesiastes 10:1 (ISV)**

DAILY EXHORTATION

This morning's scripture likens dead flies to
foolishness and perfume or ointment to a
reputation of wisdom and honor. And you know,
this is so true. When you are wearing a sweet-
smelling perfume and you enter into a room, it
can affect the way people react to you. All other
things being equal [stature, physical appearance,
character, knowledge, etc.], if two people enter
into a room and one of them wears a nice
perfume and the other does not, it is somewhat
likely that the one with the perfume will get a
better reception.

You see, when people perceive good
perfume, it conjures up a number of assumptions

in their minds. They feel "*he or she is sophisticated*" or "*he or she is wealthy*", etc. So, they want to put in extra effort to treat the person well according to the assumptions they have in their hearts. In the same manner and in fact, much more so, when you have a reputation for wisdom and honor, people will treat you well. When they see you from afar, they'll say "*look at so and so who solved that problem for so and so*" or "*look at so and so who saved so and so from this and that*". Whenever someone needs help or advice, they'll say "*why don't you call so and so. He's very wise and experienced in this kind of matter*", etc. This is what the Bible means when it compares perfume with a good reputation.

Then, we come to the other part of this scripture. No matter how expensive a bottle of perfume or cologne is, if you pour dead flies into it, they will ruin its sweet smell. Therefore, today's devotional is a warning. Foolishness or foolish behavior can ruin your reputation of wisdom and honor. Just like dead flies can cause expensive perfume to stink, wrong / immoral / sinful words and behaviors can cause you to fall from grace to grass and rob you of your hard-earned reputation. We see it everyday. On the nightly news, almost everyday, we hear of famous doctors who one day decided to molest their patients. All of a sudden, all the years of medical school and all the years of building their name goes down the drain... and they also go to prison. You hear of finance and investment wizards who have become popular for keeping and legally multiplying people's money. But one day, they decided to take one dollar, then 2, then 3, then 10,000, then $1,000,000 and so on. Pretty soon, the police is at the door. They lose everything — their name, their money, their family and they also go to prison. Ditto political office holders, teachers, pastors, etc.

For all these people, dead flies have entered into the perfume of their lives and have caused it to stink. Their foolish behavior has ruined their reputation for wisdom and honor. You have the opportunity this morning to speak to the Almighty in order to prevent this from happening in your own life. If you speak to him, He will listen to you and help you.

So, what will it be? Do you want your reputation of wisdom and honor to be preserved? Do you want to prevent dead flies from piling into the perfume of your life? If yes, get yourself ready!

TODAY'S PRAYERS

1. Father, I thank You for the revelation of this morning. I thank You for letting me know that my reputation of wisdom and honor is like perfume. Help me to keep it smelling

sweet, in the name of Jesus.

2. This morning I decree: If there be any foul spirit working against me in order to pour dead flies into the perfume of my life, your time is up: I bind you with fetters of fire that can never break. I command you: Depart from life and never ever return, in the name of Jesus.

3. Any pile of dead flies gathered against my destiny to cause the perfume of my life to stink, I set you ablaze. Be consumed by the fire of the Holy Ghost and vanish from my life forever, in the name of Jesus.

4. My God, this morning I ask that You release into my life the fruit of the Spirit of self control. With the help of Your Holy Spirit, let me gain full control of my mouth and my body so that I do not say or do anything foolish, in the name of Jesus.

5. Any foolish desire or thought or idea in my heart which if I act on will cause my perfume to stink and cause me to lose my reputation, your time is up. I command you this morning to die and never rise up again, in the name of Jesus.

6. Since I will not act on any foolish thought or

idea, the sweet smell of the perfume of my life will be preserved. My reputation of wisdom and honor will be preserved. I will never fall from grace to grass. Rather I will go higher and higher until I fulfill my destiny and my assignment on the earth, in the name of Jesus.

7. Thank You Father God for answering my prayers, in Jesus' mighty name, amen.

If you have the need and the time, please feel free to add more prayers at this point.

Blessing: May God help you to control yourself so that the sweet smell coming from your life will never go away, in the name of Jesus.

DAY 34

GOOD TIMES

"But as for you, you will go to your ancestors in peace and be buried at a good old age." — Genesis 15:15 (NET)

DAILY EXHORTATION

The "good old age" portion of our opening scripture is quite straightforward. But for the "peace" part, we'll have to dig a little deeper. Let's take a look at scriptures:

Deuteronomy 34:7 (NET) "*And Moses was an hundred and twenty years old when he died: his eye was not dim, nor his natural force abated.*"

1 Chronicles 29:26-28 (KJV) "*Thus David the son of Jesse reigned over all Israel. And the time that he reigned over Israel was forty years; seven years reigned he in Hebron, and thirty and three years reigned he in Jerusalem. And he died in a good old age, full of days, riches, and honour: and Solomon his son reigned in his stead.*"

It is good to die at a good old age but it also important to die in peace. According to the scriptures above, peaceful death means that at the time of your death, you will not be afflicted with any major illness and your senses will still be in working order. It also means leaving behind a track record of achievement, riches and honor. Finally, it means leaving behind a successor or successors who will "reign" in your stead and continue and build upon the legacy you have left behind.

So, this morning's assignment is not complicated. You are going to speak into your future. Realize that, for example, if you die and leave behind honor, it means that all your days were spent doing honorable things. Ditto if you die and leave behind riches, it means that throughout your life, you worked and God blessed your efforts. Therefore, while these verses speak about old age, death, etc., they really are about your life from now until the day God decides to call you home.

So, do you want to live a peaceful, disease-free life? Do you want to live in prosperity? Do you want your good name and legacy to continue long after you are gone just as the legacy of David continues till this day? If the answer to all these is yes, get yourself ready!

TODAY'S PRAYERS

1. Adonai, according to Your word, I want to enter into heaven in peace and be buried at a good old age. Help me and let this be my portion, in the name of Jesus.

2. I use this morning's scripture to speak against any element of untimely death that may be in my life. I decree that by reason of the manifestation of this morning's scripture in my life, I will not die young or before my time, in the name of Jesus.

3. O Lord my God, as it was for Moses, from now until my old age even until the day of my death, my eye shall not be dim neither shall my natural force be abated. Let me live a long, strong and healthy life, in the name of Jesus.

4. Mighty Father, as it was for David, let me reign in my own personal kingdom through the days of my life. Let all my days until my old age be filled with riches even until the day of my death and beyond, in the name of Jesus.

5. Holy One of Israel, let me do honorable things from now until my old age so that

from now until the day that I die, I shall live a life of honor, in the name of Jesus.

6. Jehovah God, bless me with successors who will learn from me from now until my old age and even unto the day of my death. Let my children be filled with Your word and Your will so that they will continue and build upon the legacy that I shall leave behind. Finally Lord, when my time comes, let me close my eyes with the peace and calmness that when I open them, I shall do so in Your eternal kingdom, in the name of Jesus.

7. Thank You Great and Mighty God for answering my prayers, in Jesus' mighty name, amen.

If you have the need and the time, please feel free to add more prayers at this point.

Blessing: May God bless you with a long life and with His peace even until the end, in the name of Jesus.

DAY 35
ALPHA AND OMEGA

"I am Alpha and Omega, the beginning and the ending, saith the Lord, which is, and which was, and which is to come, the Almighty." — Revelation 1:8 (KJV)

DAILY EXHORTATION

The Almighty also repeats a similar statement to our opening scripture in Revelation 22:13 (KJV) which says "*I am Alpha and Omega, the beginning and the end, the first and the last.*" One of the common occurrences at the death bed of renowned atheists and other such people is that right there in their closing hours, they ask the same God they have publicly denounced for years, for mercy. And believe it or not, because Jesus' death has paid for everyone's sins, these reputable unbelievers will be forgiven and they will make it into heaven. Let's take a look at an example of this in scripture:

Luke 23:32 (KJV) "*And there were also two other, malefactors, led with him to be put to death.*"

Luke 23:39-43 (NET) "*One of the criminals who was hanging there railed at him, saying, 'Aren't you the Christ? Save yourself and us!' But the other rebuked him, saying, 'Don't you fear God, since you are under the same sentence of condemnation? And we rightly so, for we are getting what we deserve for what we did, but this man has done nothing wrong.'* **Then he said, 'Jesus, remember me when you come in your kingdom.' And Jesus said to him, 'I tell you the truth, today you will be with me in paradise.'**"

Let's say that the 'good' criminal who repented is called "Andy". In order to be caught and crucified like this, it meant Andy was a nasty man and a hardened, merciless criminal. In the scripture above, Andy admitted that he was getting what he deserved. It is also very clear that, up till the Cross, Andy was not a born again Christian and He did not believe in Jesus. Ordinarily speaking, the moment Andy closed his eyes, he was supposed to open them in hell. But with a sentence of only 8 words "*Jesus, remember me when you come in your kingdom.*", his eternal trajectory was changed! Jesus promised him eternity in heaven. Great!

But do you know that if Andy had followers, they did not get this update? Those followers would not have known that Andy, at the last minute, crossed over to Jesus. Therefore, those followers would still be on the fast track to hell. In the same vein, there are people now who are 20 / 30 / 40 / 50 or even 100 years old who think they have all the knowledge in the world. A person that is only three decades old believes that he or she knows for a fact that there is no God and there is no heaven and there is no hell despite all the evidences in the Bible and in Israel [a physical place they can visit]. And because of the Charisma of this person, you have people following him or her.

This also happens in politics, where you find 50 / 60 / 70 year old politicians saying that the principles that God has put in place to govern the human race for thousands of years have become outdated! Can you imagine that? Someone who has lived for only 5 decades defying a God who is the beginning and the end of all things? And you have people following him or her?! When God says thou shall not kill. They say No, you can kill. When he says you should not engage in sexual perversion, they say you're free to do whatever you like. Some of these are people are still scared of the dark despite their age! And they are altering the principles of an everlasting God and people are listening to them?

The earth and the entire universe were created by a single being and His name is

Almighty God! He made you. He made everything you see or you can't see. He made everything you know about or have never heard of. He is the Alpha and Omega. Everything begins and ends with Him. No one is higher than Him. He is the greatest.

As you have seen from the example of the thief on the Cross, following a charismatic but ignorant person is the fastest way to get into hell. Do not follow people who speak against or do things which are contrary to the word and the will of God. Obey and honor God instead and it will be well with you. God loves you and within Him are great and unimaginable benefits.

So, what would it be this morning? Do you want to accept the Alpha and Omega as the all-in-all? Or do you want to believe the words of godless human beings who do not know their right from their left? If you prefer to pitch your tent with the Almighty, today is your day. Get yourself ready!

TODAY'S PRAYERS

1. Abba Father, I rededicate my life to You today, in the name of Jesus.

2. My Father and my God, I declare that I believe that You are the Alpha and the

Omega, in the name of Jesus.

3. I declare that I believe that You are beginning and the end of all things, in the name of Jesus.

4. I declare that I believe that You are the first and the last, in the name of Jesus.

5. I declare that You, O Lord, are the one who is, who was and who is to come, in the name of Jesus.

6. Therefore Lord, I bow before You. I place no one above You. I will disregard the word of anyone whose word and lifestyle are contrary to Your word. I will forever seek to obey and honor You, in the name of Jesus.

7. Thank You Lord for answering my prayers, in Jesus' mighty name, amen.

If you have the need and the time, please feel free to add more prayers at this point.

Blessing: As you have decided to honor the Almighty today, He too will honor You, in the name of Jesus.

DAY 36

THE OMNIPOTENT GOD

"And I heard as it were the voice of a great multitude, and as the voice of many waters, and as the voice of mighty thunderings, saying, Alleluia: for the Lord God omnipotent reigneth."
— Revelation 19:6 (KJV)

DAILY EXHORTATION

In Exodus 6:8 (AMP), the Bible says "*I will bring you to the land which I swore to give to Abraham, Isaac, and Jacob (Israel); and I will give it to you as a possession. I am the Lord [you have the promise of My changeless omnipotence and faithfulness].*" This verse and our opening scripture both shine the spotlight on God in His nature as the Omnipotent God. God, as the only omnipotent being, has unlimited power to do anything He wants. When He spoke the words of Exodus 6:8 to Moses and therefore to the Israelites, they were still in bondage. He was telling people in bondage that they would soon be free, they would stop being slaves, independence day was coming, that they would have their own government, they would become landlords, etc. In their condition at the time, it was hard news for the Israelites to swallow. But did God not do it? He did. He used His unlimited power to bend Pharaoh [the greatest king of his era] to submission.

God prepared and manufactured plagues which no one had ever seen before they manifested. He caused pillars of cloud and of fire to appear in the heavens and to move with the Jews. He caused the Red Sea to separate so that His children could cross to the other side in safety. He caused birds to appear from nowhere as meat for His children in the desert. He rained down food from heaven which was called Manna in order to feed His children. He produced water from a rock / stone in the desert. He fulfilled His promise and right now in the middle east is a beautiful and prosperous country called Israel — an eternal evidence of the omnipotent power of the Most High God.

So, what are you facing that is a challenge to you? What is causing you to worry? What is giving you sleepless nights? What has enslaved you and does not want to let you go? Know this, that there is an Omnipotent God for whom nothing is too hard or difficult. There is nothing that He cannot do. In the same way He did it for the Israelites, He will do it for you. Call on Him today and get a taste of His omnipotence and power!

TODAY'S PRAYERS

1. Omnipotent God, I have challenges. I need Your omnipotent power to work in my favor, in the name of Jesus.

2. Righteous Father, You gave the Children of Israel the promise of Your changeless omnipotence and faithfulness. And indeed You fulfilled Your promise to them and brought them out of Egypt with a great deliverance. Come and deliver me also today, in the name of Jesus.

3. Father, after You brought Your children out of Egypt, you performed great and mighty miracles in order to protect them and sustain them. These things You did with Your Omnipotent power. With that same power, come and work great and might miracles in my life as well, in the name of Jesus.

4. My Father, You are the omnipotent God. Deliver me from _____ [whatever you want God to deliver you from], in the name

of Jesus.

5. My God, You are the omnipotent God. I need a miracle of _____ [whatever miracle you want him to perform in your life]. Perform it for me, in the name of Jesus.

6. Alpha and Omega, use me in my generation as a human billboard to advertise Your omnipotent power on the earth, in the name of Jesus.

7. Thank You Omnipotent God for answering my prayers, in Jesus' mighty name, amen.

If you have the need and the time, please feel free to add more prayers at this point.

Blessing: May you experience the deliverance and the miracle-working power of the Omnipotent God, in the name of Jesus.

DAY 37

THE OMNISCIENT GOD

"He (Jesus) said to her, 'Go call your husband and come back here.' The woman replied, 'I have no husband.' Jesus said to her, 'Right you are when you said, 'I have no husband,' for you have had five husbands, and the man you are living with now is not your husband. This you said truthfully!' The woman said to him, 'Sir, I see that you are a prophet.'"
— John 4:16-19 (NET)

DAILY EXHORTATION

Let's take a look at a few more scriptures before we go into today's exhortation:

John 4:25 (NET) "*The woman said to Him, 'I know that Messiah is coming' (the one called Christ); 'whenever he comes, He will tell us everything.'*"

John 4:26 (NET) "*Jesus said to her, 'I, the one*

speaking to you, am He.'"

John 4:28-30 (NET) "*Then the woman left her water jar, went off into the town and said to the people, 'Come, see a man who told me everything I ever did. Surely he can't be the Messiah, can he?' So they left the town and began coming to Him.*"

The word "omniscient" means to have all knowledge in the universe. For example, in Luke 12:6-7 (KJV), the Bible says "*Are not five sparrows sold for two farthings, and not one of them is forgotten before God?* **But even the very hairs of your head are all numbered.** *Fear not therefore: ye are of more value than many sparrows.*" God knows the number of hair strands on the head of every human being who has ever lived! Can you imagine that? This means that there is nothing that He does not know or understand. In fact, the concept of "knowing" or "to know" or "to understand" were things that He created. He is a great and mighty God.

Our opening scripture takes us to a day in the life of the Messiah. On this day, He met a woman by a well whom He asked for some water and they got talking. Along the line, He revealed to her details of her marital status. The woman also acknowledged that she knew that someone was coming who knows all things and could therefore tell or teach them all things. Jesus then told her, He was the one that she and all other persons were expecting. He was the omniscient one.

You see, nothing is hidden from God the Father, the Son and the Holy Ghost. This was why, for example, when asked to pay tax, Jesus knew that there was a fish in the water nearby that had a coin in its mouth. He had knowledge of all the fish and He could therefore locate the one that had money in its mouth. Incredible!

What is great about all of this is that when Jesus died and resurrected, He opened the way for all human beings to also have access to or more appropriately, utilize this kind of knowledge. Let's take a look at this in scripture:

John 14:26 (KJV) *"But the Comforter, which is the Holy Ghost, whom the Father will send in my name, **he shall teach you all things**, and bring all things to your remembrance, whatsoever I have said unto you."*

John 16:13 (KJV) *"Howbeit when he, the Spirit of truth, is come, **he will guide you into all truth**: for he shall not speak of himself; but whatsoever he shall hear, that shall he speak: and he will shew you things to come."*

Through the Holy Spirit, God has made

available His omniscience so that we can all benefit from it. However, because this benefit can be gotten only through the Holy Spirit, it means you first have to be born again and also filled with the Spirit of God. Once you have done these, you will be qualified to benefit from this incredible advantage. It should be clear to you the advantages that divine knowledge can bring into your life. For instance, if you want to make a decision in your business or concerning your career, you can call on the Almighty to let you know which direction to go through the Holy Spirit. You can use this benefit in any area of your life in order to get knowledge about whatever it is that you want. Isn't this great? Isn't it wonderful to be a believer? Therefore, if you are ready to utilize the omniscient power of the Most High God in your life, get yourself ready!

TODAY'S PRAYERS

1. O Lord God Almighty, I come to You this morning and I rededicate my life to You, in the name of Jesus.

2. Great and Mighty God, fill me afresh with Your precious Holy Spirit, in the name of Jesus.

3. This morning, O Lord, I want to begin to tap into Omniscience so that I can utilize it in my life to Your glory. Help me, in the name of Jesus.

4. Holy Spirit of the Most High God, my life is available to You. According to the word of the Lord, come and teach me all things, in the name of Jesus.

5. Spirit of Truth, my life is available to You. According to the word of the Lord, come and guide me into all truth, in the name of Jesus.

6. Omniscient God, I need Your divine direction regarding _____ [anything or area in which you need divine direction]. Have mercy on me and reveal to me what to do, in the name of Jesus. [Repeat prayer for anything or area of your life in which you want divine direction]

7. Thank You Omniscient God for answering my prayers, in Jesus' mighty name, amen.

If you have the need and the time, please feel free to add more prayers at this point.

Blessing: May God give you knowledge that will unleash divine prosperity into any area of your life in which you need it, in the name of Jesus.

DAY 38

THE OMNIPRESENT GOD

(NET) "Where can I go to escape your spirit? Where can I flee to escape your presence? If I were to ascend to heaven, you would be there. If I were to sprawl out in Sheol, there you would be. If I were to fly away on the wings of the dawn, and settle down on the other side of the sea, even there your hand would guide me, your right hand would grab hold of me."
— Psalm 139:7-10

DAILY EXHORTATION

The word "omnipresent" refers to a person who is present wherever you go. Only one being has this quality and this is the Almighty God. In our opening scripture, David reveals that if he ran away into the heavens, God would be there. If he tried to escape to Sheol (hell), He would also be there. If he tried to run to the other side of the sea, God's hand would be there to hold and guide him. Truly God is everywhere.

This omnipresence of the Almighty should bring a lot of comfort to you as a person because it has several advantages. Let's examine a few of these from the Bible:

1. Omnipresence for Reassurance:

Joshua 1:5 (NET) "*No one will be able to resist you all the days of your life. As I was with Moses, so I will be with you. I will not abandon you or leave you alone.*"

Moses had just been called home and Joshua had just taken over as his replacement. It is possible that God saw that Joshua was overwhelmed by the responsibility of being the leader of Israel. Therefore, He gave him the promise above — that no one will be able to stand against him or resist him all the days of his life. How would this happen? Because God said He would never abandon him or leave him alone. Do you have a huge task before you? Are you concerned that you do not have the capacity to carry out your responsibility? If yes, the Omnipresent God is there with you and He will not abandon you or leave you alone.

2. Omnipresence for Protection

2 Samuel 7:8-9 (NET) *"So now, say this to my servant David: 'This is what the Lord of hosts says: I took you from the pasture and from your work as a shepherd to make you leader of my people Israel.* **I was with you wherever you went, and I defeated all your enemies before you.** *Now I will make you as famous as the great men of the earth..."*

Another application of God's omnipresence is to protect you from your enemies — physical or spiritual. The only reason David survived the deadly pursuit of Saul and all the other people who waged war against him was because God was with him everywhere he went. If you know that you are in any form of danger or you are going to a dangerous place, you can call on the Almighty to be with you and to protect you.

There are many other applications of the omnipresence of God. You can think about your own unique situation and consider how you want God to help you with His divine presence. Are you ready to do this, if yes, get yourself ready!

TODAY'S PRAYERS

1. King of kings, I believe from the bottom of my heart that there is no place in the

universe that is beyond Your reach. This causes me to be filled with joy. Give ear to my prayers this morning and answer them, in the name of Jesus.

2.   Lord of lords, let it be that no matter where I am on this earth, You will be present there with me, in the name of Jesus.

3.   Merciful Father, this morning I ask for Your omnipresence for reassurance. I need Your reassurance concerning _____ (whatever area you need reassurance). Help me. As you did for Joshua come and do for me also, in the name of Jesus.

4.   Great and Mighty God, I ask for Your omnipresence for protection. I need your protection because _____ (explain why you need divine protection). As you did for David, do for me so I can also benefit from Your divine protection, in the name of Jesus.

5.   Lord, I need Your omnipresence regarding _____ (any other area of your life where you need God's presence). Help me, in the name of Jesus.

6.   My God, in the same way Joshua and David fulfilled their divine destinies on the earth because you were with them, let Your

presence be with me all the days of my life and help me to also fulfill my divine destiny on the earth, in the name of Jesus.

7. Thank You Mighty God for answering my prayers, in Jesus' mighty name, amen.

If you have the need and the time, please feel free to add more prayers at this point.

Blessing: May God be with you wherever you go and may you only know good by reason of His presence in your life, in the name of Jesus.

DAY 39

BE KNOWN FOR GOOD

"Now they wanted to arrest him (but they feared the crowd), because they realized that he told this parable against them. So they left him and went away."
— Mark 12:12 (NET)

DAILY EXHORTATION

In Proverbs 22:1 (KJV), the Bible says "*A good name is rather to be chosen than great riches, and loving favour rather than silver and gold.*" One of the reasons why the Bible says this is because of our opening scripture. At this point, Jesus was well into His ministry. He was healing the sick, casting out demons from people, etc. In other words, He had established a name for Himself in Israel. Then one day, He spoke a parable which essentially was a heavy rebuke of the chief priests and the elders of the people. Other people thought it was just a story. However, the targets of the parable got the message. They were angry and wanted to arrest Him BUT they could not. Why couldn't they? Because they feared the crowd!

Jesus was doing good. He was supplying the people with what they wanted — healthcare, freedom from mental and spiritual oppression, spiritual enlightenment and so on... and you want to arrest such a man? On what grounds? Therefore, they had no choice but to leave Him and go away.

Herein lies a big lesson for you. It is not enough for you to worship God in your closet. In addition, you must do good in public, according to the word of the Lord. There is good fame and there is bad fame. Good fame results from doing good works under the umbrella of Messiah. Bad fame is being known for being nasty or immoral or some other negative thing.

To elucidate this further, let's take a look at one example. The word of God commands us to give and to do so consistently. If you do this, you will soon become known for giving amongst the people. Without you knowing this, you are creating a shield of witnesses around you. You are building what the Bible calls "a good name". The good name that Boaz had was what caused Naomi to push Ruth in his direction and made him an ancestor of David and of the Lord Jesus Christ:

Ruth 2:19-20 (NIV) "*Her mother-in-law asked her,*

'Where did you glean today? Where did you work? Blessed be the man who took notice of you!'' Then Ruth told her mother-in-law about the one at whose place she had been working. 'The name of the man I worked with today is Boaz,' she said. **'The Lord bless him!' Naomi said to her daughter-in-law. 'He has not stopped showing his kindness to the living and the dead.'"**

Insofar as you do not soil that name by doing something bad, a day will come when you will need to withdraw from *GoodName Savings & Trust.* God forbid, it could be that someone makes a false accusation against you. If this happens, because of your good name, people will rise up in your favor. People whom those people know will also rise up in your defense. And in no time, by God's grace, you will be off the hook and the false accuser in the dock!

You need a good name. You cannot have a good name in your closet. You have to be up and about doing good. This is the only way you will get a good name. That good name will one day save you. Are you ready to acquire a good name? Do you want to enjoy the benefits of favor with man? If yes, get yourself ready!

TODAY'S PRAYERS

1. Lord, I thank You so much for the grace You have given me to live a holy life. To You be all the glory, honor and praise, in the name of Jesus.

2. Now Lord, according to Your word, I want to have a good name and enjoy loving favor. Give ear to my prayers this morning and answer me, in the name of Jesus.

3. Father, give me wisdom and give me direction. Show me the place or places where I can serve and make maximum impact amongst Your people, in the name of Jesus.

4. As I identify my calling and go after it, my Lord and my God, give me the grace to engage it with passion and power, in the name of Jesus.

5. As I commit myself to my work, according to Your word, let me do it not for eye service or the praise of people but in response to divine instruction. Therefore, let me never seek vain glory in whatever good I am doing and let me never be filled with pride, in the name of Jesus.

6. I ask O Lord, in the same manner the chief priests feared the crowd and could not touch Jesus, let my good name by reason of my good works become a shield for me. And Lord, in the same way the good name of Boaz helped him to achieve personal fulfillment and generational relevance, let my good name also procure for me personal fulfillment and generational relevance, in the name of Jesus.

7. Thank You Father God for answering my prayers, in Jesus' mighty name, amen.

If you have the need and the time, please feel free to add more prayers at this point.

Blessing: As you do good in line with the word of God, may you acquire a good name as well as all the benefits that come with it, in the name of Jesus.

DAY 40

GATHER IN SUMMER

"He that gathereth in summer is a wise son: but he that sleepeth in harvest is a son that causeth shame."
— Proverbs 10:5 (KJV)

DAILY EXHORTATION

We will examine today's exhortation in two dimensions — literal and implied. First, let's take a look at the literal dimension of our opening verse. If you have a farm and summer is here, which is the time you should gather or reap what you have sown, and you do so, it means you will have sufficient produce for the feeding of yourself and your family. You will also have enough produce to sell in the market that will earn you money and guarantee your prosperity. However, if you refuse to gather in summer and instead decide to sleep away the season, you will have no produce. The field is heavy with produce but you refused to enter into it and begin harvesting. Therefore, all the fruits and vegetables will go to waste right there on the field. This means that when winter comes, such a person will have nothing to sell and his / her entire family will go hungry.

The shame that our opening scripture refers to is the shame that such a person will experience when they go about from house to house begging for food. This is great shame.

The implied dimension is much more far reaching. This passage is saying that there is a season of life called "summer". And in that season what people do is to gather and harvest. Some sons indeed gather and harvest while others sleep this summer away!

At the summer of life, a person is supposed to be getting a good education, making all the necessary and essential connections and relationships for a rewarding career or business. Some do this. They go to school. They get internships. They perform well during their internships. They earn recommendations or they are retained where they interned. They start from the bottom and slowly begin to work their way up until they get to the top.

On the other hand, some decide that summer is for partying, smoking and drinking alcohol. For some, summer is a time for playing video games and watching television. Pretty soon summer will be over. The people who responded to the call of summer have acquired a reputation, wealth and have brought honor to their parents. But the people who were sleeping their summer away have become a shame to their parents. They do not know anyone, they do not have a good career, good relationships or any other blessing. For them, summer is gone and the harsh winter is here!

Please, if you do not want to live in regret, recognize this morning that today is a day that you have to seize. Whatever opportunities come your way, you must go out and grab them! Become aggressive. Do the right thing at the right time. Gather and harvest in summer! If you do this, you will never have any cause to spend the rest of your life in regret.

Do you want to be able to seize the day? Do you want to prevent yourself from sleeping during summer or during harvest? Do you want to receive strength to gather? Do you want to bring honor to your parents and family? If yes, today is your day, get yourself ready!

TODAY'S PRAYERS

1. O my Father, I want to be wise for the sake of myself, my parents and my family. Help me, in the name of Jesus.

2. Blessed Redeemer, let me always recognize

the summer of life when it comes, in the name of Jesus.

3. Any spirit of sleeping and slumber assigned against me during the summer of my life, I bind you now and I cast you out of my life forever and ever, in the name of Jesus.

4. In the summer of my life, power to gather, power to harvest, power to reap, locate me and enter into my life, in the name of Jesus.

5. My Lord and my God, at every point in my life, let me become aware of what is expected of me. Then, let me perform above and beyond that which is expected of me. Let me spend the summer of my life getting equipped for life. Bless me with everything that I need to build a solid foundation for the rest of my life, in the name of Jesus.

6. Now Lord I ask: Because I have decided to be awake and to do my part in the summer of life, do not let me know what regret is. Do not let me ever do anything that will bring shame to me, my parents or my family. Instead, let me be blessed with a good reputation, with wealth and let me bring honor to my parents and my family and to You, in the name of Jesus.

7. Thank You O Lord for answering my prayers, in Jesus' mighty name, amen.

If you have the need and the time, please feel free to add more prayers at this point.

Blessing: May you never sleep your summer away. Instead, may you be awake and alert to seize all the opportunities you need in order to build a solid foundation for the rest of your life, in the name of Jesus.

DAY 41

DELIVERANCE FROM OPPRESSION

"Woe to them that devise iniquity, and work evil upon their beds! when the morning is light, they practice it, because it is in the power of their hand. And they covet fields, and take them by violence; and houses, and take them away: so they oppress a man and his house, even a man and his heritage." — Micah 2:1-2 (KJV)

DAILY EXHORTATION

In Psalm 17:8-9 (KJV), David called out to the Almighty and said *"Keep me as the apple of the eye, hide me under the shadow of thy wings, From the wicked that oppress me, from my deadly enemies, who compass me about."* And in Psalm 119:134 (NET), he said *"Deliver me from oppressive men, so that I can keep your precepts."* Oppression is real! Oppression occurs when someone with power or authority or influence over you decides to be cruel to you. This person may demonstrate his / her wickedness by depriving you of what you have a right to or by putting you in situations that may cause you suffering and pain. Ultimately, the actions of an oppressor are meant to place a physical, mental or spiritual burden on your life. The oppressor wants to see you anxious, depressed, beggarly, poor, tormented or dead.

From our opening scripture, we can see that there are certain people who devise iniquity. That is, they invent new ways to oppress. While other people are sleeping, these people stay awake and plot evil on their beds. They can't wait till daybreak to put their wicked inventions and evil plots to work in the lives of people they hate. The brand of oppression they practice does not only affect their targets but can also negatively affect the descendants of their targets.

All across the world, in different neighborhoods, towns and cities, you will find all kinds of oppressors. You will find people who collude with law enforcement or with the local legal system in order to deprive people of what rightfully belongs to them. You will find people snatching property from others and rendering them homeless and wretched. You will find people snatching other people's spouses away from them because of their money and power. You will find people concocting allegations in order to get people they hate locked up in jail.

They'll make up a story, bribe false witnesses and it's goodnight! Jail! In all the offices across the world, there are superiors and bosses who are mean for no reason or for a reason. It could be because they feel threatened by you. It could be because they feel you look better than them. It could be because they asked you for an amorous relationship and you said No. It could be because they resent your Christian faith. It could be anything. Therefore, they oppress you — malicious assessments, denied promotions, transfer to mundane departments, transfer to dead-end branches, demotion, excessive criticism of your work, public ridicule and disgrace, knocking down your ideas, making you irrelevant by assigning no work to you, recommending you for a sack, making false allegations against you, trying to get you killed using dark spiritual powers and other such terrible things. Once again, oppression is real.

So, if you are oppressed in any way, shape or form, who can help you? Let's take a look at scriptures:

Psalm 103:6 (KJV) "*The LORD executeth righteousness and judgment for all that are oppressed.*"

Psalm 72:14 (NET) "*From harm and violence he will defend them; he will value their lives.*"

The only person who can save you from the hands of a powerful, influential oppressor is Almighty God. Without wasting time, how can you access God's righteous judgment in order to be free from oppression? Again, let's find out from the Bible:

Deuteronomy 26:6-9 (KJV) *"And the Egyptians evil entreated us, and afflicted us, and laid upon us hard bondage:* **And when we cried unto the Lord God of our fathers, the Lord heard our voice, and looked on our affliction, and our labour, and our oppression: And the Lord brought us forth out of Egypt with a mighty hand, and with an outstretched arm, and with great terribleness, and with signs, and with wonders:** *And he hath brought us into this place, and hath given us this land, even a land that floweth with milk and honey."*

You can access God's righteous judgment by crying out to the Lord. If you are a born again Christian, the Almighty will hear your cry. He will then do a detailed assessment of your situation and of your oppressor. Thereafter, He will stretch out His Mighty hand and in the way He knows best, He will rescue you from the hand of your oppressor. He will also execute judgment on your oppressor for sure! Are you ready to be delivered from oppression? If yes, this is your day!

TODAY'S PRAYERS

1. Lord, I do not want to be burdened by the hand of the oppressor any longer. Come now and save me, in the name of Jesus.

2. Rock of Ages, I call out onto you today: Deliver me from the hand of those that are oppressing me, in the name of Jesus.

3. Hear my cry, O Lord. Stretch out Your Mighty hand for my sake and with great terribleness, signs and wonders, rescue me from Egypt, in the name of Jesus.

4. By the power that is in the Blood of Jesus, I arrest any man or woman who invents oppression. I arrest any person who lies awake on their bed every night in order to work evil against me. I arrest any practitioner and administrator of oppression against me and I hand them over to the Almighty for divine judgment, in the name of Jesus.

5. Right now, I speak against any physical, mental, emotional or spiritual burden and suffering that has been placed upon my life by my oppressors, COME OFF MY LIFE

NOW! and depart forever and ever, in the name of Jesus.

6. Anything that I have lost as a result of oppression, O Lord my God, let them be restored unto me multiple-fold, in the name of Jesus.

7. Thank You Mighty Father for putting an end to oppression in my life, in Jesus' mighty name, amen.

If you have the need and the time, please feel free to add more prayers at this point.

Blessing: May your oppression come to an end so that you can be free to worship your God, in the name of Jesus.

DAY 42

THE BLESSING OF THE DYING MAN

"For I rescued the poor who cried out for help, and the orphan who had no one to assist him; the blessing of the dying man descended on me, and I made the widow's heart rejoice" — Job 29:12-13 (NET)

DAILY EXHORTATION

In Job 1:1-3 (KJV), the Bible says "*There was a man in the land of Uz, whose name was Job; and that man was perfect and upright, and one that feared God, and eschewed evil. And there were born unto him seven sons and three daughters. His substance also was seven thousand sheep, and three thousand camels, and five hundred yoke of oxen, and five hundred she asses, and a very great household;* **so that this man was the greatest of all the men of the east.**"

When you read scriptures like the one above about Job, you should be curious to know how on earth a man got to be so wealthy to the extent that the Bible called him "the greatest of all the men of the east". If you are someone who wants to make clean money and have peace of mind, you should be interested in the secrets of the financial success of someone like Job. And this is what we will be looking at today very briefly.

Our opening scripture gives us a glimpse into just one of the secrets of Job's financial success. Job said that he rescued the poor who cried out to him for help. Not only that, he also rescued the orphan who had no one to assist him. He also helped out men who were about to die as well as widows. For his troubles, Job got what was called "*the blessing of the dying man*". Wow! Powerful stuff!

This dying man could have been someone who was sick and could not afford to pay for his own healthcare or it could have been someone wounded along the way whom Job decided to rescue and take care of. And in return, he got the dying man's blessing. Specifically, he said "*the blessing of the dying man descended on him*". That is, it came from above and descended into his life.

These people Job mentioned in this verse were not individuals but categories. So, when he says I rescued "the poor", he means poor people as a category. When he says "the orphan", he means many orphans. When he says "the dying man", he actually means many dying men and when he says "the widow", he means many widows. You should realize that though he singled out the blessing of the dying man, all of these different categories of people [the poor, the orphans, dying people, widows, etc] would have also blessed Job.

Herein lies a great secret of financial breakthrough and wealth accumulation. Imagine tens, hundreds or thousands of people blessing you from time to time or everyday! Imagine a group of people saying "May God replenish your pocket", "May God increase you", "May God keep evil away from you", "May God continue to prosper you" and so on. God will hear these blessings and prayers and He will answer them in your favor. Most of the wealthiest people in the world give. Perhaps this is why they never fade away?

Do you want to be wealthy? Do you want financial establishment? Do you want people praying for you and blessing you before God? Do you want to grow from strength to strength? Do you need the blessing of the dying man? If yes, get yourself ready!

TODAY'S PRAYERS

1. Almighty God, I want financial establishment. Give me the grace to put into practice the principles Job adopted in his life

which caused him to become the greatest of his time, in the name of Jesus.

2. From today, I will set aside a portion of what I have been blessed with to rescue **the poor** who cry out to me for help, in the name of Jesus.

3. From today, I will set aside a portion of what I have been blessed with to rescue **the orphans** who have no one to assist them, in the name of Jesus.

4. From today, I will set aside a portion of what I have been blessed with to help **dying people** who cannot afford to care for themselves, in the name of Jesus.

5. From today, I will set aside a portion of what I have been blessed with in order to give to **the widows** so that their hearts can rejoice, in the name of Jesus.

6. By reason of my deeds, O God, let the blessing of the dying man descend on me. Let the blessing of the poor, the orphans and the widows descend on me. As these people utter their blessings and their prayers in my favor before You, O God, hear them and bless me indeed, in the name of Jesus.

7. Thank You Mighty God for answering my prayers, in Jesus' mighty name, amen.

If you have the need and the time, please feel free to add more prayers at this point.

Blessing: May the blessing of the dying man descend on you and may God hear it and cause it to manifest in your life, in the name of Jesus.

DAY 43

A NOTE OF WARNING

"Take heed that ye do not your alms before men, to be seen of them: otherwise ye have no reward of your Father which is in heaven." — Matthew 6:1 (KJV)

DAILY EXHORTATION

Yesterday, we looked at one of the practices of Job that contributed to his greatness. Specifically, we saw that he was someone who helped out the poor, the orphans, the dying and the widows. We also saw that you could replicate the success that he had by replicating what he did.

Now, this morning, there's a warning concerning that. It is true that if you give to a dying man, he will bless you and God will answer the blessing and cause it to manifest. But there are things that could very well block the blessing of the dying man. One of these things is what is highlighted in our opening scripture. The Lord Jesus Christ is warning that when you want to give alms — such as to poor people, orphans, sick and dying people and widows — DO NOT do it publicly. For instance, do not go in with cameras and other such equipment in order to advertise to the world that you have given or you are giving. Jesus says that if you do that, even though the recipients bless you, God will not respond to the blessings and therefore, you will get nothing. That should be quite clear and straightforward.

So, what should you do then in order to ensure that the blessing of the dying man actually descends on you and works in your favor? Let's find out from our Lord and Savior:

Matthew 6:2-4 (NET) "*Thus whenever you do charitable giving, do not blow a trumpet before you, as the hypocrites do in synagogues and on streets so that people will praise them. I tell you the truth, they have their reward.* **But when you do your giving, do not let your left hand know what your right hand is doing, so that your gift may be in secret.** *And your Father, who sees in secret, will reward you.*"

Do your giving in secret and without telling anyone except perhaps your spouse. Also practically speaking, you may record your givings in your books for obvious reasons [such as accounting, etc]. BUT no publicity. If you follow the words of Christ and do as He says, any blessing that is directed at you by the recipients of your charity will be answered by God. And as a result, God will reward you. Are you ready to obey Jesus? If yes, get yourself ready!

TODAY'S PRAYERS

1. My Lord and my God, what I am after in life is not the praise of people BUT to obey Your word and to be blessed by You. Help me, in the name of Jesus.

2. According to the word of the Lord, any trumpet of hypocrisy in my hand, I smash you to pieces, in the name of Jesus.

3. Any power of the flesh in my life which is addicted to publicity and showing off, I command you to die now, in the name of Jesus.

4. Father, according to Your word, as I identify those to whom I want to give, let me go to them in secret and do my giving, in the name of Jesus.

5. Father, as I give to the poor, orphans, widows, sick and dying people and any other person in need, if they utter words of blessing in my favor, have mercy, hear their words of

blessing and answer them for my sake, in the name of Jesus.

6. My Lord and my God, let these words of blessings uttered by these people in secret, become instruments for my breakthrough, in the name of Jesus.

7. Thank You O Lord for answering my prayers, in Jesus' mighty name, amen.

If you have the need and the time, please feel free to add more prayers at this point.

Blessing: As you obey the Lord, you shall surely receive your reward, in the name of Jesus.

DAY 44

PRAY FOR EXPERIENCE

"And Pharaoh said unto Joseph, See, I have set thee over all the land of Egypt. And Pharaoh took off his ring from his hand, and put it upon Joseph's hand, and arrayed him in vestures of fine linen, and put a gold chain about his neck; And he made him to ride in the second chariot which he had; and they cried before him, Bow the knee: and he made him ruler over all the land of Egypt."
— Genesis 41:41-43 (KJV)

DAILY EXHORTATION

One of the great realities of life is that sudden greatness can be very detrimental. Many people who go from zero to hero in an instant usually lack the foundation upon which to base their new found greatness. Therefore, failure is not far from them. This is why sometimes you have to be careful what you wish for and even pray for. God knew that at some point in the future a famine would cover the whole earth. No one knows why it had to be that way. But that was the way it is. Therefore, the Almighty wanted a well-seasoned descendant of Abraham to become the "savior" of the human race at that time. The only way He could save humanity was to get this person into Egypt. Therefore, Joseph began to behave in ways that ultimately inspired his brothers to dispose of him. They sold him off to traders going to Egypt. God then arranged everything so that Joseph would have a path to the palace of Pharaoh.

But because saving the world required a person with administrative skills and experience, God also arranged it for Joseph to acquire all the administrative skills and experience he would need. Let's take a look at Joseph's resume:

Genesis 39:1&4 (KJV) "*And Joseph was brought down to Egypt; and Potiphar, an officer of Pharaoh, captain of the guard, an Egyptian, bought him of the hands of the Ishmeelites, which had brought him down thither... And Joseph found grace in his sight, and he served him:* **and he made him overseer over his house, and all that he had he put into his hand.**"

Genesis 39:5-6 (KJV) "*And it came to pass from the time that he had made him overseer in his house, and over* *all that he had, that the Lord blessed the Egyptian's house for Joseph's sake; and the blessing of the Lord was upon all that he had in the house, and in the field.* ***And he left all that he had in Joseph's hand; and he knew not ought he had****, save the bread which he did eat. And Joseph was a goodly person, and well favoured."*

Genesis 39:19-20 (KJV) *"And it came to pass, when his master heard the words of his wife, which she spake unto him, saying, After this manner did thy servant to me; that his wrath was kindled. And Joseph's master took him, and put him into the prison, a place where the king's prisoners were bound: and he was there in the prison."*

Genesis 39:21-23 (KJV) *"But the Lord was with Joseph, and shewed him mercy, and gave him favour in the sight of the keeper of the prison. And the keeper of the prison committed to Joseph's hand all the prisoners that were in the prison; and whatsoever they did there, he was the doer of it. The keeper of the prison looked not to any thing that was under his hand; because the Lord was with him, and that which he did, the Lord made it to prosper."*

Genesis 41:39-43 (KJV) *"And Pharaoh said unto Joseph, Forasmuch as God hath shewed thee all this, there is none so discreet and wise as thou art:* ***Thou shalt be over my house, and according unto thy***

word shall all my people be ruled: only in the throne will I be greater than thou. And Pharaoh said unto Joseph, See, I have set thee over all the land of Egypt. And Pharaoh took off his ring from his hand, and put it upon Joseph's hand, and arrayed him in vestures of fine linen, and put a gold chain about his neck; And he made him to ride in the second chariot which he had; and they cried before him, Bow the knee: and he made him ruler over all the land of Egypt."

What a wonderful track record! What a fantastic resume. And this is just the beginning part of Joseph's resume! In the house of Potiphar, God ensured that he was made the overseer. Then, even when he was in prison, he was made the overseer of all the prisoners and he was in this position for many years doing this job. Therefore, when Pharaoh made him ruler, he had already acquired several years of administrative experience.

Great lives take time to build. If you want something that will last for a very long time, you need experience. You have to pray to God to provide you with opportunities for experience as much as you pray for him to bless you with anything else.

Experience will put your mind at ease. It will ensure that any challenge that comes your way will be surmountable. It will make problems that are so difficult for others become routine for you to solve. It is so crucial and so vital.

Now, there are some other things to consider regarding Joseph. In order to make Joseph's experience worthwhile, God also helped with certain things. From the scriptures above, some of these things include: **causing Joseph to find grace and favor in the sight of his masters, being blessed with the aptitude for service, blessing his masters with the blessing of the Lord by reason of Joseph's presence, causing his masters to give him more responsibilities so that he could gain experience quicker, causing Joseph to have accountability and integrity, inspiring people to behave in ways that caused Joseph to move to the next level, causing him to have people management skills in spite of his amateurish relationship with his brothers in the past, miraculously helping him get to the pinnacle of his career where he could use his experience to the maximum, etc.**

Do you want to be great? Do you want God to provide you with opportunities that will equip you with the experience you need in order to handle greatness? If yes, get yourself ready!

TODAY'S PRAYERS

1. Messiah, I want to be great. And now, I realize that I need experience in order to become great and to last. Therefore, I come to You this morning to ask for Your help. Give ear to my prayers and answer me, in the name of Jesus.

2. Lord God, have mercy on me. Inspire people to create circumstances that will push me into or get me into the places I need to get to in order to acquire the experience that I need, in the name of Jesus.

3. My God, when I get into these places, let me find grace and favor in the eyes of my employers. Make me develop people skills so that I can relate with the high, the middle and the low and any other person successfully, in the name of Jesus.

4. Father, unleash in me the aptitude for service so that I can give my best to my employers. Fit me with accountability and integrity so that my reputation will always speak for me. Even as I work, inspire my employers to give me more responsibilities so that I can acquire all the knowledge and experience that I need quicker, in the name of Jesus.

5. O Lord God, whomever I work for or work with, let it become clear that it is because of my presence there that they are being blessed, in the name of Jesus.

6. King of kings, after You know that I have had all the training and experience that I need, create miraculous events that will take me from wherever I am to the pinnacle of my career so that I can unleash what I have learned for the benefit of mankind and to Your glory, in the name of Jesus.

7. Thank You Excellency for answering my prayers, in Jesus' mighty name, amen.

If you have the need and the time, please feel free to add more prayers at this point.

Blessing: May God help you to acquire the experience that will prepare you to make impact in your generation, in the name of Jesus.

DAY 45

CURSES ARE REAL

"...Now Balak son of Zippor was king of the Moabites at this time. And he sent messengers to Balaam son of Beor at Pethor, which is by the Euphrates River in the land of Amaw, to summon him, saying, 'Look, a nation has come out of Egypt. They cover the face of the earth, and they are settling next to me. So now, please come and curse this nation for me, for they are too powerful for me. Perhaps I will prevail so that we may conquer them and drive them out of the land. For I know that whoever you bless is blessed, and whoever you curse is cursed.'"
— Numbers 22:4B-6 (NET)

DAILY EXHORTATION

News of the miraculous events that God performed in the land of Egypt in order to rescue His people from oppression had gone far and wide. Most of the kings of the countries in the

Middle East had heard about the stories of a race of people who had been saved through signs and wonders from the hands of Pharaoh.

Therefore, as Moses led his people toward Canaan, the promised land, you'd think that these neighboring kingdoms would just leave them alone. But this was not the case. In some cases, without any provocation, a king would hear that the Israelites were about to reach his country. He would then gather his army in order to fight them BUT the former slaves would completely defeat them. In one case, the Israelites sent word to a king to please let them through but the king refused and instead brought out his entire army to destroy the Jews. This was a mistake because he and his country were completely annihilated by the Israelites.

So, the kings of other kingdoms in the region began to get apprehensive and one of them was Balak, son of Zippor, king of Moab. His own turn too had arrived. The Israelites came and camped nearby. Balak was quite intelligent. He knew that those kings that had confronted Israel using pure military force were already in the grave. So, he decided to try a hybrid approach — spiritual warfare and then military warfare. It is at this point that we get to our opening scripture. Balak knew of a man who heard from God. This man had a strange reputation. Whomever he blessed would certainly be blessed BUT whomever he cursed would certainly be cursed. So, he sent for Balaam to come and help him. He wanted Balaam to first curse the Jews then after they had been weakened by the curse, he would then go in with military force to conquer them and drive them away from his country.

This was a very nice strategy but these were the chosen people of the Most High and that made it a strategy of failure. When the messengers arrived at Balaam's house, this was what God told Balaam:

Numbers 22:12 (KJV) "*And God said unto Balaam, Thou shalt not go with them;* ***thou shalt not curse the people: for they are blessed.***"

Balak again sent another batch of messengers and this time Balaam went with them. However, on the way, his donkey began to misbehave. It was misbehaving because he saw what Balaam could not see — an angel of the Lord with a sword drawn out. The donkey twisted and turned and did all kinds of things to avoid the angel. Balaam thought it was just being stubborn and so he beat his dear donkey. Then, all of a sudden, the Lord also opened Balaam's own eyes and this was what happened:

Numbers 22:31-33 (NET) "*Then the Lord opened Balaam's eyes, and he saw the angel of the Lord standing in the way with his sword drawn in his hand; so he bowed his head and threw himself down with his face to the ground. The angel of the Lord said to him, 'Why have you beaten your donkey these three times? Look, I came out to oppose you because what you are doing is perverse before me. The donkey saw me and turned from me these three times.* **If she had not turned from me, I would have killed you** *but saved her alive.'*"

God ultimately let Balaam go to Balak but rather than curse the Israelites, he used their enemy's resources to bless them multiple times. We will examine these blessings further tomorrow and the day after. But back to the scriptures we have examined for today.

You see, a curse is a matter of fact. It is a real thing. Negative words spoken by anyone [especially one who has spiritual power or some kind of authority] against another person can come to pass. You can see for yourself the trouble Balak took in order to get someone who could curse a whole nation. You can also see that God did not just dismiss the entire episode. God took the episode very seriously and this is was why He personally intervened in the matter. In Proverbs 18:21 (KJV), the Bible says "*Death and life are in the power of the tongue ...*" If Balaam had been allowed by God, for instance, to say "*O Israel, I decree failure upon you, I curse your bodies. May each one of you be consumed with sickness and disease until you become a forgotten people.*", believe it or not, those words would have come to pass in reality. This is why you also have to take the issue of curses seriously.

Just like the Israelites were a threat to Balak, it is possible that you are a threat to someone. It could be that someone is concerned that your presence in your office would soon lead to you taking their position or being promoted instead of them or above them. It could be that someone hates you because of your race, looks, Christian faith, natural beauty, natural gifts, natural endowments, etc. and they just want you paralyzed, removed or destroyed. Therefore, they themselves could purchase books on curses and magic in order to curse you. Or, as Balak did, they could locate a medium or an evil prophet of some kind in order for him or her to curse you. And just as Israel was unaware of the efforts of Balak at the time, how do you know that someone is not currently going about seeking to lay a curse on you as you read this?

Now, what do you do to protect yourself from the curse of the Balaks and the Balaams of today. The first thing that you have to do is to ask for the blessing of God upon your life. In Numbers 22:12 above, this was the first thing that prevented Balaam from cursing the Jews. The second thing is that you have to realize that today, there are no more neutral prophets. A prophet is either of God or of the devil.

Therefore, if God is on your side, He will do to any evil prophet today what He threatened to do to Balaam in Numbers 22:33 "... *If she [the donkey] had not turned from me, I would have killed you* ..." To be safe from curses, you need to be blessed and you need God to execute any judgment that He desires upon any enemy who is stubbornly seeking to do you evil. If these two things are not in place, the curse of the enemy will manifest against you. If these two are in place, you will be completely safe. Do you want to fortify yourself against curses? If yes, get yourself ready!

TODAY'S PRAYERS

1. My heavenly Father, I thank You for the **natural endowments** that You have blessed me with, in the name of Jesus.

2. Almighty God, I thank You for all the **spiritual endowments** that You have blessed me with. To You be all the glory and praise, in the name of Jesus.

3. O Lord, I thank You for all the achievements I have had and everything that I have accumulated in life thus far by reason of the natural and spiritual endowments that You have blessed me with. Receive my praises and my adoration, in the name of Jesus.

4. My Lord and my God, if there is any person out there who is going from place to place in order to attack my life because of any advantage they believe I have over them, according to Your word, let their actions become perverse before You, in the name of Jesus.

5. Almighty God, through the death and resurrection of Jesus Christ, I too am now connected to the same blessing of Abraham that natural born Jews are connected to. Therefore, let this blessing of Abraham and Your direct blessing upon me speak against any curse issued against me in order to nullify it and cause it to come to nothing, in the name of Jesus.

6. Great Judge of the universe, if there be anyone out there, an evil Balak or an evil Balaam, seeking to curse me in order to weaken me, to remove me or to destroy me, I arrest this person and I hand them over to

You for Your divine judgment. As I do this, let any attempt to curse me be eradicated forever and ever, in the name of Jesus.

7. Thank You Blessed Father for answering my prayers, in Jesus' mighty name, amen.

If you have the need and the time, please feel free to add more prayers at this point.

Blessing: May the blessing of God work for you and may He judge anyone who seeks your hurt through a curse, in the name of Jesus.

DAY 46

BLESSINGS TOO ARE REAL - PART 1

"And Balaam said unto Balak, Stand by thy burnt offering, and I will go: peradventure the LORD will come to meet me: and whatsoever he sheweth me I will tell thee. And he went to an high place."
— Numbers 23:3 (KJV)

DAILY EXHORTATION

Yesterday, we learned that, despite the hindrances God put in Balaam's way, he eventually let Balaam go to Balak. However, rather than curse the Israelites, Balaam used Balak's resources to bless them multiple times.

Today, we will be examining one of such times that Balaam blessed Israel. You will also have the opportunity to personalize these blessings upon your own life. We will do the same thing tomorrow with another set of blessings uttered by Balaam.

So, from our opening scripture, Balaam

went up to a high place, deceiving Balak as if he wanted to curse the Jews. But this is a feedback of blessing he brought back with him from the high place [in this case, Pisgah]:

Numbers 23:20-24 (KJV) "*Behold, I have received commandment to bless: and He [God] hath blessed; and I cannot reverse it. He hath not beheld iniquity in Jacob, neither hath he seen perverseness in Israel: the Lord his God is with him, and the shout of a king is among them. God brought them out of Egypt; he hath as it were the strength of an unicorn. Surely there is no enchantment against Jacob, neither is there any divination against Israel: according to this time it shall be said of Jacob and of Israel, What hath God wrought! Behold, the people shall rise up as a great lion, and lift up himself as a young lion: he shall not lie down until he eat of the prey, and drink the blood of the slain.*"

This morning, you have the opportunity to personalize these blessings so they will manifest in your life. Get yourself ready!

TODAY'S PRAYERS

1. O Lord my High Tower, examine me and by reason of the sacrifice of Your son, Jesus Christ, find no iniquity in me, in the name of Jesus.

2. O Lord my refuge, examine me and by Your grace and mercy, see no perverseness in me, in the name of Jesus.

3. Everlasting God, be with me and let shouts and proclamations of You, my King, be found in me, in the name of Jesus.

4. Great Deliverer, give me the strength of an unicorn and of a wild ox so that no one will be able to stand against me all the days of my life, in the name of Jesus.

5. Rock of Ages, let any attempt to use enchantments, divination, sorcery, dark magic, witchcraft, curses, omen or any other evil means against me, always come to nothing, in the name of Jesus.

6. Jehovah, cause me to be like a lion so that anyone who rises against me will be completely defeated, in the name of Jesus.

7. Thank You Father for answering my prayers, in Jesus' mighty name, amen.

If you have the need and the time, please feel free to add more prayers at this point.

Blessing: May the blessings you have prayed upon yourself this morning manifest in your favor, in the name of Jesus.

DAY 47

BLESSINGS TOO ARE REAL - PART 2

"And when Balaam saw that it pleased the Lord to bless Israel, he went not, as at other times, to seek for enchantments, but he set his face toward the wilderness. And Balaam lifted up his eyes, and he saw Israel abiding in his tents according to their tribes; and the spirit of God came upon him." — Numbers 24:1-2 (KJV)

DAILY EXHORTATION

Yesterday, you had the opportunity to review some of the blessings Balaam was forced to declare upon the Jews. You also got the chance to personalize them for your own sake. Today, we will be looking at a second batch of blessings. Let's take a quick look at what they are from the word of God:

Numbers 24:2-4 *(KJV) "And Balaam lifted up his eyes, and he saw Israel abiding in his tents according to* *their tribes; and the spirit of God came upon him. And he took up his parable, and said, Balaam the son of Beor hath said, and the man whose eyes are open hath said: He hath said, which heard the words of God, which saw the vision of the Almighty, falling into a trance, but having his eyes open:*

Numbers 24:5-9 *(KJV) How goodly are thy tents, O Jacob, and thy tabernacles, O Israel! As the valleys are they spread forth, as gardens by the river's side, as the trees of lign aloes which the Lord hath planted, and as cedar trees beside the waters. He shall pour the water out of his buckets, and his seed shall be in many waters, and his king shall be higher than Agag, and his kingdom shall be exalted. God brought him forth out of Egypt; he hath as it were the strength of an unicorn: he shall eat up the nations his enemies, and shall break their bones, and pierce them through with his arrows. He couched, he lay down as a lion, and as a great lion: who shall stir him up? Blessed is he that blesseth thee, and cursed is he that curseth thee. "*

Once again, you have the opportunity to personalize these blessings so they will manifest in your life. Get yourself ready!

TODAY'S PRAYERS

1. Omnipotent God, make my place of dwelling a goodly place, in the name of Jesus.

2. Father, let my life be like gardens by the river's side. Let it be like trees of aloes which You Yourself have planted. Let my life be like cedar trees beside divine waters, in the name of Jesus.

3. Elohim, because You shall send down Your divine rain upon my life, I shall always pour water out of my buckets and my seed and my descendants will be in many waters, in the name of Jesus.

4. Eternal King, make me higher than Agag and let my household be exalted, in the name of Jesus.

5. Great and Mighty God, I ask once again that You give me the strength of an unicorn and of a wild ox so that no one will be able to stand before me for evil all the days of my life, in the name of Jesus.

6. My Lord and my God, let anyone who blesses me be blessed and let any curse issued against me come to nothing but return to its sender, in the name of Jesus.

7. Thank You Dear Father for answering my prayers, in Jesus' mighty name, amen.

If you have the need and the time, please feel free to add more prayers at this point.

Blessing: May the blessings you have prayed upon yourself this morning manifest in your favor, in the name of Jesus.

DAY 48

THE BELLY CHALLENGE

"'When my life was ebbing away, I called out to the Lord, and my prayer came to your holy temple. Those who worship worthless idols forfeit the mercy that could be theirs. But as for me, I promise to offer a sacrifice to you with a public declaration of praise; I will surely do what I have promised. Salvation belongs to the Lord!' Then the Lord commanded the fish and it disgorged Jonah on dry land."
— Jonah 2:7-10 (NET)

DAILY EXHORTATION

God wanted Jonah to deliver a message of warning to the people of Nineveh. Jonah wanted to avoid the assignment. He tried to run away by boat to some other city but God made the waters rumble against him. Ultimately, Jonah found himself in the mouth of a huge fish.

Our opening scripture comes from Jonah

while he was in the belly of the fish. For three days and nights, Jonah was in this fish. He began to feel that this could be the end of his life, so, he called out in prayer to the Lord.

Amongst other things, he acknowledged that God listens to prayer. He mentions that idol worship does not include mercy and mercy can only be found in the Almighty. He promised to offer a sacrifice to God with thanksgiving. He also made a vow to the Lord. Finally, he declared that salvation or deliverance comes only from God. When God heard this cry of repentance, He commanded the fish to release Jonah on dry land.

One more thing about this episode in Jonah's life is that he was on a three-day fast while he was in the fish's belly. When Jonah recovered from his ordeal, he proceeded to Nineveh and carried out the task that was assigned to him. What an ordeal!

Imagine being in that fish's belly not knowing what wild creature it would swallow next that could come in and attack you. Imagine sitting down in darkness [with momentary flashes of light] for three days. Imagine the trauma. And all this could have been averted if Jonah had simply obeyed the Lord from the beginning.

This episode also shows that "anything" you see or indeed any creature made by God can be commanded against you, if you act contrary to the word of God. In order to get Jonah to repent, God simply commanded the fish: "locate Jonah and swallow him". In the same way, because of a sin you are committing, God can command a human being to begin to oppose you. He can command the weather to work against you because of your sin. He can use anything!

So, this morning, you need to examine your life and your circumstances. Do you have a sin that you are committing? Or is there a good deed that you should do but you are not doing? Are you experiencing serious challenges in your life? If yes to all these, there could be a link between your sin or what you have neglected to do and the challenge you are having. In this case, you can put an end to the challenge by doing as Jonah did. That challenge is your own belly of fish. Like Jonah, acknowledge that God listens to prayer. In your prayer to God, confess your sin or the thing you are neglecting to do and ask God for mercy and forgiveness. Offer unto God a sacrifice of praise and thanksgiving in words and in songs. Make a promise or a vow to the Lord which you have every intention of keeping. Declare unto the Lord that He is the only source of salvation and deliverance.

If you do all of this, in the same manner God commanded the fish to vomit Jonah from its belly, He will also put an end to your challenge.

So, do you want deliverance from the challenge you are facing? Do you want to make peace with your creator? If yes, get yourself ready!

TODAY'S PRAYERS

1. Everlasting God, if the challenges I am facing are as a result of my sins or a consequence of something I failed to do, have mercy on me, in the name of Jesus.

2. Mighty God, if like Jonah, I have found myself in my own belly of fish as a result of disobedience, forgive me, have mercy on me and deliver me from the belly of the fish, in the name of Jesus.

3. Now, pick 3 praise and worship songs. Concentrate on God the Father and sing these songs to Him once each. Accept my praise and worship, in the name of Jesus.

4. O God, I declare this morning that You are the source of all salvation and deliverance, in the name of Jesus.

5. My Lord and my Savior, save me from my challenges so that I can be free to do Your will, in the name of Jesus.

6. Great Deliverer, deliver me from my challenges so that I can be free to execute Your divine instructions to the letter, in the name of Jesus.

7. Thank You Father God for answering my prayers, in Jesus' mighty name, amen.

If you have the need and the time, please feel free to add more prayers at this point.

Blessing: As you do the will of God, may He lift you up exceedingly, in the name of Jesus.

DAY 49
CLEARING YOUR CONSCIENCE

"The Holy Spirit is making clear that the way into the holy place had not yet appeared as long as the old tabernacle was standing. This was a symbol for the time then present, when gifts and sacrifices were offered that could not perfect the conscience of the worshiper."
— Hebrews 9:8-9 (NET)

DAILY EXHORTATION

In Hebrews 9:22 (NET), the Bible says "*Indeed according to the law almost everything was purified with blood, and without the shedding of blood there is no forgiveness.*" Therefore, in the old testament, there was a tabernacle. It had an outer room and an inner room known as the Holy of Holies. Regular priests could enter into the outer room to perform different kinds of duties. However, on "Yom Kippur" or the "Day of Atonement" [which is still observed in Israel till this day], after extensive prior preparations with the blood of animals, the high priest would enter into the Holy of Holies in order to seek forgiveness for his owns sins and the sins of every person in Israel. The high priest always had to make sure that he entered into the Holy of Holies with animal blood because, as we just read, blood is required for forgiveness. Once Yom Kippur was over, the people were free to pray and expect the blessings of God until the following year.

Our opening scripture says that in setting up this process at that time, the Holy Spirit was making it clear that, for regular, everyday people, the way into the Holy of Holies had not yet manifested or appeared. As an individual, you could not at the time approach God directly in the Holy of Holies. To do that was to be destroyed. You needed a human high priest to intervene. But even he himself had to ask for the forgiveness of his own sins!

Our opening scripture also says that even with this process, the day of atonement did not clear the conscience of the sinner. It cleared people on the outside but their hearts were still beleaguered with the guilt and conscience of their sins. Therefore, a change was needed. "The way" as referred to in our opening scripture had to appear. A change that would give everyone in the world access to the Holy of Holies and at the same time clear one's conscience was badly needed. Did this change come? Let's find out from scripture:

Hebrews 9:11-12 (KJV) "*But Christ being come an high priest of good things to come, by a greater and more perfect tabernacle, not made with hands, that is to say, not of this building; Neither by the blood of goats and calves, but by his own blood he entered in once into the holy place, having obtained eternal redemption for us.*"

Hebrews 9:13-14 (KJV) "*For if the blood of bulls and of goats, and the ashes of an heifer sprinkling the unclean, sanctifieth to the purifying of the flesh: How much more shall the blood of Christ, who through the eternal Spirit offered himself without spot to God, purge your conscience from dead works to serve the living God?*"

"The way" eventually appeared. The way is Jesus Christ. No wonder He said of Himself "*I am the way, the truth, and the life: no man cometh unto the Father, but by me*" (John 14:6, KJV). As the scriptures above reveal, all the beatings Jesus suffered and His crucifixion on the Cross caused Him to lose blood. The blood of this innocent man who never committed any sin thus became the perfect blood of atonement. And because the tabernacle he entered into upon His death was not a physical one but heaven itself, His blood of atonement was sufficient enough to obtain eternal redemption [not a yearly atonement] for anyone who believes in Him.

Further, His blood, working with God's Holy Spirit, has all the power and potency to wash your heart and clear your conscience. It is for this reason that, no matter what sin you commit as a believer, your sins will be forgiven and your conscience should be clear.

Jesus has paid the once and for all price for your sins. All you need to do is to ask Him for forgiveness and you will get it. This is good news because it means that you will not lose fellowship with God, you will enjoy His blessings and you will be able to walk everyday of your life without fear of your eternal destination.

So, do you want to live a life free from a guilty conscience? Do you want to feel outwardly and inwardly clean? If yes, get yourself ready!

TODAY'S PRAYERS

1. Lord Jesus, I thank You for coming to the earth to shed Your blood and to die for my sins. I praise You.

2. My Savior, it is because of Your blood, Your death and Your resurrection that I have hope in this life. I give You all the glory.

3. Great Redeemer, it is because of Your holy sacrifice that I have obtained eternal redemption and access to the heavenly tabernacle of the Most High God. Be forever glorified.

4. Father God, this morning, I confess all my sins to You and I forsake them. By reason of the blood of Jesus, have mercy on me and forgive me. Let my fellowship with You be restored, in the name of Jesus.

5. Lord, let the blood of Jesus flow into my life right now and purify my flesh and everything concerning me, in the name of Jesus.

6. Messiah, let the blood of Jesus flow into my heart, my spirit and my soul and cleanse my conscience from all dead works so that I can be free to serve You, in the name of Jesus.

7. Thank You Father for answering my prayers, in Jesus' mighty name, amen.

If you have the need and the time, please feel free to add more prayers at this point.

Blessing: May the purpose of Christ's sacrifice be fulfilled in your life, in the name of Jesus.

DAY 50

GREAT
EXPECTATIONS

**"And Lamech lived an hundred eighty and
two years, and begat a son: And he called
his name Noah, saying, This same shall
comfort us concerning our work and toil
of our hands, because of the ground which
the Lord hath cursed."
— Genesis 5:28-29 (KJV)**

DAILY EXHORTATION

Noah's parents were disillusioned by the amount
of work and toil they had to contend with in
order to make a living. Therefore, they poured all
their hopes for some comfort and a better life into
their baby boy, Noah. It was their hope that,
when he grew up, he would help them and make
their lives easier.

In the same manner, most committed
parents have hopes and expectations regarding
their children. These expectations may be like
that of Noah's folks, that is, helping them at some

point in the future. Or it may reflect a desire to see a child become a certain kind of person in life. Many parents who are wealthy hope that their offspring would at least be like them or exceed them in every way. No committed parent wants their offspring to do bad in life. But the reality is that there are many uncommitted parents. These kinds of people are too busy struggling with the battles of their lives and have no time to think about the "now" or the "later" of any child. Some realize this and give their children up for adoption or walk away. Others, keep the child in place and make his or her life a living hell.

If you have or had committed parents, good for you. If they had hopes and expectations for you which are in line with your own interests, by all means, do all you can to meet those expectations. If you do not or did not have committed parents, there is also good news for you. In Psalm 27:10 (NET), the Bible says "*Even if my father and mother abandoned me, the LORD would take me in.*" When the Lord takes you in, it means He will do everything that a parent should do for you and even go above and beyond. He will make human and material provision for you that will ensure you turn out well in life. Before we pray, let's examine one more passage from the Bible:

Hebrews 10:7 (NET) "*Then I said, 'Look, I have*

come. It is written about me in the scroll of a book; to do your will, God.'"

You see, everyone has a destiny. Whether you had committed parents or not, there is something that has been written concerning you which you must fulfill on the earth. Whether your parents were poor, rich, influential, humble, sophisticated, crass, etc., it doesn't matter. There is a destiny that God has put in place for you. If you fulfill it, you will please the Lord. If you please God, He will see to it that you will not lack anything that you truly need in this life.

Even if you were born humble, fulfillment of your destiny will see to it that there is no difference between you and someone born with a silver spoon. In fact, that is not quite accurate. Fulfillment of your destiny, will place you so high that the difference between you and those who are not committed to God will be remarkably great! This was what happened in the life of Gideon in the Bible.

So, in closing, it is great to fulfill the expectations of your parents. However, it is more important to fulfill the expectations God has put in place for you. Do you want to do this and reap the benefits all the days of your life? Do you want the hand of God to be with you and everything you lay your hands on? If yes, get yourself ready!

TODAY'S PRAYERS

1. Holy One of Israel, I thank You for the opportunity to come into this world in order to carry out Your will and demonstrate Your power on the earth. Accept my praises and my adoration, in the name of Jesus.

2. I Am that I Am, give me the determination and everything that I need to carry out the good hopes and expectations that my parents have for me, in the name of Jesus.

3. My Lord and my God, make me the solution to the problems of my parents so that their joy may be full, in the name of Jesus.

4. I declare unto You, O God, that I am committed to You and to the divine plan that You have for my life. Visit me through any means You desire and reveal to me the plan that You want me to execute in this life, in the name of Jesus.

5. Messiah, this morning I ask: Provide me with the human, material, mental, spiritual, emotional, physical and every other resource that I need in order to go about and fulfill my destiny, in the name of Jesus.

6. Almighty God, as I demonstrate my commitment to Your divine plan and as I carry it out each day of my life, let me find grace in Your sight. Bless me and let me have all that I need so that I too can become an instrument of blessing and of destiny fulfillment to others, in the name of Jesus.

7. Thank You O God for answering my prayers, in Jesus' mighty name, amen.

If you have the need and the time, please feel free to add more prayers at this point.

Blessing: May you fulfill the expectations of your parents and may you execute God's special plan for your life, in the name of Jesus.

DAY 51

THE PALM TREE AND THE CEDAR

"The righteous shall flourish like the palm tree: he shall grow like a cedar in Lebanon." — Psalm 92:12 (KJV)

DAILY EXHORTATION

The palm tree is a magnificent tree. If you are familiar with the variety of things that can be produced from palm trees, you would claim our opening scripture everyday of your life.

On a basic level, from palm trees you can get brooms (for sweeping floors), palm wine, palm oil (edible and as raw material for several industrial products such as body creams, soaps, margarine), palm kernel (for food or industrial raw material), palm fruit (for food or raw material), planks (for making sheds, etc.). When processed, various parts of the palm tree can be used to make doormats, brushes, mattresses, ropes, dyes, varnishes, incense, bio-diesel (to power vehicles and engines), biscuits, chocolates, cookies, sweets, edible cream, peanut butter, milk, cereals, cakes, cosmetics, soaps, lotions and gels, shampoo, detergents, toothpaste, waxes, lubricants, ink, paper and so on.

Do you know that certain countries with very large economies such as Indonesia and Malaysia depend on the palm tree for a huge portion of their GDP?! In fact, if you withdraw the palm tree from these two countries, their economies would collapse immediately and this would cause a multi-year recession in the whole of Asia and around the world! Palm tree!

The Lebanon Cedar tree, on the other hand, is an intimidating presence. It is an evergreen tree that can grow to about 40 meters or 130 feet. To put that into perspective, that is, a little under the length of 3 basketball courts put together! Imagine yourself as tall as that! Therefore, when our opening scripture says that you will grow like a cedar in Lebanon, it means you will tower high above compatriots, competitors, principalities and powers, above problems that easily overwhelm or overcome the unrighteous and above all evil. It means you will be a financial giant, spiritual giant, marital giant and a giant in every area of your life. It means your life will remain ever green and youthful even with advancing age!

When you put these two together, this scripture simply means that you will be extremely productive, wealthy, healthy and unstoppable. What great benefits!

That said, the scripture says that you have to be righteous in order to access these benefits. Hopefully, at this point you have become born again. As a born again Christian, living a righteous life means living according to the word of God. It means avoiding sin. It means forsaking evil thought patterns and habits. Righteousness means living and walking with the Holy Spirit so that you can know what's on God's mind with the result that your ways will always be pleasing to Him. If you do this, your life will flourish like a palm tree and grow like a cedar in Lebanon.

Do you want all these glorious benefits in your life? If yes, get yourself ready!

TODAY'S PRAYERS

1. O Lord, I want the blessings that You have specially reserved for your children to manifest in my life. Help me, in the name of Jesus.

2. Father, I am aware that Your blessings are reserved for the righteous. I want to live a righteous life. Come to my aid, in the name of Jesus.

3. My God, let me live my life according to Your word. Let me always avoid sin and help me to forsake my evil thought patterns and habits, in the name of Jesus.

4. King of kings, let me live and walk with Your precious Holy Spirit so that I can always know what is on Your mind and so that my ways can always please you, in the name of Jesus.

5. Lord of lords, by reason of my commitment to You, let me flourish like a well-watered palm tree. Let this flourishing be made manifest in my life in as many ways as possible, in the name of Jesus.

6. Alpha and Omega, by reason of my commitment to You, let me grow like a Cedar in Lebanon. Let this growth be made manifest in my life in every way possible, in the name of Jesus.

7. Thank You Mighty God for answering my prayers, in Jesus' mighty name, amen.

If you have the need and the time, please feel free to add more prayers at this point.

Blessing: May God Almighty look upon your commitment to Him and indeed cause you to flourish like a palm tree and grow like a Cedar in Lebanon, in the name of Jesus.

DAY 52

THIS IS TOUGH

"I have smitten you with blasting and mildew: when your gardens and your vineyards and your fig trees and your olive trees increased, the palmerworm devoured them: yet have ye not returned unto me, saith the LORD."
— Amos 4:9 (KJV)

DAILY EXHORTATION

Many Christians believe that if they are facing a certain kind of challenge, it must be that they are being attacked by the devil or his myriad of agents. This is usually true. However, our opening scripture reveals another source of adversity — God Almighty.

Now, if you are living a holy life, this scripture should not bother you in any way. But if you know that you desire to live in sin, this scripture is probably something to worry about. Already, we know that anyone who sins opens himself or herself up to the devil for a spiritual attack and now there's the possibility that you may be punished by God? If the devil is after you, you can run to God for deliverance and for safety and you will be delivered and protected. BUT, if God is on your case, who will you appeal to?

Our opening scripture talks about people who have refused to return to God. In other words, unrepentant backsliders. It says that these people will be smitten with blasting and mildew. It says that palmerworms will be unleashed upon these people, thus causing destruction on their gardens, vineyards, fig trees and olive trees. Gardens signify beauty. So, this implies that backsliders will suffer damage to their appearance in some way or form. Vineyards, fig trees and olive trees are all revenue earners. This implies that backsliders will suffer some sort of great economic loss. This is tough stuff.

God has a right to do any or all of these because He is our creator. The way out is to stay with God or if you have already backslidden, return to Him. If you do either of these, none of these problems will ever find their way to you. Instead of suffering damage to your appearance, you will look better and better even as you get older. And you will go from strength to strength financially. Everything we need is in the Lord — fame, money, rest, etc.— they are all in the Lord. If you are in God, you can have all of these and still live in such a manner as to please him.

Are you ready to stay in the Lord and be spared all kinds of problems? If yes, today is your day. Get yourself ready!

TODAY'S PRAYERS

1. Adonai, I declare this morning that I am with You of my own free volition and because of my love for You. I know that You created me and therefore only You know what is best for me. Let my love for You continue to burn bright throughout the days of my life, in the name of Jesus.

2. By reason of my love for God, blasting and mildew will never be my portion throughout the days of my life, in the name of Jesus.

3. By reason of my love for God, the palmerworm of judgment shall not know its way to the door of my life, in the name of Jesus.

4. By reason of my love for God, the gardens of my life will continue to flourish, in the name of Jesus.

5. By reason of my love for God, my vineyards, my fig trees and my olive trees will continue

to increase and will grow from strength to strength. Throughout the days of my life, they will continue to be instruments of blessing to me and bring me great returns, in the name of Jesus.

6. By reason of my love for God, I will never go down. I will only go up, in the name of Jesus.

7. Thank You Father God for answering my prayers, in Jesus' mighty name, amen.

If you have the need and the time, please feel free to add more prayers at this point.

Blessing: By reason of your love for God, you will never ever experience His wrath but only His love, in the name of Jesus.

DAY 53
DIVINE PANIC

"And they said unto Joshua, Truly the LORD hath delivered into our hands all the land; for even all the inhabitants of the country do faint because of us."
— Joshua 2:24 (NET)

DAILY EXHORTATION

The spies Joshua sent out to Jericho had returned and they were eager to give him good news. They told him "*Truly the LORD hath delivered into our hands all the land*". Why were they so confident that Jericho had been delivered into their hands? The answer lies in their next statement "...*for even all the inhabitants of the country do faint because of us.*"

Today's opening scripture introduces us to a powerful instrument or weapon God uses to win battles and wars for His beloved children. This instrument is called "Panic". To panic means to be afraid, to feel terrorized, to be alarmed, to be dismayed, to be discomfited or to be horrified. God Almighty can and does scare, terrorize, alarm, dismay, discomfit and horrify enemies of His children in order to give them victory. Let's consider a few examples from scriptures:

1 Samuel 14:15,22-23 (NET) "***Then fear overwhelmed those who were in the camp, those who were in the field, all the army in the garrison, and the raiding bands. They trembled and the ground shook. This fear was caused by God...*** *When all the Israelites who had hidden themselves in the hill country of Ephraim heard that the Philistines had fled, they too pursued them in battle. So the Lord delivered Israel that day, and the battle shifted over to Beth Aven.*"

1 Samuel 14:18-19 (NET) "*So Saul said to Ahijah, 'Bring near the ephod,' for he was at that time wearing the ephod. While Saul spoke to the priest,* **the panic in the Philistines' camp was becoming greater and greater...**"

Psalm 48:4-7 (NET) "*For look, the kings assemble; they advance together.* **As soon as they see, they are shocked; they are terrified, they quickly retreat. Look at them shake uncontrollably, like a woman writhing in childbirth.** *With an east wind you shatter the large ships.*"

Joshua 10:7-10 (KJV) "*So Joshua ascended from Gilgal, he, and all the people of war with him, and all the mighty men of valour.* **And the Lord said unto Joshua, Fear them not: for I have delivered them into thine hand; there shall not a man of them stand before thee.** *Joshua therefore came unto them suddenly, and went up from Gilgal all night.* **And the Lord discomfited them before Israel**, *and slew them with a great slaughter at Gibeon, and chased them along the way that goeth up to Bethhoron, and smote them to Azekah, and unto Makkedah.*"

Here are some very important lessons to learn from these passages: God is biased in favor of His children. He will do whatsoever is necessary to turn things in their favor. God can cause fear to overwhelm anyone that has made himself or herself an enemy of His children. That person will suddenly be filled with an inexplicable fear of you to the extent that whenever they see you, they will begin to physically tremble or shake. It is then left to you to do whatever you like with that enemy.

God can also modulate the intensity of the panic with which He afflicts your enemies. In 1 Samuel 14:18-19 above, the Bible says "... *the panic in the Philistines' camp was becoming greater and greater...*" This means that for example, if you feel someone who hates you but who you have been merciful to is back trying to harm you again, you can ask God to increase the intensity of panic in that person's life! God can also use panic to cause an enemy to retreat from pursuing after you. And finally, if they refuse to stop their pursuit of your life, your career, your marriage, your children for evil, He can remove that enemy from your vicinity completely.

So, do you have someone who is tormenting you for no just cause? Do you have someone who is threatening you for no just cause? Do you have someone whose evil activities have caused your peace to depart from you? Do you want to turn the tables around and become a terror to that enemy? Do you want to obtain complete victory over your enemies? If yes, get yourself ready!

TODAY'S PRAYERS

1. Father God, Your word says that I should love my enemies and pray for them. This morning, I pray that You will have mercy upon any person who has made himself or herself into my enemy but who wishes to change, in the name of Jesus.

2. Mighty Warrior, if there be any enemy that refuses to repent and has decided to come

after my life or anything that pertains to me, let the weapon of Panic be unleashed against that person now, in the name of Jesus.

3. My Lord and my God, let my unrepentant enemies be filled and overwhelmed with the fear of me to the extent that whenever they see me they will physically tremble, in the name of Jesus.

4. Mighty God, according to Your word, if an enemy decides that he or she will not let me go, let the intensity of the spirit of panic be increased in that person's life, in the name of Jesus.

5. O Lord God, use the spirit of panic to cause my unrepentant enemies to retreat from me, my loved ones and anything that has to do with me, in the name of Jesus.

6. Messiah, if an enemy that has been chased away from me decides to once again attack me or seek my physical or spiritual hurt, use the spirit of panic to remove that person away from my vicinity completely and permanently, in the name of Jesus.

7. Thank You O God for answering my prayers. Thank you for the opportunity to benefit from this unique weapon of spiritual

warfare, in Jesus' mighty name, amen.

If you have the need and the time, please feel free to add more prayers at this point.

Blessing: May God use the weapon of panic against your enemies in order to obtain peace of mind for you, in the name of Jesus.

DAY 54

THE HUMBLING BUT

"...Therefore, so that I would not become arrogant, a thorn in the flesh was given to me, a messenger of Satan to trouble me— so that I would not become arrogant. I asked the Lord three times about this, that it would depart from me."
— 2 Corinthians 12:6-8 (NET)

DAILY EXHORTATION

If you were perfect in every way, it is very likely that you would be overwhelmed with pride. The Bible says *"Pride goeth before destruction, and an haughty spirit before a fall."* (Proverbs 16:18, KJV). Throughout history, many people who were born extremely good looking, extremely intelligent, extremely gifted with some talent, etc. succumbed to pride and therefore to a fall and destruction.

Many people who are extremely intelligent, good looking, gifted and are alive today have been preserved because they have what you can call a "BUT" in their lives. For example, *"Josh is tall, dark and handsome BUT he is not good at Math"*, *"Mary is so pretty BUT she is so shy"*, *"Adam is so bright. Look at how easily he programs computers BUT he is a very short guy. "*, *"Eva is the best case researcher in our law firm BUT she stutters"* and so on. These BUTs will make Josh, Mary, Adam and Eva humble despite their remarkable gifts.

Even the very righteous amongst us are not free from these BUTs. The words in our opening scripture are from Apostle Paul. As great as the apostle was, he had a BUT in his life. How did he come about such a thing. In 2 Corinthians 12, he writes that he was taken into heaven and heard so many amazing things that humans are not allowed to know about. And because this incredibly rare episode might make him arrogant, he was given a BUT in his life which he called "a thorn in the flesh" or "a messenger of Satan". Paul mentioned that he prayed to the Almighty to remove this BUT three times. How did God answer Paul's prayer? Let's find out:

2 Corinthians 12:8-9 (KJV) *"For this thing I besought the Lord thrice, that it might depart from me. And he said unto me,* ***My grace is sufficient for thee: for my strength is made perfect in weakness.****"*

In other words, God refused to remove the

BUT from his life in order to save his life and keep him humble. So, there are two very important lessons here: First, if God has endowed you with some special feature or ability that other people do not have, if you do not want a BUT in your life, you've got to speak to yourself. You will need to command your flesh and your human instincts to bury themselves under the will of God. You will have to develop the mentality that everything you have is from God and is for carrying out His word and will. You should do special things with the abilities He has given you but you should not seek the glory for yourself. If you can do this, you may be spared BUTs. If you cannot do this, God will assess you and He might introduce "a humbling but" into your life.

If you notice that you have an issue in your life that is not a threat to your life but is at the same time making you uncomfortable, you should pray to God to remove it. If God replies and tells you that He put it there, just like Paul, it means He has assessed you and determined that pride is likely to overwhelm you. Therefore, you would have to learn to live with it as it is there to prevent you from a fall and from destruction. This morning's prayers will focus on living in such a way as to prevent a BUT from being introduced into your life. Get yourself ready!

TODAY'S PRAYERS

1. Lord Jesus, Conqueror of sin, come and conquer sin, the flesh and my basic human instincts today, in the name of Jesus.

2. Father Lord, I do not want a thorn in my flesh. Deliver me from the spirit of pride, in the name of Jesus.

3. Abba Father, I do not want any messenger of satan to trouble me. Save me from arrogance, in the name of Jesus.

4. O God, today, I acknowledge that everything I have and that I am is from You and You alone, in the name of Jesus.

5. Jehovah, teach me to use the special features and abilities You have blessed me with to do special things and to give all the glory to You, in the name of Jesus.

6. Merciful Father, even as I continue to live in complete humility everyday of my life, by reason of my humility, do not let a 'humbling but' be introduced into my life, in the name of Jesus.

7. Thank You Father God for answering my prayers, in Jesus' mighty name, amen.

If you have the need and the time, please feel free to add more prayers at this point.

Blessing: May God help you and may your life so align with His will that He will see no need to give you a thorn in your flesh, in the name of Jesus.

DAY 55

NEPOTISM

"Now Abimelech son of Jerub-Baal went to Shechem to see his mother's relatives. He said to them and to his mother's entire extended family, 'Tell all the leaders of Shechem this: 'Why would you want to have seventy men, all Jerub-Baal's sons, ruling over you, when you can have just one ruler? Recall that I am your own flesh and blood.'' His mother's relatives spoke on his behalf to all the leaders of Shechem and reported his proposal. The leaders were drawn to Abimelech; they said, 'He is our close relative.' ... All the leaders of Shechem and Beth Millo assembled and then went and made Abimelech king by the oak near the pillar in Shechem."
—Judges 9:1-3,6 (NET)

DAILY EXHORTATION

Gideon [a.k.a Jerub-Baal] had just passed away. Gideon had been raised by God to deliver His children from the bondage of the Midianites. The Midianites were wasting powers, who would wait until the crops of the Jews were ready to be harvested. However, instead of grabbing the crops for themselves, they would destroy the whole lot. This introduced oppression into the lives of the Israelites and eventually led to the rise of Gideon. Through the power of God, Gideon delivered the Israelites from the hand of their oppressors.

So, you'd think that after he died, his children would be treated with the utmost care, consideration and respect. This probably would have been the case BUT there was a problem. Gideon had 70 legitimate sons and one illegitimate son called "Abimelech" [or Abimelek]. Abimelek was the son Gideon had with his maid who was from a place called Shechem.

While there was a vacuum of power, Abimelek took the opportunity to approach his people with a proposal for him to become king. If he did not do this, some sort of arrangement would have been put in place for all 70 of Gideon's legitimate sons to rule over Israel. But Abimelek did. Notice the words he used when he spoke with his relatives "*Recall that I am your own flesh and blood*" and when his relatives went to meet the leaders of Shechem, the leaders agreed to his proposal saying "*He is our close relative*". Afterward, they supplied him with money with which Abimelek hired assassins in order to murder all his brothers except Jotham, who was fortunate to escape.

There are a few lessons to learn from this episode. First, whenever you commit sin, it may come back to hurt you someday in your future. When Gideon's legitimate wives were giving birth to his 70 boys, there must have been great rejoicing and happiness in his household. He must have carried each boy and projected his wishes into the boy's life — "you will be great", "you will be prosperous", "you will be fruitful", etc. As the boys grew up, he would have thought to himself "wow, look at my small army". When he was about to die, he must have looked around and felt fulfilled that he was leaving behind a massive population of descendants. Unfortunately, the one son that resulted from his adulterous union with his slave was the one who extinguished all his dreams for his children. Abimelek killed them all. This is why we need the grace of God so that we do not fall into the kind of sin that would rise up later in life to destroy all that we have worked for.

The second lesson to learn from today's opening scripture is that Nepotism is real. Many people go to meet their relatives who occupy places of authority and influence to tell them "*Recall that I am your own flesh and blood*" and those powerful relatives would reply "*Yes, you are my close relative*". In so doing, these powerful relatives would disregard due process, deprive qualified people opportunity and give their relatives positions or opportunities that they are not qualified for.

If you know that people are using or may use nepotism to deprive you of what should be yours, you need to be ready for strategic prayers. Gideon's 70 sons were eligible to become rulers but nepotism blocked their path to power forever. But can God nullify the power of nepotism? Let's find out from scripture:

Judges 9:22-23 (KJV) "*When Abimelech had reigned three years over Israel, Then God sent an evil spirit between Abimelech and the men of Shechem; and the men of Shechem dealt treacherously with Abimelech.*"

Judges 9:24 (NET) "*He did this so the violent deaths of Jerub-Baal's seventy sons might be avenged and Abimelech, their half-brother who murdered them, might have to pay for their spilled blood, along with the leaders of Shechem who helped him murder them.*"

So, as you can see, God can nullify the power of nepotism. He can break any kind of bond when that bond is responsible for oppression and wickedness. If Gideon's 70 sons had prayed to God before Abimelek could act against them, they would have been spared. What God did in the verses above was instead the fulfillment of the prayer of Jotham, the son that managed to escape.

This should give you the confidence that if you are currently a victim of nepotism, God can correct the situation so that you can get what is rightfully yours.

So, are you a victim of nepotism? Do you want to see an end to oppression in your life? Do you want to ensure that sin does not sow a seed of danger in the soil of your life? If yes to all these, today is your day. Get yourself ready!

TODAY'S PRAYERS

1. Merciful God, I come before You this morning to confess all my sins and to forsake them. Have mercy on me and forgive me, in the name of Jesus.

2. God of grace, let any seed of sin in the soil of my life be destroyed now. Do not let the consequences of my sins rise up in the future to extinguish my dreams or to destroy everything that I have worked for, in the

name of Jesus.

3. My Lord and my God, do not let me become a victim of nepotism, in the name of Jesus.

4. Great and Mighty God, do not let me suffer irreversible loss by reason of nepotism as the sons of Gideon suffered, in the name of Jesus.

5. Jehovah Nissi, anytime any close relative or friend of anyone in a place of authority approaches them with a proposal to put them in a position they are not qualified for and which will block my own legitimate and deserved path to progress, as it was between Abimelek and the men of Shechem, let there be a stirring up of disagreement between them for my sake, in the name of Jesus.

6. Father God, let my work always yield fruit. Let my path of progress always be clear. Let me always move forward and do not let the greed and selfishness of men stop me as I fulfill my destiny, in the name of Jesus.

7. Thank You Father for answering my prayers, in Jesus' mighty name, amen.

If you have the need and the time, please feel free to add more prayers at this point.

Blessing: May God save you from sinful blasts from the past and from the wickedness of nepotism, in the name of Jesus.

DAY 56

WHAT WILL YOU DO WHEN THE TRAVELER COMES?

"And the Lord sent Nathan unto David. And he came unto him, and said unto him, There were two men in one city; the one rich, and the other poor. The rich man had exceeding many flocks and herds: But the poor man had nothing, save one little ewe lamb, which he had bought and nourished up: and it grew up together with him, and with his children; it did eat of his own meat, and drank of his own cup, and lay in his bosom, and was unto him as a daughter. And there came a traveller unto the rich man, and he spared to take of his own flock and of his own herd, to dress for the wayfaring man that was come unto him; but took the poor man's lamb, and dressed it for the man that was come to him. And David's anger was greatly kindled against the man; and he said to Nathan, As the Lord liveth, the man that hath done this thing shall surely die: And he shall restore the lamb fourfold, because he did this thing, and because he had no pity."
— 2 Samuel 12:1-6 (KJV)

DAILY EXHORTATION

Yesterday, we examined the injustice of nepotism. Today, we will be looking at something of a flip side to that. That is, if you find yourself in a position of power and you could do almost anything, how would you handle yourself?

One day, when Israel was at war and all its men of war were at the war-front, king David decided to stay home. That evening, as he was loitering around, he saw a naked woman bathing in the distance. He found out who she was. Despite being told she was married to a solider — Uriah the Hittite — David still went ahead and slept with her. It could have been a perfect 'one night stand' but sometime later, the woman [Bathsheba] sent word to him that she was pregnant.

This was the perfect scandal waiting to happen! David must have imagined how the rumors would spread all around Israel and around the region "King David Commits Adultery with Serving Soldier's Wife", "Randy King Impregnates Solider's Lonely Wife", etc. Therefore, David decided to take action.

First, he had Uriah brought back from war under the pretext that he wanted him to bring him news about the war. After Uriah told him the goings-on at the war-front, David told him to go home. His calculation was that, a man who had been away from home for so long would very earnestly desire to be with his wife and to sleep with her. However, Uriah refused to go home. To him, while all the able-bodied warriors of Israel were fighting for their country, it was absurd to go home, rest and 'be with' the Mrs. If all the boys were back from war, it would have been great and appropriate. But Uriah felt that in the context of the time, going home was a shameful thing to do. So, David tried another tactic. He invited Uriah to a kind of banquet and they both ate and drank. David's aim was to get him drunk enough so that he would go home to be with his wife. But even when fully drunk, Uriah remained in the palace, on duty, with the king's servants.

At this point, David saw very clearly that Uriah was committed to his philosophy and this is when David did something he would regret for the rest of his life. Let's find out what this is from the Bible:

2 Samuel 11:14-17 (KJV) "*And it came to pass in the morning, that David wrote a letter to Joab, and sent it by the hand of Uriah. And he wrote in the letter, saying,* **Set ye Uriah in the forefront of the hottest battle, and retire ye from him, that he may be smitten, and die.** *And it came to pass, when Joab observed the city, that he assigned Uriah unto a* *place where he knew that valiant men were. And the men of the city went out, and fought with Joab: and there fell some of the people of the servants of David; and Uriah the Hittite died also."*

2 Samuel 11:26-27 (KJV) *"And when the wife of Uriah heard that Uriah her husband was dead, she mourned for her husband. And when the mourning was past, David sent and fetched her to his house, and she became his wife, and bare him a son. But the thing that David had done displeased the Lord."*

You can see how one sin can lead to another and to another and to another. In trying to cover his sin of adultery, David brought shame upon a valiant man. He then got him drunk. He then got him killed. In the process, he soiled the hands of Joab [who had to carry out his instruction] with innocent blood and his action also caused collateral damage as some other soldiers besides Uriah also died at that forefront because of David's directive.

If someone had told you before this episode that David could do something like this, you'd say "Never!". But this is David killing an innocent man. Why? Because, as our opening scripture says "a traveler" came to him and David did not know how to handle the traveler.

Do you know that many of the assassinations

carried out in our cities are ordered by people who hitherto were law-abiding citizens? But because they find themselves stuck in a rut [such as blackmail, threat of exposure, challenge to position, etc], they decide to eliminate their opponents!

The traveler can come to anyone just as it did to David and many do not know how to handle it. What is this traveler that Nathan was referring to in his parable to David? The Traveler is anything that comes to you and makes demands on you. In the case of David, the traveler was his sexual urge. While he was loitering around on his rooftop, it came and unfortunately, David did not have the self-control to subdue it. For some other person, it could be the that a vacancy became available. The traveler would be the urge to become the person to fill that vacancy 'by all means' [including offering bribes, offering to sleep with someone to get it, or the willingness to kill for it].

The Traveler is pressure of any kind that wants to be satisfied. But as you can see from the scripture above, because David tried to use 'any means' to hide his sin of adultery including the killing of an innocent man, God was greatly displeased and this was why He sent the prophet Nathan to David to tell him the proverb in our opening scripture. God spared David's life BUT a curse was placed upon his household. In addition, the son resulting from his night with Bathsheba died. See 2 Samuel 12:7-19 for details.

The question this morning is this: If David, an anointed man, a national hero, a generally good and much-beloved child of God, could arrange for someone to be killed because he was desperate, what will YOU do when your own traveler comes and you have power to do anything you like? If you had a lot of money, power and influence and you find yourself in a situation of great pressure, how will you handle yourself? Will you be able to control yourself and save yourself from divine judgment OR will you satisfy your urges and incur God's wrath as David did?

This morning you have the opportunity to seek the face of God for His grace and for strength for when your own traveler comes. If this is something you would like to do, get yourself ready!

TODAY'S PRAYERS

1. El Olam, this morning, I ask for Your grace and Your mercy. Let them never depart from me, in the name of Jesus.

2. Messiah, if David could commit a sin as

grievous as he did, it means anyone else can do the same or even much worse. Therefore, I ask You to ever be my guide and never leave my side, in the name of Jesus.

3. My Lord and my God, through the power of Your Holy Spirit who lives in me, let self-control be unleashed into every area of my life now so that I can have the supernatural power to say No when I need to say No and to say Yes when I should say Yes, in the name of Jesus.

4. Father, when the Traveler comes as it comes or will come to everyone that is alive, do not let me fail you. Let me satisfy the Traveler with what rightfully belongs to me and not with what belongs to another person, in the name of Jesus.

5. Holy One of Israel, when the Traveler leaves me, let my hands remain clean and my soul remain innocent, in the name of Jesus.

6. Lord, by reason of my action of righteousness, let me spared curses and divine judgment. Instead, let me be a beneficiary of Your great and mighty blessings, in the name of Jesus.

7. Thank You Father for answering my prayers,

in Jesus' mighty name, amen.

If you have the need and the time, please feel free to add more prayers at this point.

Blessing: May God's grace be with you so that you will pass the test of the Traveler, in the name of Jesus.

DAY 57

SOME PEOPLE NEVER FORGET

"Her brother Absalom said to her, 'Was Amnon your brother with you? Now be quiet, my sister. He is your brother. Don't take it so seriously!' Tamar, devastated, lived in the house of her brother Absalom. Now King David heard about all these things and was very angry. But Absalom said nothing to Amnon, either bad or good, yet Absalom hated Amnon because he had humiliated his sister Tamar."
— 2 Samuel 13:20-22

DAILY EXHORTATION

David had many children. Today's devotional covers a situation that affected three of them namely Amnon, his half-sister Tamar and her brother Absalom. Even though Prince Amnon could have any woman he liked in the land of Israel, he made his half-sister, Tamar, his love interest. He became so obsessed with her that when he concluded that he could not have her, he became depressed. Then, one day his cousin Jonadab confronted him and asked him to tell him what his problem was. Upon hearing his story, this was the advice Jonadab gave Amnon:

2 Samuel 13:4-5 (NET) "*He asked Amnon, 'Why are you, the king's son, so depressed every morning? Can't you tell me?' So Amnon said to him, 'I'm in love with Tamar the sister of my brother Absalom.' Jonadab replied to him, 'Lie down on your bed and pretend to be sick. When your father comes in to see you, say to him, 'Please let my sister Tamar come in so she can fix some food for me. Let her prepare the food in my sight so I can watch. Then I will eat from her hand.'*"

So Prince Amnon foolishly followed his cousin's advice and did everything he told him to. When Tamar came to his bed to feed him the bread she had made for her supposedly sick brother, he grabbed her. And despite all her pleas, he raped her and then drove her away!

Poor Tamar's life had been turned upside down and damaged in a few minutes. Her carefully preserved virginity had been stolen from her by her own half-brother! She tore her robe of purity, poured ashes on her head and began weeping and wailing as she headed toward her brother's [Absalom's] house. This is where it gets negatively interesting. According to our opening scripture, Absalom consoled her and told her not to take the rape too seriously. And he himself never said anything to Amnon. But the Bible says that from that day, he hated his half-brother for what he did to his sister.

Month after month went by and Absalom did absolutely nothing. The first year went by and Absalom still did nothing. At this point, Amnon must have been thinking that all was well with him... and at the very worst, they would have a fight and that would be all. But had Absalom actually forgiven Amnon? Had he forgotten about the rape of his sister and the shame she was suffering? The answer to this question came two years after the rape. Let's find out what this was from scripture:

2 Samuel 13:23-27 (NET) "*Two years later Absalom's sheepshearers were in Baal Hazor, near Ephraim. Absalom invited all the king's sons. Then Absalom went to the king and said, 'My shearers have begun their work. Let the king and his servants go with me.' But the king said to Absalom, 'No, my son. We shouldn't all go. We shouldn't burden you in that way.' Though Absalom pressed him, the king was not willing to go. Instead, David blessed him. Then Absalom said, 'If you will not go, then let my brother Amnon go with us.' The king* *replied to him, 'Why should he go with you?' But when Absalom pressed him, he sent Amnon and all the king's sons along with him.*"

2 Samuel 13:28-29 (NET) "*Absalom instructed his servants,* **'Look! When Amnon is drunk and I say to you, 'Strike Amnon down,' kill him then and there.** *Don't fear! Is it not I who have given you these instructions? Be strong and courageous!'* **So Absalom's servants did to Amnon exactly what Absalom had instructed.** *Then all the king's sons got up; each one rode away on his mule and fled.*"

As you can see, Absalom never forgot and he never forgave Amnon, even after two full years had passed. Today's devotional offers a number of very important life lessons.

1. WATCH WHAT YOU THINK ABOUT:
Of all the things to think about as a prince, Amnon's daily focus was on how to sleep with his half-sister. If he did not have thoughts of this nature, his relationship with his half-siblings would have been preserved and he would have lived to a good old age. Here are scriptures to help you with your thoughts:

Proverbs 4:23 (KJV) *"Keep thy heart with all diligence; for out of it are the issues of life."*

Philippians 4:8 (KJV) *"Finally, brethren, whatsoever things are true, whatsoever things are honest, whatsoever things are just, whatsoever things are pure, whatsoever things are lovely, whatsoever things are of good report; if there be any virtue, and if there be any praise, think on these things."*

2. WATCH WHO INFLUENCES YOUR THOUGHTS AND YOUR ACTIONS:

Instead of Jonadab, Amnon's cousin, to rebuke him and snap him out of his negative thinking, he encouraged him by providing him with tips and tricks to use to get his sister into bed. Here are scriptures to help you in this regard:

1 Corinthians 15:33 (NET) *"Do not be deceived: 'Bad company corrupts good morals.'"*

Proverbs 13:20 (KJV) *"He that walketh with wise men shall be wise: but a companion of fools shall be destroyed."*

Psalm 1:1 (KJV) *"Blessed is the man that walketh not in the counsel of the ungodly, nor standeth in the way of sinners, nor sitteth in the seat of the scornful."*

3. SOME PEOPLE NEVER FORGET THE HARM THAT YOU CAUSE THEM: As you can see, there are some people, no matter how long it takes, they will get their own pound of flesh. If you harm someone like this, be sure that they would come back to get you and it is possible that their payback will far outweigh what you did to them. Therefore, it is better to not ever think of hurting or harming anyone if you want your career, your family, your life to be preserved. Here are some scriptures to help you:

2 Timothy 2:22 (KJV) "*Flee also youthful lusts: but follow righteousness, faith, charity, peace, with them that call on the Lord out of a pure heart.*"

Proverbs 17:14 (NET) "*Starting a quarrel is like letting out water; stop it before strife breaks out!*"

Psalm 34:14 (NET) "*Turn away from evil and do what is right! Strive for peace and promote it!*"

So, do you want to be a person who filters out negative thoughts from his or her mind? Do you want to be careful about who you associate with or who influences your thoughts and actions? Do you want to prevent yourself from being the source of sorrow or tragedy in anyone's life? Do you want to be spared from the burning rage of vengeance? If yes, get yourself ready!

TODAY'S PRAYERS

1. Heavenly Father, I do not want to die an untimely death by reason of my foolish actions. Come to my aid this morning, in the name of Jesus.

2. Holy Spirit of God, teach me to guard my heart with all diligence. Help me to always think only about things that are true, honest, just, pure, lovely, things that are of good report, that are virtuous and that are praiseworthy, in the name of Jesus.

3. My Lord and my God, let any fountain of evil thoughts and desires in my heart be destroyed and let the flow of evil thoughts into my mind be terminated, in the name of Jesus.

4. Father, teach me to push away from my life anyone who constitutes bad company. Let me no longer be a companion of fools. Remove me from the way of sinners and raise me up from the seat of the scornful. Let me know how to walk with wise men so that I too can be wise, in the name of Jesus.

5. From today, O God, with Your help, I will flee all youthful lusts to which I have hitherto given myself. From today, with Your help, I will start avoiding any kind of quarrel or trouble that can backfire into my life. And from today, with your help, I will turn away from evil. Instead, I will begin to follow righteousness, faith, charity, peace, with them that call on the Lord out of a pure heart. I will not let strife break out wherever I am. I will begin to do what is right, to strive for peace and to promote it, in the name of Jesus.

6. Jehovah Shalom, with all these commitments that I have made today and the prayers that I have said, let my journey in life never be cut short. Let me never be the victim of vengeance. Let me experience Your peace all the days of my life so that I can always live to glorify You, in the name of Jesus.

7. Thank You Father God for answering my prayers, in Jesus' mighty name, amen.

If you have the need and the time, please feel free to add more prayers at this point.

Blessing: May you never do anything that will cause violent vengeance to be unleashed against you, in the name of Jesus.

DAY 58

NOT EVERY SITUATION IS PERMANENT

"And Solomon did evil in the sight of the LORD, and went not fully after the LORD, as did David his father."
— 1 Kings 11:6 (KJV)

DAILY EXHORTATION

In 1 Kings 5:2-4 (KJV), the Bible says *"And Solomon sent to Hiram, saying, Thou knowest how that David my father could not build an house unto the name of the Lord his God for the wars which were about him on every side, until the Lord put them under the soles of his feet. But now the Lord my God hath given me rest on every side, so that there is neither adversary nor evil occurrent."*

David had just died and Solomon was sending a message to his father's friend, king Hiram, for assistance so that he could build the temple his father was not allowed to. In the scripture we just read, Solomon clearly states that the rest he was enjoying as well as his immunity from adversaries and evil threats were gifts from God Almighty. Even with the sins that David committed, he was always quick to repent and to forsake his sins. His total desire in life was to please God.

When you read the Book of Psalms [written by David] and then Proverbs, Ecclesiastes and Songs of Solomon [written by Solomon], you will find that the Psalms appear to have been written by someone with a deep and thorough longing for God.

With regard to the rest and the peace that Solomon enjoyed, even he himself said "*When a man's ways please the LORD, he maketh even his enemies to be at peace with him.*" (Proverbs 16:7, KJV). But writing about something and living that thing are two different things. Solomon's ways which pleased the Lord at the beginning of his reign as king took a turn for the worse. According to our opening scripture, Solomon began to do evil in the sight of the Lord. What does this mean — "do evil"? Let's find out from scripture:

1. UNHOLY MARRIAGES TO STRANGE WOMEN

1 Kings 11:1-2 (KJV) "*But king Solomon loved many strange women, together with the daughter of Pharaoh, women of the Moabites, Ammonites, Edomites, Zidonians,* *and Hittites:* **Of the nations concerning which the Lord said unto the children of Israel, Ye shall not go in to them, neither shall they come in unto you***: for surely they will turn away your heart after their gods:* **Solomon clave unto these in love***."*

2. IDOL WORSHIP

1 Kings 11:4-7 (KJV) *"For it came to pass, when Solomon was old, that his wives turned away his heart after other gods: and his heart was not perfect with the Lord his God, as was the heart of David his father. For Solomon went after Ashtoreth the goddess of the Zidonians, and after Milcom the abomination of the Ammonites. And Solomon did evil in the sight of the Lord, and went not fully after the Lord, as did David his father. Then did Solomon build an high place for Chemosh, the abomination of Moab, in the hill that is before Jerusalem, and for Molech, the abomination of the children of Ammon."*

These were the two great evils Solomon did before the Lord. He was disobedient in that he married foreign idolatrous women and he rejected the living God by pursuing the worship of idols. The great king Solomon, who had been blessed with uncommon wisdom, was now bowing to man-made sculptures filled with demonic spirits! Very unfortunate.

In any case, just as Solomon himself had

written, his ways no longer pleased the Lord and therefore, he would have to suffer consequences. He would have to see changes to his erstwhile blissful existence.

How did God judge Solomon? Let's take a quick look at scriptures:

1 Kings 11:11-12 (KJV) "*Wherefore the Lord said unto Solomon, Forasmuch as this is done of thee, and thou hast not kept my covenant and my statutes, which I have commanded thee, I will surely rend the kingdom from thee, and will give it to thy servant. Notwithstanding in thy days I will not do it for David thy father's sake: but I will rend it out of the hand of thy son.*"

1 Kings 11:14 (KJV) "*And the Lord stirred up an adversary unto Solomon, Hadad the Edomite: he was of the king's seed in Edom.*"

1 Kings 11:23,25 (KJV) "*And God stirred him up another adversary, Rezon the son of Eliadah, which fled from his lord Hadadezer king of Zobah... And he was an adversary to Israel all the days of Solomon, beside the mischief that Hadad did: and he abhorred Israel, and reigned over Syria.*"

1 Kings 11:26 (KJV) "*And Jeroboam the son of Nebat, an Ephrathite of Zereda, Solomon's servant, whose mother's name was Zeruah, a widow woman, even he* *lifted up his hand against the king.*"

If you look at the consequences Solomon suffered, was it worth it to turn away from God? The Almighty took away the kingdom from Solomon [eventually leaving only one tribe for the sake of David]. He then inspired three men [Hadad, Rezon and Jeroboam] to become tormentors unto Solomon for the rest of his days. The peace and rest he wrote to Hiram about was now gone and his descendants had been deprived of their "once great" royal inheritance! The blessings Solomon thought were permanent were now gone!

The lesson for you here is straightforward: Be faithful to God and you will continue to enjoy his benefits. On the other hand, if you turn away from God, it is certain that you will suffer consequences such as loss of position or assets as well as loss of peace.

If you are currently under attack by human tormentors, who are doing all they can to see to it that you have no peace of mind, it may be because there is something you are doing that is against the word of God. And if you are currently enjoying prosperity and peace, let the story of Solomon inspire you today to remain in the narrow way of righteousness so that your situation can be preserved or enhanced. This morning you have a golden opportunity to rededicate your life to God concerning these issues. Get yourself ready!

TODAY'S PRAYERS

1. Be merciful unto me, O Lord. Let the blessings that You have given me be permanent and cause them to even increase more and more, in the name of Jesus.

2. My King and my God, forgive me for any sin of conscious or unconscious disobedience I have committed against you. As I confess my sin of disobedience today, give me the fortitude to forsake this sin now and forever, in the name of Jesus.

3. Father, if I am addicted to anything or anyone which or whom I have given my heart and my life to instead of You, be merciful unto me today and forgive me. Break the negative influence of that person or that thing over my life. This morning, I declare that You are the priority of my life and the greatest object of my devotion, in the name of Jesus.

4. O Righteous Father, do not let me suffer any loss to my position or my assets. Rather, look

upon my renewed devotion and open the windows of heaven for my sake, in the name of Jesus.

5. My Lord and my God, do not let the peace and rest that You have blessed me with be withdrawn from me. And if any adversary has been stirred up against me already in order to torment me, in Your mercy, cause that adversary to lose interest in me now and forever, in the name of Jesus.

6. Finally, Lord, I ask: let me go fully after You in the manner that David did. Give me a heart that will enthrone You forever as the Lord of my life, in the name of Jesus.

7. Thank You Almighty God for answering my prayers, in Jesus' mighty name, amen.

If you have the need and the time, please feel free to add more prayers at this point.

Blessing: May you enjoy the peace, rest and blessings of God even as You make him the Alpha and Omega of your life, in the name of Jesus.

DAY 59

GIVE THEM AN INCH, THEY'LL TAKE A YARD

"And Benhadad the king of Syria gathered all his host together: and there were thirty and two kings with him, and horses, and chariots; and he went up and besieged Samaria, and warred against it. And he sent messengers to Ahab king of Israel into the city, and said unto him, Thus saith Benhadad, Thy silver and thy gold is mine; thy wives also and thy children, even the goodliest, are mine. And the king of Israel answered and said, My lord, O king, according to thy saying, I am thine, and all that I have."
— 1 Kings 20:1-4 (KJV)

DAILY EXHORTATION

Without provocation, you rose up suddenly one day and besieged another nation. Then, you sent their king a message: "*I want your gold, I want your silver, I want the best of your wives and your children.*"

and the king of the besieged nation replied: "*Yes sir. I am yours and everything I have is also yours*".

You'd think that, that would be enough for this Benhadad, right? Unfortunately, it wasn't because shortly after, he sent a new message to king Ahab. Let's find out what it was from scripture:

1 Kings 20:5-6 (KJV) "*And the messengers came again, and said, Thus speaketh Benhadad, saying, Although I have sent unto thee, saying, Thou shalt deliver me thy silver, and thy gold, and thy wives, and thy children; Yet I will send my servants unto thee to morrow about this time, and they shall search thine house, and the houses of thy servants; and it shall be, that whatsoever is pleasant in thine eyes, they shall put it in their hand, and take it away.*"

By agreeing to the first demand, Ahab had given Benhadad an inch of allowance. Therefore, Benhadad felt emboldened and thought that he could also proceed to take a yard. How can you say that you would come into another person's palace and search his house and that of his servants and anything that person values, you would take away. Anything? Benhadad had clearly overstepped his bounds and something needed to be done.

Do you know that this is exactly the

approach the devil takes when he wants to destroy a person's life? For example, first, he could attack a person with the spirit of lust. Once he sees that his victim's defenses are weak, he may then try to introduce addiction to pornography. If he sees that his victim agrees with this, he could then inspire the victim to sleep with prostitutes. From there, the victim may contract a terminal disease and die OR the prostitute could resort to blackmail and ruin the victim's reputation, career and family.

However, if the so-called victim had stopped the devil at the point where he attacked him with lust, he or she would never have had to suffer any negative consequences. And this is similar to what Ahab did in response to Benhadad's ridiculous demand. Let's check out the details from scripture:

1 Kings 20:7-9 (KJV) "*Then the king of Israel called all the elders of the land, and said, Mark, I pray you, and see how this man seeketh mischief: for he sent unto me for my wives, and for my children, and for my silver, and for my gold; and I denied him not. And all the elders and all the people said unto him, Hearken not unto him, nor consent. Wherefore he said unto the messengers of Benhadad, Tell my lord the king, All that thou didst send for to thy servant at the first I will do:* **but this thing I may not do**. *And the messengers departed, and brought* *him word again."*

Ahab refused to comply and Benhadad threatened him with annihilation. It is at this point that God decided to step in. You see, God wants to see your heart and your determination to not allow evil to take control of your life. Notice that the first time Ahab complied, heaven said nothing. But this second time, on seeing Ahab's decision to not be dominated by an evil enemy, God stepped in.

What happened and especially was Ahab's refusal to submit to oppression worth it? Let's find out from scripture:

1 Kings 20:13-16 (KJV) *"And, behold, there came a prophet unto Ahab king of Israel, saying, Thus saith the Lord, Hast thou seen all this great multitude? behold, I will deliver it into thine hand this day; and thou shalt know that I am the Lord. And Ahab said, By whom? And he said, Thus saith the Lord, Even by the young men of the princes of the provinces. Then he said, Who shall order the battle? And he answered, Thou. Then he numbered the young men of the princes of the provinces, and they were two hundred and thirty two: and after them he numbered all the people, even all the children of Israel, being seven thousand. And they went out at noon. But Benhadad was drinking himself drunk in the pavilions, he and the kings, the thirty and two kings that helped him."*

1 Kings 20:17-21 (KJV) *"And the young men of the princes of the provinces went out first; and Benhadad sent out, and they told him, saying, There are men come out of Samaria. And he said, Whether they be come out for peace, take them alive; or whether they be come out for war, take them alive.* **So these young men of the princes of the provinces came out of the city, and the army which followed them. And they slew every one his man: and the Syrians fled; and Israel pursued them: and Benhadad the king of Syria escaped on an horse with the horsemen. And the king of Israel went out, and smote the horses and chariots, and slew the Syrians with a great slaughter.**"

The army of the king of Syria who had boasted to destroy the king of Israel was wasted. The enemy of God's children was put to flight! Never ever give the devil a chance in your life. If he comes against you with temptation, refuse to submit to it. If he comes to you with disease or sickness, refuse to submit to it. If he comes against you with a spiritual attack, refuse to submit to it. If you submit to any of all of these things, he will attempt to go deeper in order to ruin your life. However, if, from the bottom of your heart, you are determined to never submit to the wiles and caprices of the enemy, and you call upon the living God to help you, in the same manner He came through for His children the Israelites, He will also come through for you.

Do you want to declare your stand against oppression? Are you willing to not give an inch of your life to the devil? Do you want to be a spiritual victor? If your answer to all these is Yes, get yourself ready!

TODAY'S PRAYERS

1. My Father and my God, I want to become a spiritual champion. Help me, in the name of Jesus.

2. Lord, I recognize today that if I give even an inch of my life to the devil and his agents, he will attempt to take a yard of my life and then my entire my life. I am determined to not let this happen. Come to my aid, in the name of Jesus.

3. Now Lord, anytime the devil comes to me through any means be it sickness, temptation, spiritual attack or any other way, give me the grace and the strength to never submit to him, in the name of Jesus.

4. At that instant, when I recognize that the devil's hand is at work, O Lord, let me take a

stand of righteousness and refuse, from the bottom of my heart, to submit to him, in the name of Jesus.

5. Eternal King, when I take my stand, in accordance with Your word, come to my aid. Make spiritual provision available for my sake so that I can have the resources to fight the battle of righteousness, in the name of Jesus.

6. Jehovah, in the same manner You secured a mighty victory for Your children against Benhadad and his cohorts, always help me to defeat any agent of darkness sent my way, in the name of Jesus.

7. Thank You Precious Father for answering my prayers, in Jesus' mighty name, amen.

If you have the need and the time, please feel free to add more prayers at this point.

Blessing: May you never submit to the enemy and may God always rise to your defense whenever you need Him, in the name of Jesus.

DAY 60

THE THORNBUSH'S CHALLENGE

"Then Amaziah sent messengers to Jehoash son of Jehoahaz son of Jehu, king of Israel. He said, 'Come, let's meet face to face.' King Jehoash of Israel sent this message back to King Amaziah of Judah, 'A thornbush in Lebanon sent this message to a cedar in Lebanon, 'Give your daughter to my son as a wife.' Then a wild animal of Lebanon came by and trampled down the thorn. You thoroughly defeated Edom and it has gone to your head! Gloat over your success, but stay in your palace. Why bring calamity on yourself? Why bring down yourself and Judah along with you?'" — 2 Kings 14:8-10 (NET)

DAILY EXHORTATION

In the game of boxing, it is very common for someone who has had recent success in the form of an unbeaten run to begin to challenge the champion of his weight class. So, this person would go on the screen and boast that because he beat this person and beat that person, he was now calling out the champion. He would challenge the champion to a fight! The champion, on the other hand, sometimes doesn't say much and might accept the challenge. Usually, people like the challenger in our example are knocked out within the first few rounds of such boxing matches. This is very similar to what happened to Amaziah, king of Judah.

The Bible reveals that Amaziah, when he became king of Judah, tried to serve God faithfully but his heart was not 100% right with God. Nevertheless, God was with him for the sake of David, his ancestor. He was once went to war against 10,000 Edomites and defeated them all. That was fine. However, without any provocation or threat of any sort, he sent a bizarre message to Jehoash, king of Israel asking for a battle. Jehoash's response to the challenge is recorded in our opening scripture.

Jehoash referred to Amaziah as a thornbush and he as a Cedar. A thornbush would on average be as high as 3 - 4 feet. A Lebanon Cedar, on the other hand, is an intimidating presence. It is an evergreen tree that can grow to about 40 meters or 130 feet. To put that into perspective, that is, a little under the length of 3 basketball courts put together! In other words, he was telling Amaziah that he was a nobody. Jehoash went further and told Amaziah that if he persisted in his taunting of him, a wild animal would be unleashed which will trample the thorn. Amaziah did not listen and therefore Jehoash decided to take action. Let's find out what happened in scripture:

2 Kings 14:11-14 (KJV) "*But Amaziah would not hear. Therefore Jehoash king of Israel went up; and he and Amaziah king of Judah looked one another in the face at Bethshemesh, which belongeth to Judah. And Judah was put to the worse before Israel; and they fled every man to their tents.* **And Jehoash king of Israel took Amaziah king of Judah**, *the son of Jehoash the son of Ahaziah, at Bethshemesh, and came to Jerusalem, and brake down the wall of Jerusalem from the gate of Ephraim unto the corner gate, four hundred cubits.* **And he took all the gold and silver, and all the vessels that were found in the house of the Lord, and in the treasures of the king's house, and hostages, and returned to Samaria**."

Amaziah, by reason of his recent victory against Edom, was puffed up with pride. He thought there was nothing he could not do and no one he could not face.

When God blesses you with anything — spiritual gifts, money, promotions, business growth, children, etc., there is no need to become a show-off. More importantly, there is no need to taunt other people and provoke them to arguments, quarrels, feuds and fights. Be thankful to God and enjoy whatever He has given you. This is necessary because you do not know the kind of power or ability the other person has. If you challenge people and taunt them in a competition, the worst that could happen is that you will be disgraced when the person defeats you. But, how do you think you would fare if you taunt someone and that person resorts to using dark, demonic powers against you? Since God is clearly not in support of His children causing offense, the dark powers may work against you.

Therefore, if you do not want to suffer the fate of Amaziah or worse [that is public disgrace, dispossession, loss of your loved ones and of property], please stay humble. Do you want to let go of pride this morning? Do you want to preserve what and whom God has blessed you with? If yes, get yourself ready!

TODAY'S PRAYERS

1. This morning, I reject the spirit of arrogance. You the spirit of arrogance, I bind you and I

cast you out of my life. Depart now and depart forever, in the name of Jesus.

2. My Lord and my God, this morning, I bow before You in order to thank You for the people and the things that You have blessed me with. Accept my thanks and praises, in the name of Jesus.

3. Lord, whatever might be in me that will cause me to go about provoking people and taunting them until they are riled up and ready to fight me, take it away from my life, in the name of Jesus.

4. Redeemer, cover me with the cloak of humility and let me never take it off. Do not let me do anything that will bring calamity upon me or that will bring me down, in the name of Jesus.

5. Father, bless me with ambition and the aggression that I need in order to tackle the tasks that You have placed in my own destiny. Let me never go out of the path that You have designed for me. Raise me up from a thornbush and make me as the Cedar of Lebanon, in the name of Jesus.

6. Messiah, by reason of my humbled heart and my willingness to obey Your word, let my life

be filled with achievements. Let everything and everyone dear to me as well as myself be protected and preserved by Your mercy and Your grace, in the name of Jesus.

7.   Thank You Excellency for answering my prayers, in Jesus' mighty name, amen.

If you have the need and the time, please feel free to add more prayers at this point.

Blessing: May you be humble and may you reap the rewards of humility, in the name of Jesus.

Encourage Yourself, Your Loved Ones & Friends
With Our KEEP ON PRAYING™ T-shirt

*This T-shirt currently only ships to readers in the United States.

GET THIS T-SHIRT FOR YOURSELF AND YOUR LOVED ONES

BUY THE KEEP ON PRAYING T-SHIRT NOW ON AMAZON

www.amazon.com/dp/B077FB2PMC

THANK YOU FOR GETTING THIS BOOK. BY GOD'S GRACE, MORE BOOKS ARE ON THE WAY THAT WILL LIKELY COVER MORE AREAS OR THEMES OR TOPICS OF INTEREST TO YOU. THE BEST WAY TO KNOW WHICH BOOKS ARE BEING RELEASED IS BY GETTING AN ALERT OR A NOTIFICATION FROM US. IF YOU WANT TO GET ACCESS TO THE LATEST UPDATES ON NEW BOOKS AS WELL AS OTHER ESSENTIAL INFORMATION FROM BROTHER MILLER, PLEASE JOIN OUR READERS' MAILING LIST (FOR EMAIL UPDATES), LIKE OUR FACEBOOK PAGE (FOR FACEBOOK UPDATES) AND FOLLOW US ON TWITTER. GOD BLESS YOU.

VISIT THIS PAGE TO JOIN NOW

http://johnmillerbooks.com/signup/

LIKE JOHN'S FACEBOOK PAGE AT:

facebook.com/johnmillerauthor

FOLLOW JOHN ON TWITTER AT:

twitter.com/johnmillerbooks

DAY 61 TO 90

DAY 61

PERSONALIZING HOLY METAPHORS

"You uprooted a vine from Egypt; you drove out nations and transplanted it. You cleared the ground for it; it took root, and filled the land. The mountains were covered by its shadow, the highest cedars by its branches. Its branches reached the Mediterranean Sea, and its shoots the Euphrates River." — Psalm 80:8-11 (NET)

DAILY EXHORTATION

Today's devotional takes us on a metaphorical journey as authored by king David. It begins with Israel's deliverance from the land of Egypt and ends with its establishment as a mighty, independent nation.

Our task this morning is simple and straightforward; In the same manner David applied the metaphors he used in this scripture to Israel, you will also personalize these metaphors and use them in prayer for yourself. Get yourself ready!

TODAY'S PRAYERS

1. Yahweh, by Your mighty hand, uproot me from Egypt, in the name of Jesus.

2. Mighty God, drive out the nations from the place You have assigned to me and plant me firmly in it, in the name of Jesus.

3. Messiah, clear the ground for me and make room for me in my place of destiny, in the name of Jesus.

4. Ah Lord God, help me so that I can take root and fill out my place of destiny, in the name of Jesus.

5. Alpha and Omega, let the mountains be covered by my shadow and the highest cedars by my branches, in the name of Jesus.

6. Adonai, let my branches be so great that they will reach the sea of greatness and my shoots so powerful that they will reach the river of power, in the name of Jesus.

7. Thank You All-Powerful God for answering my prayers, in Jesus' mighty name, amen.

If you have the need and the time, please feel free to add more prayers at this point.

Blessing: May all the words you have declared this morning manifest in your favor, in the name of Jesus.

DAY 62

THE KING'S INITIATIVE

"Who can tell if God will turn and repent, and turn away from his fierce anger, that we perish not?" — Jonah 3:9 (KJV)

DAILY EXHORTATION

Today is an update to what we learned on Day 48. On that day, we saw that after Jonah repented, the Lord forgave him and commanded the fish that had swallowed him to release him on dry land in Nineveh. Upon landing, Jonah began to preach that judgment was coming to the city. For three days, he went through the length and breadth of Nineveh until his message reached the ears of its king. Here's what happened when the king heard Jonah's dire warning:

Jonah 3:6-9 (KJV) "*For word came unto the king of Nineveh, and he arose from his throne, and he laid his robe from him, and covered him with sackcloth, and sat in ashes. And he caused it to be proclaimed and published*

through Nineveh by the decree of the king and his nobles,
saying, Let neither man nor beast, herd nor flock, taste any
thing: let them not feed, nor drink water: But let man and
beast be covered with sackcloth, and cry mightily unto God:
yea, let them turn every one from his evil way, and from the
violence that is in their hands. Who can tell if God will
turn and repent, and turn away from his fierce anger, that
we perish not?"

The king was devastated and remorseful
upon hearing the negative news. His behavior
suggests that he had been expecting divine
judgment by reason of the sins of the people he
was governing. Therefore, he proclaimed a
nationwide dry fast for both people and their
animals. He commanded his people to cry to the
Lord for mercy and to turn from their evil ways
and the violence in their hands.

The people of Nineveh obeyed their king.
However, when God sent Jonah to deliver His
message, He did not include mercy in the
message. These were the specific words of Jonah:
"At the end of forty days, Nineveh will be overthrown!"
(Jonah 3:4b). There was no option of repentance
in the message. The fasting, the praying and the
repentance mandate by the king were common-
sense solutions he felt 'might' solve their problem.
This is why the king said "*Who can tell if God will*
turn and repent, and turn away from his fierce anger, that

we perish not?"

So, what was the result of the king's initiative? Did it work? Let's find out from scripture:

Jonah 3:9 (KJV) "*And God saw their works, that they turned from their evil way; and God repented of the evil, that he had said that he would do unto them; and he did it not.*"

The king's initiative worked! God spared Nineveh His divine judgment! This episode in history is very important for us as believers and here's why: The people of Nineveh were fortunate in the sense that Jonah was sent to them to warn them of impending judgment. What if he did not go there? It meant that 40 days from that day some form of calamity would have befallen Nineveh. Their neighbors would have thought "*Poor Nineveh... they were consumed by sudden destruction*". Their neighbors would not have realized that the judgment had been prepared against them several days in advance. Nothing is sudden in this regard!

If you are noticing an unusual change in your circumstances that you do not like and you do not know why, please imitate the king's initiative. This is more so if you know from the bottom of your heart that you are doing something that you should not be doing. As you can see, the king's initiative works and can bring about the mercy of God and a restoration of God's loving favor.

So, to recap, what is the king's initiative? Whenever you feel a change in your circumstances, develop genuine remorse from the bottom of your heart, go on a 1 or 2 or 3 day dry fast [meaning no food or water], repent of your sins [or abandon your evil ways in your heart], drop the violence in your hands [or stop doing bad things] and cry to Almighty God for mercy. If you genuinely follow this king's initiative and put it into practice, in the same way God showed Nineveh mercy, He will show you mercy. Are you ready to put this into practice so that you can be restored unto God's kind favor? If yes, get yourself ready!

TODAY'S PRAYERS

1. O Righteous Father, I want to live a life that pleases You everyday. Help me, in the name of Jesus.

2. My Father, I do not want divine judgment to be executed on me neither do I want to endure an unfavorable change in the positive circumstances of my life, in the name of

Jesus.

3. Merciful God, I want to adopt the king's initiative so that I can find favor with You. Come to my aid today, in the name of Jesus.

4. In accordance with the king's initiative, this morning, O Lord, with genuine remorse in my heart, I have decided to embark on a ____ day dry fast [choose either 1 / 2 / 3 days]. Look upon my fast with mercy, in the name of Jesus.

5. In accordance with the king's initiative, this morning, O Lord, I confess and repent of my sins. I drop the violence in my hands or the bad things that I know that I do. And I ask You to have mercy on me, in the name of Jesus.

6. Great and Mighty God, by reason of my actions, spare me divine judgment and let me experience Your divine restoration, in the name of Jesus.

7. Thank You Father for answering my prayers, in Jesus' mighty name, amen.

If you have the need and the time, please feel free to add more prayers at this point.

Blessing: May you benefit from God's grace and mercy by reason of the genuineness of your heart, in the name of Jesus.

DAY 63

THE MEANING
OF MY DREAM

**"Now while Peter doubted in himself what
this vision which he had seen should
mean, behold, the men which were sent
from Cornelius had made enquiry for
Simon's house, and stood before the gate"
— Acts 10:17 (KJV)**

DAILY EXHORTATION

The great apostle Peter once had a trance or a
daydream and it went as follows:

Acts 10:11-16 (NET) "*He saw heaven opened and an
object something like a large sheet descending, being let
down to earth by its four corners. In it were all kinds of
four-footed animals and reptiles of the earth and wild
birds. Then a voice said to him, 'Get up, Peter; slaughter
and eat!' But Peter said, 'Certainly not, Lord, for I have
never eaten anything defiled and ritually unclean!' The
voice spoke to him again, a second time, 'What God has
made clean, you must not consider ritually unclean!' This*

happened three times, and immediately the object was taken up into heaven."

According to our opening scripture, after Peter saw this trance or dream, he began to wonder about the meaning of what he had just seen. What does this dream mean that I just saw? What is this large sheet? What do these four-footed animals, the reptiles and the wild birds represent? What did God mean when He said he had made them clean and that I should eat them? Remember that this is Apostle Peter, the right hand man of the Lord Jesus Christ and the foundation of the Christian church. This fact is important because it shines a spotlight on persons who purport to know the interpretation of every dream in the universe.

The truth is that while person A may have the same dream as person B, the interpretation may be the same or may be different. So, that you saw yourself wearing a white garment and your best friend or coworker or relative also wore the same garment in their own dream does not mean that the white garment means the same thing for both of you.

Many people have applied strange interpretations to the dreams that they have had which have led them to take unnecessary or even harmful actions. The kind of dream God showed

Peter is not one that He showed anyone else. It was a highly symbolic dream. This dream was significant because it would herald a new era in the body of Christ.

Similarly, if you are a child of God, walking according to His plan and purpose for your life, you too will also have unique dreams from time to time that aren't recorded in any book or manual. This was the case with the dreams of Joseph, son of Jacob, Joseph, father of Jesus, Daniel and other such people.

So, you might be wondering what you should do in order to get the meaning of your dream, if it is a significant, symbolic dream. Let's find out from scripture:

1 . **Ask God for the interpretation of the dream:** When Daniel wanted to interpret the dream of Nebuchadnezzar, here's what he did: "*So Daniel went in and requested the king to grant him time, that he might disclose the interpretation to the king. Then Daniel went to his home and informed his friends Hananiah, Mishael, and Azariah of the matter.* **He asked them to pray for mercy from the God of heaven concerning this mystery** *so that he and his friends would not be destroyed along with the rest of the wise men of Babylon.* **Then in a night vision the mystery was revealed to Daniel. So Daniel praised the God of heaven**"

(Daniel 2:16-19, NET).

Through prayer, God revealed to Daniel what every symbol in Nebuchadnezzar's dream meant.

2. Wait for it to Manifest: "*And the Lord answered me, and said, Write the vision, and make it plain upon tables, that he may run that readeth it. For the vision is yet for an appointed time, but at the end it shall speak, and not lie: though it tarry, wait for it; because it will surely come, it will not tarry.*" (Habakkuk 2:2-3, KJV)

The above two scriptures apply to symbolic dreams. For dreams of straightforward warning, nightmares, instruction, inspiration, etc. you should get up immediately and pray accordingly to address the dream [We have a large library of of books for these, with more coming soon]. BUT for symbolic dreams, you can only ask for the interpretation or wait. The latter, that is, waiting was what Peter did and it wouldn't be long before he understood the vision that God had shown him:

Acts 10:19-23 (NET) "*While Peter was still thinking seriously about the vision, the Spirit said to him, 'Look! Three men are looking for you. But get up, go down, and* *accompany them without hesitation, because I have sent them.' So Peter went down to the men and said, 'Here I am, the person you're looking for. Why have you come?' They said, 'Cornelius the centurion, a righteous and God-fearing man, well spoken of by the whole Jewish nation, was directed by a holy angel to summon you to his house and to hear a message from you.' So Peter invited them in and entertained them as guests. On the next day he got up and set out with them, and some of the brothers from Joppa accompanied him."*

When Peter got to the house of Cornelius and met the man, he saw a large crowd of people there, all of whom were gentiles. Then, the dream began to click in Peter's mind and he made the following statement:

Acts 10:28 (KJV) *"And he said unto them, Ye know how that it is an unlawful thing for a man that is a Jew to keep company, or come unto one of another nation; but God hath shewed me that I should not call any man common or unclean."*

After Cornelius revealed to him that God asked him to send for him [Peter] through a dream, Peter again made the following statement:

Acts 10:34-35 (KJV) *"Then Peter opened his mouth, and said, Of a truth I perceive that God is no respecter of* *persons: But in every nation he that feareth him, and worketh righteousness, is accepted with him."*

Then, as Peter began to minister to the large gathering of gentiles, suddenly something strange happened:

Acts 10:44-46 (KJV) "*While Peter yet spake these words, the Holy Ghost fell on all them which heard the word. And they of the circumcision which believed were astonished, as many as came with Peter, because that on the Gentiles also was poured out the gift of the Holy Ghost. For they heard them speak with tongues, and magnify God.*"

So, it was that the dream or the vision that Peter had seen, interpreted itself right before his eyes. Through the situations and circumstances that God orchestrated, Peter understood what the large sheet of cloth was, what the animals were and what it meant to eat them. The large sheet represented the world. The animals represented all human beings in every nation of the world [including you] and eating them meant accepting these people with all of his heart.

In what book would you have found an interpretation like this? And to confirm all of this, right in front of Peter's eyes, God poured out His Holy Spirit on all the gentiles that were in that room and in the process ushered into the world the beginning of a new era.

Beloved, it is sweet to have a symbolic dream, to wait and to have God interpret the dream to you through real-life events that would unfold right before your very eyes. These dreams could be about your relationships, your career, your health, etc. No matter the kind of dream, and as long as it is for good, if you anticipate its manifestation, God will cause it to be interpreted right before your very eyes. Is this something that you desire? If yes, get yourself ready!

TODAY'S PRAYERS

1. Everlasting Father, make me a candidate of Your symbolic dreams today, in the name of Jesus.

2. Eternal King, I declare to You that just as it was for Peter, I too am available for Your powerful dreams. Transmit them into my life, in the name of Jesus.

3. Messiah, from today, whenever I have a symbolic dream, let me stop bothering myself about its meaning or its interpretation, in the name of Jesus.

4. O God, as it was for Daniel, whenever I have

a symbolic dream and I call unto You for its meaning, visit me and reveal the meaning to me, in the name of Jesus.

5. O Lord, as it was for Peter, whenever I have a symbolic dream and I decide to wait for its manifestation, let it be that the dream will interpret itself before my very eyes for my benefit, in the name of Jesus.

6. Creator of heaven and earth, use dreams to reveal to me Your plans for me and for others that You love so that I and them can continue to be in the center of Your plans, in the name of Jesus.

7. Thank You Excellency for answering my prayers, in Jesus' mighty name, amen.

If you have the need and the time, please feel free to add more prayers at this point.

Blessing: May you dream dreams including symbolic dreams and may God, in His own way, reveal their meanings to you, in the name of Jesus.

DAY 64
THE SOLDIER

"No man that warreth entangleth himself with the affairs of this life; that he may please him who hath chosen him to be a soldier." — 2 Timothy 2:4 (KJV)

DAILY EXHORTATION

In 2 Corinthians 10:3-6 (KJV), the Bible says "*For though we walk in the flesh, we do not war after the flesh: (For the weapons of our warfare are not carnal, but mighty through God to the pulling down of strong holds;) Casting down imaginations, and every high thing that exalteth itself against the knowledge of God, and bringing into captivity every thought to the obedience of Christ...*" According to this scripture, as a believer, whether you like it or not, you are in a war. You are a soldier but a special kind of soldier.

Amongst other things, your assignment is to cast down ungodly imaginations as well as anything that exalts itself against the knowledge of God. It is also to bring into captivity every thought to the obedience of Christ. But it doesn't end there. In Ephesians 6:12 (KJV), again the Bible says "*For we wrestle not against flesh and blood, but against principalities, against powers, against the rulers of the darkness of this world, against spiritual wickedness in high places.*" So, you will also have to fight against principalities, powers, dark powers and authorities and spiritual wickedness in high places.

Taken together, these verses tell you that there are internal wars as well as external wars to fight. As a solider of Christ, you must master how to control your imagination, how to submit your emotions to the divine authority of the Almighty and how to control your thoughts.

After you have done these, be aware that there are dark powers in our world. Evil people are everywhere as well as demonic forces. Towns, cities, and nations have different dark powers that rule over them [such as the demonic prince and the king of Persia in the days of Daniel]. There are people who use fetish powers to manipulate and control people in order that they may love them, submit to them or some other dark reason. There are astrologers and false prophets who make evil prophesies on behalf of their clients against innocent people and see to it that they come to pass. There are occultic masters who create effigies that represent people, businesses, families, etc. and they speak to these effigies, torture them, burn them, etc. Whatever they do to these objects begin to happen to the persons or entities which are their targets. Dark powers!

These are the kinds of things believers face as soldiers of Christ. This is why in our opening scripture, Paul told Timothy that a solider does not entangle himself or herself with the affairs of this life. Other versions say "the affairs of civilian life". You cannot be on the warfront and be distracted by thoughts of "who's picking the trash today?", "I have to go shopping today", "should i wear this watch or that watch?", "what kind of shirt do I put on today?", "I want to go to the cinema", etc. If you think like that, the Bible says you will not please "Him" who has chosen you to be a soldier... and in fact, if you think like that, you will most likely get killed on the warfront.

Therefore, you have to learn to live by the military code. Our military code is the word of God. You cannot afford to live like sinners. Sinners are overwhelmed by their imaginations, thoughts, emotions, etc. Sinners are easy prey to the powers of darkness. However, if you live according to the word of God, your victory in the battles of life is assured.

Do you want to be certain of victory as a Child of God over the things you are facing or will face? If yes, get yourself ready!

TODAY'S PRAYERS

1. Heavenly Father, I accept with all gladness my enlistment in Your divine army. To You be all the glory and honor forever, in the name of Jesus.

2. O Lord, my strength and my fortress, bless me with divine focus so that I can never be distracted by iniquity or sin or other affairs of civilian life, in the name of Jesus.

3. Jehovah, put in my heart this day a thorough love for Your military code. Let me long to study the Bible in order to learn what I need to be a perfect solider of Christ, in the name of Jesus.

4. Great General, equip me with the weapons that I need to cast down imaginations and every high thing that exalts itself against Your knowledge. Give me the tools of war that I need to bring into captivity every thought to the obedience of Christ, in the name of Jesus.

5. Eternal King, through Your word, teach me how to defeat principalities, powers, rulers of darkness of this world and spiritual wickedness in high places, in the name of Jesus.

6. Finally Lord, I ask: You have chosen me as Your soldier. Help me so that, according to Your word, my ways will always please You, in the name of Jesus.

7. Thank You Great and Mighty God for answering my prayers, in Jesus' mighty name, amen.

If you have the need and the time, please feel free to add more prayers at this point.

Blessing: May the Lord make you a perfect solider of Christ, in the name of Jesus.

DAY 65

THE ATHLETE

"Also, if anyone competes as an athlete, he will not be crowned as the winner unless he competes according to the rules." — 2 Timothy 2:5 (NET)

DAILY EXHORTATION

Yesterday, we examined Paul's instructions to Timothy concerning living one's life as a solider of Christ. Today, we will continue with more of the instructions he passed on to Timothy. This time Paul talks about believers as athletes.

As you know, there are many sports in the world. There is no interesting sport on earth that lacks rules. Every single sport has a set of rules. Apart from meeting the physical requirements, if you want to participate in a particular sport, you must master the rules. So, for example, if you want to win a wrestling match, you would have to pin down your opponent long enough for the referee to tap the canvas three times. If he taps 2 1/2 times only and your opponent gets up his back, the match continues. In boxing, you cannot hit below the belt, you cannot kick your opponent, etc. In soccer, if you bring down one of your opponents in your side's 18-yard box, a penalty will be awarded against you. These are just a few of the rules from a handful of sports. There are several sports and several rules.

Now, according to our opening scripture, you may be the greatest boxer in the world BUT if you say "*I will hit my opponent below the belt*", the first time you try it, you might get a warning. However, if you do it again or a couple more times, you will be disqualified and the match will be awarded to your opponent. As a believer, you are an athlete. And as an athlete, you are competing for a crown. If you do not compete according to the rules, you will not be crowned as a winner. BUT, if you are spiritually fit and you compete according to the rules, with God's help, you will be crowned the winner.

But where are the rules for Christian athletes? They are all right there in the word. All the commands of Christ [for instance, "love your neighbor as yourself] as well as those from His apostles written under the unction of the Holy Spirit are the rules you need to familiarize yourself with in order to be the winner.

The more you read the word of God, the more you master the rules and the easier it will be for you to get your crown.

If you want to win and you want to get God's crown of victory, get yourself ready!

TODAY'S PRAYERS

1. My King and my God, I accept with all joy my role as an athlete in Your kingdom. Receive all the glory and honor forever, in the name of Jesus.

2. Lord, I understand that in order me to win and to receive the crown of victory, I need to be spiritually fit and I need to master the rules of the game. Come to my aid so that I can be successful in this task, in the name of Jesus.

3. As I study Your word, Father, let it sink down into my spirit, soul and body until it becomes part of every cell in my body and every fiber of my being, in the name of Jesus.

4. Rock of Ages, let Your word automatically begin to change my thoughts, emotions and my behavior for better to Your glory, in the name of Jesus.

5. Messiah, following my mastery of Your divine rules through the study of Your word,

give me the grace to win in the competition of life and of destiny, in the name of Jesus.

6. Eternal Father, by reason of my victory in the competition of life, let my head be crowned with the crown of glory, in the name of Jesus.

7. Thank You Father for answering my prayers, in Jesus' mighty name, amen.

If you have the need and the time, please feel free to add more prayers at this point.

Blessing: May you master the rules, compete, win and receive Your crown of glory, in the name of Jesus.

DAY 66

THE FARMER

**"The farmer who works hard ought to
have the first share of the crops."
— 2 Timothy 2:6 (NET)**

DAILY EXHORTATION

In other words, in order for you to reap, you have
to sow. Today, the Apostle Paul is likening
believers to farmers. Therefore, as a believer, you
are a farmer.

Back in the day, to be a farmer, you had to
have a piece of land to do your farming, you had
to have been an apprentice under someone who'd
teach you the essentials of farm management and
specifically, the nitty-gritty of the crop(s) you want
to deal in such as what time of the year to plant it
and what time of the year to harvest it. You'd also
need to know how to till the soil, different ways of
planting different kinds of seeds, water
requirements of each type of plant, etc. You also
have to put in a lot of hard work.

This is also how it is in Christianity.

Christianity is spiritual agriculture. The farm is life on earth. Life is a platform for you to demonstrate what you have learned from your teacher [Almighty God]. Every time you read the Bible, you are working hard on the farm. Whenever you exercise the fruit of the spirit [love, joy, peace, patience, kindness, goodness, faithfulness, gentleness, and self-control], you are hard at work on the farm. When you give alms to the less privileged and the poor and the orphans, you are working on the farm. When you pray or sing in the spirit, you are hard at work on the farm. When you fast and pray, you are hard at work on the farm. When you resist all manner of temptation, seductions and provocations, you are hard at work on the farm. And so on.

If you put in your best in all of these activities, the Almighty will see to it that you have the first share of the crops. This means good health [mental, emotional, physical and spiritual]. It means financial blessings and breakthrough upon the work of your hand. It means enjoying the fullness of God's goodness and mercy. It also means security with regard to Your eternal life — you will have peace of mind from the knowledge that your spiritual farming activities and your sowing will help you to reap an eternity in the kingdom of heaven.

So, do you want to accept your role as a

farmer today? Are you willing to work hard as a farmer in order to get the first share of the crops? If yes, get yourself ready!

TODAY'S PRAYERS

1. Most High God, I am glad to embrace my role as a farmer in Your kingdom. To You be all the glory, in the name of Jesus.

2. I know that in order for me to get the first share of Your divine crops, I have to work hard. Help me, in the name of Jesus.

3. O Lord my God, let Your Holy Spirit fill my life with enthusiasm and with energy so that I can be a successful farmer in Your kingdom, in the name of Jesus.

4. Great Redeemer, as I study Your word, let Your Holy Spirit reveal to me everything that I need to know in order to be successful in my role as a spiritual farmer, in the name of Jesus.

5. King of kings, as I sow, let my seeds be blessed so that I can reap multiple-fold harvests during the season of harvest, in the name of Jesus.

6. Lord of lords, preserve me so that I will see the day of harvest. When that day comes, according to Your word, let me get the first share of the crops so that my joy can be full, in the name of Jesus.

7. Thank You Precious Father for answering my prayers, in Jesus' mighty name, amen.

If you have the need and the time, please feel free to add more prayers at this point.

Blessing: May the good Lord bless you. When you sow in the farm of life, may you reap good and may you receive the first share of the crops, in the name of Jesus.

DAY 67

THE WEALTHY HOME AND ITS VESSELS

"Now in a wealthy home there are not only gold and silver vessels, but also ones made of wood and of clay, and some are for honorable use, but others for ignoble use. So if someone cleanses himself of such behavior, he will be a vessel for honorable use, set apart, useful for the Master, prepared for every good work."
— 2 Timothy 2:20-21 (NET)

DAILY EXHORTATION

Anytime you visit the house of a great or wealthy person, you will find all kinds of vessels in that house. For sure, you will find highly valuable vessels made of gold and silver in that house. However, regardless of their level of wealth, you will also find wooden vessels as well as those made of clay. Further, you will find some vessels that have been set apart for honorable uses and others dedicated to ignoble or dishonorable uses.

Do you know what? This is exactly how the Christian church is. The "vessels" Apostle Paul is referring to here are actually human beings and the 'wealthy home' is actually the church of God. What he is saying is that in the church of God, there are some people who are so valuable that in God's eyes they are like gold and silver.

A gold and silver believer is someone who is totally committed to the service of the Almighty. This is someone who has identified his or her gifts and has decided in what department of the body of Christ to use that gift. This is the kind of person who becomes glad when they say "let us go into the house of the Lord". Gold and silver Christians are people who have decided to become choristers, evangelists, missionaries, counselors, intercessors, prayer warriors, etc. and who are genuinely carrying out their service to the glory of God.

A wood and clay believer is someone who might be doing all of the above but with not as much commitment as the gold and silver believer. Then we also have believers who are honorable and those who are not. Quite simply, an honorable believer is someone whose words or deeds bring glory and honor to the Lord. An ignoble believer will call himself or herself a Christian but doesn't bear the fruits.

The presence or not of integrity, character

and sin delineates a honorable Christian from an ignoble one. People who spread rumors in the church, who steal church money, who seduce and cause the fall of others, who cause division amongst brethren, who mislead new believers, who spread false doctrines, who never practice anything they are taught in church, etc. are all examples of vessels of dishonor.

Today's devotional serves two purposes. First, it is showing you that not everyone in the church is really a child of God. Therefore, be careful. In your interactions with people in the church, ask God for the spirit of discernment and for the ability to test every spirit so that you can know who is who and prevent the derailment of your Christian walk.

Second, it is to show you who you currently are in the house of God. Based on what you have read thus far, you should be able to tell what kind of vessel you are. If you are gold or silver or a honorable vessel, good for you. Keep it up!

However, if you are wood or clay or a dishonorable vessel, there is hope for you. Our opening scripture says "*So if someone cleanses himself of such behavior, he will be a vessel for honorable use, set apart, useful for the Master, prepared for every good work.*" This means that you can change levels and go from wood / clay / dishonorable to gold / silver / honorable. You can make this divine transition by genuinely cleansing yourself of all your dishonorable deeds. If you do this, the Bible says that God will set you apart, make you useful for the Master [God Almighty] and prepare you for every good work. If you desire to be a gold / silver / honorable vessel, today is your day. Get yourself ready!

TODAY'S PRAYERS

1. O Lord of hosts, I want to be a gold / silver / honorable believer in Your great house. Help me, in the name of Jesus.

2. This morning, Father, I ask that You purge my heart with the fire of the Holy Ghost so that any insincerity in it will be removed once and for all, in the name of Jesus.

3. Great Deliverer, if there is anything in me that is causing me to behave in ways that show that I am a wood / clay / dishonorable believer, come now and remove that thing from my life, in the name of Jesus.

4. Today, I set aside any kind of behavior that I know is dishonorable. I apply the Blood of Jesus upon my spirit, soul and body so that I can be cleansed from the spirit of the wood, of clay and of dishonor, in the name of Jesus.

5. Merciful Father, by reason of my action today and according to Your word, make me a vessel for honorable use, set me apart, make me useful for Your service and prepare me for every good work, in the name of Jesus.

6. From today, I decree and declare that I am now a gold / silver / honorable vessel and I shall remain like this throughout my days, in the name of Jesus.

7. Thank You O Lord for answering my prayers, in Jesus' mighty name, amen.

If you have the need and the time, please feel free to add more prayers at this point.

Blessing: May you indeed become a vessel of honor, in the name of Jesus.

DAY 68

MAN IN THE MIRROR

"For if someone merely listens to the message and does not live it out, he is like someone who gazes at his own face in a mirror. For he gazes at himself and then goes out and immediately forgets what sort of person he was."
—James 1:23-24 (NET)

DAILY EXHORTATION

Imagine for a minute that you have a very important presentation before very important people. Naturally, you would be concerned about how you present yourself before them. This means you'll take special care to dress sharp and you'll also check yourself out in the mirror.

Now, how would it be, if after checking yourself out in the mirror a couple of times, you then step out of your house but you, for some reason, cannot remember how you looked when you were in front of the mirror? It would be unsettling and depending on the kind of person you are, this kind of situation might affect your presentation.

Today's opening scripture says that this is how it is in the spirit when you listen to the word of God BUT you do not do it or live it out or put it into practice. You are not just the physical 'you' that we see, that is, your body, you are also a spirit and a soul. That spirit and soul need a mirror to reveal their true state. The mirror of the soul and the spirit is the word of God. It reveals to you who you are right now. If you are spiritually OK, you will see it through the word of God. If you are not OK, you will also see it and therefore know what you need to do. Without this spiritual mirror, you will not know who you truly are, the kind of power that you carry, what you can do and the blessings you are eligible to receive from heaven.

At this point, you probably want to know how you can get God's divine mirror working for you? So, let's find out from scripture:

James 1:25 (NET) "*But the one who peers into the perfect law of liberty and fixes his attention there, and does not become a forgetful listener but one who lives it out—he will be blessed in what he does.*"

To get God's divine mirror working for you, you would need to pick up the Bible [as well as audio / video sermons / Christian books] and read it. This reading cannot be casual. You must completely focus on the word you are reading and fix your entire attention there. When you choose to listen to a live sermon or prepackaged ones that you watch or listen to, concentrate completely on it and be determined to do or live out what you have read, watched or listened to. You have to tell yourself that the word of God is the only way to be sure that you are on the right track in life and therefore you just have to read it as regularly as possible and do what it says. If you do this, not only will you see how you really are and secure the opportunity to make necessary changes, the word of God says that you will also be blessed in whatever you do. In this regard, studying, memorizing and doing the word of God is a powerful channel of God's blessing in your life.

So, do you want to see who you truly are? Do you want to use the information God's divine mirror gives you about yourself to become a better person? Do you want to receive blessings upon whatever you do? If yes, get yourself ready!

TODAY'S PRAYERS

1. Jehovah God, I need Your divine mirror to be available to me everyday of my life. Help

me, in the name of Jesus.

2. Father God, I want to see what I truly am. I want to know the state of my soul and my spirit at all times. Therefore, come to my aid so that I can get Your divine mirror working in my life, in the name of Jesus.

3. O God, whatever is in my life that may be causing me to have spiritual amnesia, that is, to study / watch / hear Your word and then to not do it, let that thing be cast out of my life, in the name of Jesus.

4. O my Father, from this day forward, whenever I am in a live ministration or I am listening to or watching a prepackaged sermon or I am reading Your word, let me bring my complete self to that place, in the name of Jesus.

5. From today, O God, let me look into Your perfect law of liberty and fix my attention there. Let me memorize whatever I am studying and hearing so that it can be retained within my heart, in the name of Jesus.

6. Great and Mighty God, give me the grace to take Your word that I have memorized and let me do it, live it out and put into practice.

And by reason of this, according to Your word, let me be blessed in whatever I do, in the name of Jesus.

7. Thank You El Shaddai for answering my prayers, in Jesus' mighty name, amen.

If you have the need and the time, please feel free to add more prayers at this point.

Blessing: May God give you the fortitude to become a hearer and doer of His word so that you can reap the associated benefits, in the name of Jesus.

DAY 69

HOUSE ON A ROCK

"Therefore whosoever heareth these sayings of mine, and doeth them, I will liken him unto a wise man, which built his house upon a rock."
— Matthew 7:24 (KJV)

DAILY EXHORTATION

Beginning from Matthew Chapter 5, Jesus Christ began an epic sermon which is popularly referred to as the Sermon on the Mount. This sermon contained a powerful set of exhortations which, if put into practice, are certain to benefit any life.

Then, when He reached the end of the main gist of the sermon, He began to speak out the words of our opening scripture. You'll notice that the words in our opening scripture appear to somewhat mirror a scripture we saw yesterday which says *"But the one who peers into the perfect law of liberty and fixes his attention there, and does not become a forgetful listener but one who lives it out—he will be blessed in what he does."* (James 1:25, NET).

In our opening scripture for today, Jesus is again saying that if you hear this Sermon on the Mount and do it, you will be like a wise man who built his house on a rock. Yesterday, the reward for living out or doing the word of God was that you will be blessed in whatever you do. So, is the reward for doing the sayings of Christ in today's devotional the same as yesterday's? In other words, what is the benefit of building your house on a rock? Let's find out from scripture:

Matthew 7:24-25 (KJV) "*Therefore whosoever heareth these sayings of mine, and doeth them, I will liken him unto a wise man, which built his house upon a rock:* **And the rain descended, and the floods came, and the winds blew, and beat upon that house; and it fell not: for it was founded upon a rock.**"

The Lord Jesus Christ is promising you this morning that if you listen to / read His word and you decide in your heart to do it, your "house" will never fall.

What is your "house"? Your house is everything that you are and that you have. This will include your spirit, soul and body, your name, your reputation, your spouse and kids, your career or business, the assets that you have accumulated, etc. He is saying that surely the rain of life will descend on your house, the floods of life will come and the winds of life will blow upon your house BUT by reason of the word of God which you have listened to / read and put into practice, your "house" will be preserved. This means that no matter the spiritual attack the devil and his agents may launch against you or any attempt by anyone to bring you down, you and whatever pertains to you will not fall but will instead remain standing on the rock! And Jesus Christ Himself is this rock. He is this firm foundation! Glory to God! Can you see the powerful benefits that you are eligible to receive as a child of God?!

Now, just out of curiosity, is there a flip side to this? For example, with respect to one's "house", what will happen to those who listen to / read the word of God and fail to practice it? Let's find out in scripture:

Matthew 7:26-27 (KJV) "*And every one that heareth these sayings of mine, and doeth them not, shall be likened unto a foolish man, which built his house upon the sand: And the rain descended, and the floods came, and the winds blew, and beat upon that house; and it fell: and great was the fall of it.*"

As you can see, regardless of whether or not you do the word of God, you will be faced with the same tests and trials. Both the wise man and the foolish man will have rain descending, floods coming and winds blowing and beating on their houses. However, while the wise man's house is built on a rock, the foolish man's house is built on sand. Therefore, while the wise man's house will survive anything, the foolish man's house will fall.

The choice is yours to make this morning. Do you want to be a hearer and a doer or not? If you want to be a hearer and a doer so that you can enjoy the benefits of divine preservation, get yourself ready!

TODAY'S PRAYERS

1. O God of heaven and earth, make me a hearer and doer of Your word, in the name of Jesus.

2. Creator of the Universe, if by reason of my ignorance in the past, I have not heard or practiced Your word and my house has been built on sand, have mercy on me. Send Your mighty angels to reconstruct my foundation so that the sand can be removed and replaced with Your solid rock, in the name of Jesus.

3. O Lord my God, by reason of my rock solid

foundation, **when the rains of life descend on my house**, according to Your word, **let my house remain standing**, in the name of Jesus.

4. Eternal King, by reason of my rock solid foundation, **when the floods of life come**, according to Your word, **let my house remain standing**, in the name of Jesus.

5. Rock of Ages, by reason of Your presence in my life as my rock, **when the winds of life blow and beat upon my house**, according to Your word, **let my house remain standing**, in the name of Jesus.

6. Father God, let my wise action to hear and to do Your word be sustained throughout all the days of my life so that my house will be preserved forever, in the name of Jesus.

7. Thank You Wonderful God for all the amazing benefits that You have made available to me, in Jesus' mighty name, amen.

If you have the need and the time, please feel free to add more prayers at this point.

Blessing: May you be wise to hear and to do the word so that, come what may, your house will remain standing, in the name of Jesus.

DAY 70

THIS COULD BE YOURS

"Now when the Pharisee who had invited him saw this, he said to himself, 'If this man were a prophet, he would know who and what kind of woman this is who is touching him, that she is a sinner.'"
— Luke 7:39 (NET)

DAILY EXHORTATION

A Pharisee by the name Simon invited Jesus to dinner at his house. Jesus agreed to attend. When he got there, suddenly, a woman also appeared there. This woman then went behind Jesus at his feet and began to weep. As she was weeping, her tears began to fall on the feet of Jesus. Instead of wiping Christ's feet with a piece of cloth, she decided to use her hair. Afterward, she brought out an alabaster jar of perfume, kissed his feet and anointed them with the perfume.

According to our opening scripture, it was this sight that Simon the Pharisee saw that made him doubt Jesus in his heart. The woman who was carrying out this action of penitence was known in the area as a great sinner. Simon felt that by allowing her touch Him, it must be that Jesus had no spiritual power to discern the true nature of the woman. In his heart, he concluded that Jesus was just an ordinary man and was no prophet. But notice what happened next:

Luke 7:39-43 (NET) "*Now when the Pharisee who had invited him saw this, he said to himself, 'If this man were a prophet, he would know who and what kind of woman this is who is touching him, that she is a sinner.' So Jesus answered him, 'Simon, I have something to say to you.' He replied, 'Say it, Teacher.' 'A certain creditor had two debtors; one owed him five hundred silver coins, and the other fifty. When they could not pay, he canceled the debts of both. Now which of them will love him more?' Simon answered, 'I suppose the one who had the bigger debt canceled.' Jesus said to him, 'You have judged rightly.'*"

Please understand the scene: Pharisee invited Jesus. Woman came and began weeping and anointing his feet. Pharisee knew woman as a sinner and began to think doubt-filled thoughts in his heart about the spiritual condition of Christ. However, he never uttered a word. Yet, because Jesus Christ carried the omniscient power of the

Almighty, He heard what Simon was thinking in his heart. And He publicly replied to Simon's thoughts with the illustration He gave above of the two debtors. Can you imagine this kind of power — the ability to hear a person's thoughts? Remarkable! Fantastic!

By giving this particular illustration, Jesus Christ not only confirmed to Simon that He knew about the sinful nature of the woman at his feet, He was also telling Simon that He had scanned his own heart as well and found sin it, howbeit not as much as the woman's.

In reality, the two debtors Jesus was referring to were Simon and the woman at His feet! Talk about going above and beyond! If you are a child of God, who is filled to the brim with the Holy Spirit, the Almighty can give you this kind of ability as well. Really? If you're in doubt, let's find out from scripture:

John 14:11-14 (NET) "*Believe me that I am in the Father, and the Father is in me, but if you do not believe me, believe because of the miraculous deeds themselves. I tell you the solemn truth, the person who believes in me will perform the miraculous deeds that I am doing, and will perform greater deeds than these, because I am going to the Father. And I will do whatever you ask in my name, so that the Father may be glorified in the Son. If you ask me anything in my name, I will do it.*"

Jesus, your Lord and Savior, is right now in heaven with the Father. Through the power of His Holy Spirit, if you ask Him to do 'anything', insofar as that thing is necessary, He will do it for you. You will be able to replicate every miracle Jesus performed and do even greater than He did while He was on the earth. This includes the ability to hear the thoughts of other people when it is expedient for you to do so. This should not be surprising to you because even in the old testament, Elisha had the ability to intercept secret conversations between people several miles away or in other countries! It was also how he was able to see Gehazi's greedy requests to Naaman from the comfort of his house. The power of the Most High!

You have to realize that these benefits will only be available to people who are serious and who need them for kingdom purposes. Do you want divine abilities to be deposited in your life from God's throne? If yes, get yourself ready!

TODAY'S PRAYERS

1. Omnipotent God, I bow before You this morning, in the name of Jesus.

2. Omnipresent God, I bow before You this morning, in the name of Jesus.

3. Omniscient God, I bow before You this morning, in the name of Jesus.

4. Alpha and Omega, I want to become a complete Christian. Help me, in the name of Jesus.

5. This morning, Lord, I ask You to fill me afresh with Your supernatural enabler on the earth — Your precious Holy Spirit, in the name of Jesus.

6. Lord, Your word says that as a believer, I will be able to repeat all the miracles Jesus performed while He was here on the earth and I will also be able to do even greater. Scan my heart, O God, and see that I am serious and ready for a complete Christian experience. Let this word come to pass in my life. Give me power and ability so that whenever it is expedient for me to do so, I will be able to perform miracles that will bring You glory and honor including hearing the inner thoughts of people. Teach me to use any aspect of the supernatural power You have made available to believers in order to bring comfort to the ailing, solutions to the confused, restoration to the broken and justice. Let this be my experience and my testimony even as I continue in my walk of

destiny, in the name of Jesus.

7. Thank You Almighty and All-Powerful God for answering my prayer, in Jesus' mighty name, amen.

If you have the need and the time, please feel free to add more prayers at this point.

Blessing: May God empower You so that You can enjoy the complete Christian experience, in the name of Jesus.

DAY 71

HE IS NOT AGAINST IT

"But God said to him, 'You fool! This very night your life will be demanded back from you, but who will get what you have prepared for yourself?'"
— Luke 12:20 (NET)

DAILY EXHORTATION

Many people read the "parable of the rich fool" as recorded in Luke 12 and they do not understand why God struck the man down on the night of the same day he 'appeared' to make what could be regarded as a wise investment decision.

For the purpose of clarity, let's take a look at the parable:

Luke 12:16-20 (NET) "*He then told them a parable: 'The land of a certain rich man produced an abundant crop, so he thought to himself, 'What should I do, for I have nowhere to store my crops?' Then he said, 'I will do this: I will tear down my barns and build bigger ones, and there I will store all my grain and my goods. And I will* *say to myself, 'You have plenty of goods stored up for many years; relax, eat, drink, celebrate!" But God said to him, 'You fool! This very night your life will be demanded back from you, but who will get what you have prepared for yourself?'"*

It was shortly after the rich man said all of the foregoing that he died. The man had a surplus of farm produce and since there was no space to store them, he decided to build bigger barns that could accommodate his produce. So far so good.

Then, the rich man defined the absolute scope and purpose of the surplus storage. He said "*I will say to myself, 'You have plenty of goods stored up for many years; relax, eat, drink, celebrate!*'". And this is where his life unraveled. What this man was saying is that the entire purpose of the abundant produce he was about to store was so that he could relax, eat, drink and celebrate. Nothing or no one else factored in his investment strategy. And this is where God got angry with him. We know this because of what Jesus said in verse 21 which says:

Luke 12:20-21 (NET) "*But God said to him, 'You fool! This very night your life will be demanded back from you, but who will get what you have prepared for yourself?'* **So it is with the one who stores up riches**

for himself, but is not rich toward God.'"

The crime of the rich man and what made him a fool is that he was storing up riches for himself alone BUT he was not rich toward God. Without wasting time, what does it mean to be rich toward God? Let's find out from scripture:

Matthew 25:34-36 (NET) "*Then the king will say to those on his right, 'Come, you who are blessed by my Father, inherit the kingdom prepared for you from the foundation of the world. For I was hungry and you gave me food, I was thirsty and you gave me something to drink, I was a stranger and you invited me in, I was naked and you gave me clothing, I was sick and you took care of me, I was in prison and you visited me.'"*

Matthew 25:37-41 (NET) "*Then the righteous will answer him, 'Lord, when did we see you hungry and feed you, or thirsty and give you something to drink? When did we see you a stranger and invite you in, or naked and clothe you? When did we see you sick or in prison and visit you?'* **And the king will answer them, 'I tell you the truth, just as you did it for one of the least of these brothers or sisters of mine, you did it for me.'** *Then he will say to those on his left, 'Depart from me, you accursed, into the eternal fire that has been prepared for the devil and his angels!*"*

To be rich toward God is to give to the less-privileged especially poor Christians. As you can see, being rich toward God is in fact a powerful element in entering the kingdom of heaven. Therefore, it should be very clear to you today that God is not against rich people or against you becoming wealthy. However, when you do become rich, include others in your plans and investment strategies. As you make plans to relax, eat, drink and celebrate for yourself and your family, also make simultaneous plans to give to the poor, to feed the hungry, to succor the thirsty, to house the homeless, to clothe the naked, to take care of the sick and to visit the incarcerated.

If you embed this in the core of your life and you practice it without wavering, God will multiply your financial success beyond your wildest dreams and yet, your place in heaven will be secured. Is this something you want? If yes, get yourself ready!

TODAY'S PRAYERS

1. O Great and Mighty God, I thank You for the refreshing perspective I have received on my finances this morning. Accept my thanks, in the name of Jesus.

2. Father, I do not want to be a rich fool. I want

to be wealthy and wise. Help me today, in the name of Jesus.

3. According to Your word, from today, Father, let the consciousness be in me that even as my finances grow, my richness toward You must also grow, in the name of Jesus.

4. My Shepherd, as I make investment decisions with a view to establishing myself and securing my future, let me also make plans to actively and consistently help the less-privileged around me especially those that are in the body of Christ, in the name of Jesus.

5. O God, I am willing to obey Your word to the fullest. Therefore, guide me as I embark on a lifelong journey of feeding the hungry, providing drink to the thirsty, providing housing for the homeless, clothing the naked, caring for the sick and visiting the incarcerated, in the name of Jesus.

6. Emmanuel, by reason of my commitment and my actions, let the spirit of untimely death be far from me and let my place in Your kingdom be secured, in the name of Jesus.

7. Thank You Father God for the opportunity and for answering my prayers, in Jesus'

mighty name, amen.

If you have the need and the time, please feel free to add more prayers at this point.

Blessing: May God keep you and prosper you even as you obey His word, in the name of Jesus.

DAY 72

THE TIMING OF HUMAN JUDGMENT

"He (Jesus) answered them, 'Do you think these Galileans were worse sinners than all the other Galileans, because they suffered these things?'"
— Luke 13:2 (NET)

DAILY EXHORTATION

What we are looking at this morning is one of the scariest portions of scripture in the Bible in that it provides answers to questions such as "why them?", "why now?" or even "why me?". Please read and master today's devotional for your own good and for the sake of your loved ones.

One day, some persons came to Jesus and gave Him news about how Pilate murdered some Galileans who were offering sacrifices. Jesus then took that news report and opened a window into one of the deep mysteries of life, that is, the timing of divine judgment. Let's take a look at this in scripture:

Luke 13:2-5 (NET) "*He answered them, 'Do you think these Galileans were worse sinners than all the other Galileans, because they suffered these things? No, I tell you! But unless you repent, you will all perish as well! Or those eighteen who were killed when the tower in Siloam fell on them, do you think they were worse offenders than all the others who live in Jerusalem? No, I tell you! But unless you repent you will all perish as well!'*"

Jesus was aware of the deaths at Galilee and He added another report of some 18 people who also died when a tower in Siloam fell on them. In both cases, He warned the people present [and by extension the whole world] that they should repent or the same fate that befell the people at Galilee and at Siloam would befall them as well. He did not stop there. Jesus decided to give a parable in order to shed more light on the mystery of sin and the timing of divine judgment. Let's examine this parable in scripture:

Luke 13:6-9 (NET) "*Then Jesus told this parable: 'A man had a fig tree planted in his vineyard, and he came looking for fruit on it and found none. So he said to the worker who tended the vineyard, 'For three years now, I have come looking for fruit on this fig tree, and each time I inspect it I find none. Cut it down! Why should it continue to deplete the soil?' But the worker answered him, 'Sir, leave it alone this year too, until I dig around it and put* *fertilizer on it. Then if it bears fruit next year, very well, but if not, you can cut it down.'"*

You see the earth is the vineyard. The owner of the vineyard is the Almighty, the worker or dresser who tended the vineyard is Jesus and the fig tree in the vineyard represents individual human beings.

This parable is telling us that from time to time, God visits His vineyard to assess different fig trees. He knows each and every fig tree. You can tell because He knew for exactly how long the particular fig tree in the parable had been without fruit. Different fig trees are assessed at different times. A tree might have fruit and it will be left alone. On the other hand, a tree that used to bear fruit could become barren.

The tree in the parable had not borne any fruit for three years and the owner felt it was time to cut it down. But the worker interceded on its behalf and bought it more time. Here's the thing: How do you know that you are not being assessed right now by God? What Jesus is saying through this parable is that the people who Pilate murdered at Galilee and those who died at Siloam had been assessed. They were found to have no fruit and therefore, they were cut down! When you hear news of people who die in tragic circumstances [like the people in Galilee and

Siloam], this divine assessment could be the reason for their demise.

This is a powerful realization because no one knows whether they have been assessed and found to have no fruit. No one knows whether the grace period negotiated for them has expired and still their tree has been found to have no fruit.

The reason why divine judgment happens at different times to different people all over the world is because the time of assessment is different for everybody. Ditto the period of grace. This is why Jesus Christ told those people "*do you think they were worse offenders than all the others who live in Jerusalem? No, I tell you! But unless you repent you will all perish as well!*" Those people who perished had been assessed BUT the day of assessment of every other person would come at some point in time. If there were sinners amongst those people Jesus was talking to, the reason they were still alive was probably because they had not been assessed by the owner of the vineyard or their grace period had not yet expired. If the grace period of anyone expires and they are found to still have no fruit or to still be living in sin, that person will surely perish.

However, the good news is that, even though a sinner is assessed and found to be in sin, if he or she repents from that sin before the grace period expires, he or she will not perish neither will he or she be cut down! Hallelujah! This is the hope that we have for ourselves and for our loved ones. That is, by repenting of sin and forsaking it and allowing the Holy Spirit to help us bear fruit, we can be spared divine judgment and instead enjoy the fullness of God's grace and favor. Do you want to be spared divine judgment? Do you want to make sure that you are never cut down before your time? If yes, get yourself ready!

TODAY'S PRAYERS

1. Merciful God, I know that I am not perfect. This is why this morning, I have come to ask You to have mercy on me, in the name of Jesus.

2. Almighty, I know that You are the owner of the vineyard of life, Jesus is the keeper of the vineyard and I am a fig tree in Your vineyard. Father, let Your expectations concerning my life become the reality of my life, in the name of Jesus.

3. Messiah, if there is any sin in my life, I repent of it and forsake it this morning. Let the blood of Jesus that was shed for me on the Cross of Calvary and which speaks better things than the blood of Abel begin to speak

mercy and grace for me now, in the name of Jesus.

4. Holy Spirit of God, it is only through You that a person can bear fruit that will satisfy the divine assessment of the owner of the vineyard. Therefore, I ask that You fill me up to the brim today. Take my thoughts, my emotions and my behavior and cause Your fruit to manifest through them so that the fig tree of my life in the vineyard of life can bear fruit, in the name of Jesus.

5. Lord Jesus, keeper of the vineyard of life, I am ready to bear fruit. According to Your word, dig around my fig tree and put fertilizer on me. I will bear fruit, in the name of Jesus.

6. Great and Mighty God, whenever I am assessed again, let it be that fruit will be found on the fig tree of my life. By reason of this, let me be preserved and saved from divine judgment and from perishing, in the name of Jesus.

7. Thank You Father God for answering my prayers, in Jesus' mighty name, amen.

If you have the need and the time, please feel free to add more prayers at this point.

Blessing: *May you bear fruit that will satisfy the owner of the vineyard, in the name of Jesus.*

DAY 73

HOW THE HARVEST COMES

"He also said, 'The kingdom of God is like someone who spreads seed on the ground. He goes to sleep and gets up, night and day, and the seed sprouts and grows, though he does not know how. By itself the soil produces a crop, first the stalk, then the head, then the full grain in the head. And when the grain is ripe, he sends in the sickle because the harvest has come.'"
— Mark 4:26-29 (NET)

DAILY EXHORTATION

In Matthew 6:33 (NET), the Bible says "*But above all pursue His [God's] kingdom and righteousness, and all these things will be given to you as well.*" But how exactly does this happen? Today's opening scripture is meant to supply us with a mechanism through which the things we need are given to us. God knows the needs of all His children. For some people, it might be making more money, getting married, having children, better accommodation, academic excellence, workplace promotion and having business success. For other people, it might be things like getting funding for evangelism and for missionary work, receiving the ability to be a better public speaker so that they can more effectively share God's word with others, receiving the ability to pray for more hours, a need for the fruit of the Spirit to manifest in their lives, a need to receive one or more gifts of the Spirit, making heaven, etc. Whatever the need is, the Bible says you should seek first or pursue the kingdom of God and you will have it.

Now, the question is what happens after you genuinely begin to seek or pursue after God's kingdom? The answer lies in our opening scripture. You see, your commitment to putting God's Kingdom first is akin to planting seeds in the ground. As you consistently study the Bible, do your praise and worship, sing to God both with understanding and in the Spirit, pray both with understanding and in the Spirit, talk about Jesus to others, refuse to fall into temptation, refuse to sin, show kindness and generosity to others, etc., you are putting God's kingdom first. These deeds we just enumerated are the seeds you are spreading on the "ground" of God's kingdom. And that's all you need to do. Once the seeds get into the ground, God takes over. It doesn't matter whether you are awake or asleep, or whether it is night or day, God will speak growth into your seeds. In ways that only God Himself understands, your seed will produce a crop.

First, the stalk of the crop will emerge, then the head and then the full grain in the head. These steps show God at work in putting in place the people, the physical and spiritual situations and everything else that is necessary for your needs to manifest in reality.

Does your need require money? God will arrange it. Does you need require connections to certain kinds of people? God will somehow arrange it. Does your need require that you develop some kind of trait or skill? God will go to work in order to infuse it into your life over time. These steps also show why some things cannot happen immediately. Sometimes, certain steps must be followed before the final product is developed.

Now, according to our opening scripture, after the full grain of the crop is in the head, all that remains is for the grain to be ripe. When this happens, the harvest has come and you can put in your sickle and reap the rewards. This is how God converts your prioritization of His kingdom into meeting the needs of your life. This is how your devotion to God will lead to the manifestation of the money you need, the workplace promotion, marriage, kids, academic excellence, accommodation, business success, etc.

This mechanism shows how you can get your need to evangelize or to do mission work met. This is how you can receive the fruit of God's Spirit or any of His gifts in your life or any other spiritual blessing that you desire. This is the mechanism that will ensure that you make heaven when the rapture happens or when you are called home in your old age.

So, do you want the harvest? Do you want your needs met? If yes, get yourself ready!

TODAY'S PRAYERS

1. Almighty Father, I have needs. These are the things that I need most in my life right now: _____ [Tell God what you need at this point in time]. Help me make them a reality in my life, in the name of Jesus.

2. Lord, according to Your word, I have decided from the bottom of my heart to put You first. From today, I will make sure that the matters of Your kingdom will become the priority of my life. Help me, in the name of Jesus.

3. O God, as I begin to demonstrate my commitment to You and to Your kingdom, let the righteous thoughts of my heart and my deeds be converted into seeds that can grow in the ground of Your kingdom, in the name of Jesus.

4. Yahweh, as I cast my seeds into the ground of Your kingdom, let them enter into the soil. Once they are in the soil, Lord, do what only You can do. Speak life and speak growth into my seeds, in the name of Jesus.

5. Jehovah God, by reason of the word of life that You shall speak into my seeds, at the right time, cause the stalks to show up. At the right time, cause the heads to show up. At the right time, cause the full grains to appear in the heads of my crops. Father, put in place the conditions, the situations, the circumstances, the people, the resources and everything else that is necessary for my needs to be met, in the name of Jesus.

6. Then Lord, when the crop is ripe, according to Your word, cause the harvesting sickle to appear in my hands. The harvest is come! Empower me to go forth and reap the rewards of my devotion and my total commitment to You. Lord, let the needs that

I have harbored in my heart, through the mystery of Your kingdom, manifest right in front of my eyes to Your glory, in the name of Jesus.

7. Thank You Father God for answering my prayers, in Jesus' mighty name, amen.

If you have the need and the time, please feel free to add more prayers at this point.

Blessing: May God Almighty reward your devotion to Him and to His kingdom, in the name of Jesus.

DAY 74

WHAT ARE YOU DOING IN THE SEA?

"Again, the kingdom of heaven is like a
net that was cast into the sea that caught
all kinds of fish. When it was full, they
pulled it ashore, sat down, and put the
good fish into containers and threw the
bad away. It will be this way at the end of
the age. Angels will come and separate the
evil from the righteous and throw them
into the fiery furnace, where there will be
weeping and gnashing of teeth."
— Matthew 13:47-50 (NET)

DAILY EXHORTATION

The way God sees His creations is quite different
from how we see ourselves. For example, while
we may see ourselves as handsome or beautiful or
some other trait, spiritually-speaking [at least
according to our opening scripture], we are fish in
the sea! Ah! And there are only two kinds of fish
— good or bad. This is very interesting because

the scripture doesn't talk about how good-looking a fish is or how ugly it is, it only talks about good fish or bad fish [something to think about].

Whether we like it or not, we are all in the sea of life. And the fisherman and His men are on their way. They'll be here very soon. When they come, they will cast their net into the sea, wait till its full and drag us all to the shore. They will then put those of us that are good fish into special containers and we will be taken to the fisherman's home, where we will be taken care of forever and ever. BUT, for the bad fish that are amongst us, the fisherman's men will throw them away. Not into the sea but into a fiery furnace!

Friend, heaven is real, hell too is real. Jesus is coming soon. His angels too are coming soon. The day of the Rapture is at hand. Do not be carried away by the advancements man has made. Some people actually believe that it is impossible for anything to nullify the earth as it is now. Ah! Do you know that certain countries have already developed weapons that can reach any point on the earth and cannot be stopped by any defense system? These weapons can take out entire states in a few minutes. Only one of them is needed to do this! This means that with only a few of these weapons, entire countries can be wiped out. With a few thousand of these weapons, the whole earth can be destroyed in a few days. If this happens, all the technology we see around us today will stop functioning and we will be back in the stone age. If this is what human inventions can do today, how much more the power of the Creator of the Universe. This is why we need to fear God and make Him our focus.

Now, the question is when the fisherman's men sit at the shore in order to examine the net, how do you make sure that you are selected as good fish? The answer to that lies in what you are currently doing in the sea. What are you doing in the sea of life right now? Are your ways evil or are they righteous? What you do on a daily basis, does it glorify God or not? Are you a good representative of Christ on the earth? Are you doing God's will or not? Your answer to these questions will determine whether you are put into God's special containers or you are cast away. If you are reading this devotional, certainly, it must be that it is because you want to live right before God. It must be that you want to be rapture-ready.

Therefore, you have an opportunity this morning to again examine yourself and approach God for the grace to meet the criteria of selection for entry into His kingdom. You have an opportunity to manage yourself in the sea of life so that when the net comes, you will find favor with the Lord Jesus Christ. Would you like to do this? If yes, get yourself ready!

TODAY'S PRAYERS

1. My Father and my God, I know that the end of the age is coming. I want to be ready for it. Come to my aid, in the name of Jesus.

2. Great and Mighty God, I acknowledge that, according to Your word, I am a fish in the sea of life. I acknowledge that very soon You and Your angels will soon cast a net into the sea for eternal selection. Help me O Lord, in the name of Jesus.

3. Lord, You are my Rock. Right now, as I am in the sea of life, give me the grace to live a life that is righteous before You, in the name of Jesus.

4. O God, let the Blood of Jesus that was shed for me on Calvary purify me and make my life as white as snow so that I can stand holy before You. Let the Blood of Jesus wash my heart clean so that my thinking, my feelings and my behavior can always be in line with Your expectations for me, in the name of Jesus.

5. By reason of Your mercy and Your grace, O God, when You send your fishermen to the sea of life—when You send Your angels to the world—to catch all the fish in it, and when they drag us to the shore of judgment, let me be found to be righteous, in the name of Jesus.

6. By reason of the righteousness procured for me by the sacrifice of Your son, Jesus Christ, O God, on that day and on that shore of judgment, let me be spared from the fiery furnace where there is eternal weeping and gnashing of teeth. Instead, let Your angels put me in the special container reserved for the righteous so that I can be taken into Your heavenly home to be with You forever and ever, in the name of Jesus.

7. Thank You Mighty God for Your grace and Your mercy and for answering my prayers, in Jesus' mighty name, amen.

If you have the need and the time, please feel free to add more prayers at this point.

Blessing: May you be found to be good fish! And may the sacrifice of Jesus and His Blood speak for you and save you forever, in the name of Jesus.

DAY 75
ACTS OF PERFECTION

"Be ye therefore perfect, even as your
Father which is in heaven is perfect."
— Matthew 5:48 (KJV)

DAILY EXHORTATION

As you know, ordinarily speaking, it is not
possible for a human being to be perfect. So,
what did Jesus mean in our opening scripture
when He said we should be perfect even as our
Father in heaven is perfect? The answer to that
lies in the phrase "*even as your Father in heaven*".
Jesus is simply saying that You should imitate the
holy acts of God. Here are a few more scriptures
to back up this spiritual reality:

John 5:19 (NET) "*So Jesus answered them, 'I tell you
the solemn truth, the Son can do nothing on his own
initiative, but only what he sees the Father doing. **For
whatever the Father does, the Son does
likewise**.*'"

1 Corinthians 11:1 (NET) "*Be imitators of me, just as I also am of Christ.*"

John 8:38 (NET) "*I am telling you the things I have seen while with the Father;* **as for you, practice the things you have heard from the Father!**"

The first passage above reveals to us that even Jesus Christ Himself, our Lord and Savior, was an imitator of God the Father. The second and third passages reveal how to imitate God. That is, by imitating Jesus Christ and by practicing the things you hear from the Father. So, our task has become very simple. In order to be perfect, all you need to do is to read about the things Jesus Christ did while He was on the earth and do them all. In addition, to be perfect, read everything written in the Bible which is said to be from the Father and begin to practice it. Do these things and you will become 'perfect'. So, is there an example of something you can do which reflects the acts or deeds of God? Yes, there are several. Let's take a look at one of them in scripture:

Matthew 18:23-27 (NET) "*For this reason, the kingdom of heaven is like a king who wanted to settle accounts with his slaves. As he began settling his accounts,* *a man who owed ten thousand talents was brought to him. Because he was not able to repay it, the lord ordered him to be sold, along with his wife, children, and whatever he possessed, and repayment to be made. Then the slave threw himself to the ground before him, saying, 'Be patient with me, and I will repay you everything.' The lord had compassion on that slave and released him, and forgave him the debt."*

The king in this parable is God. The original judgment against the debtor was that his entire family and possessions be sold to repay his debt but because he appeared to humble himself by throwing himself on the ground and saying *'Be patient with me, and I will repay you everything.'*, God released him and forgave him the debt. This act of God is an example of an act that we should all imitate. According to the scriptures we have read thus far, anytime we forgive people who ask us to have compassion on them for any wrong they have done to us, we are imitating God. And by doing it, we are carrying out an act of perfection. Carrying out multiple acts of this kind will cause us in the long run to become perfect just as our Father in heaven is perfect.

Now, this man in Christ's parable, was he given an opportunity to imitate God? And if yes, what did he do with the opportunity? Let's find out the answer to these questions from scripture:

Matthew 18:28-31 (NET) "*After he went out, that same slave found one of his fellow slaves who owed him one hundred silver coins. So he grabbed him by the throat and started to choke him, saying, 'Pay back what you owe me!' Then his fellow slave threw himself down and begged him, 'Be patient with me, and I will repay you.' But he refused. Instead, he went out and threw him in prison until he repaid the debt. When his fellow slaves saw what had happened, they were very upset and went and told their lord everything that had taken place.*"

Unfortunately, the man blew his chance at perfection! God gave him an immediate opportunity to imitate Him but he failed. When his own turn came to show compassion, he did not. So, is imitating God optional? As believers, can we go through life and refuse to imitate God? The answer lies in God's reaction to this man who refused to imitate Him. Let's take one final look in the Bible for today:

Matthew 18:32-35 (NET) "*Then his lord called the first slave and said to him, 'Evil slave! I forgave you all that debt because you begged me! Should you not have shown mercy to your fellow slave, just as I showed it to you?' And in anger his lord turned him over to the prison guards to torture him until he repaid all he owed. So also my heavenly Father will do to you, if each of you does not forgive your brother from your heart.*'"

As you can see, imitating God is not an option. God is holy and everything He does is perfect! God will never cause you to do anything that will be deleterious to yourself or that will cause you to be a menace to those that are around you. If you imitate God, the windows and gates of heaven will be open to you BUT if you do not, there may be repercussions. If you want to be perfect and at the same time honor your maker, get yourself ready!

TODAY'S PRAYERS

1. O Lord, You are my God. according to Your word, I want to be perfect just as You are perfect. Help me, in the name of Jesus.

2. My Father and my God, from today, as I read the Bible, particularly about the words and deeds of Your Son, Jesus Christ, open my understanding so that I can completely comprehend all of His words and deeds, in the name of Jesus.

3. Most High God, from today, as I read the Bible, especially about things You Yourself said in it, open my understanding so that I can comprehend them all, in the name of Jesus.

4. El Shaddai, give me the divine unction to take my knowledge of the words and deeds of Jesus and to successfully imitate them in my own generation, in the name of Jesus.

5. Yahweh, empower me to take the things that I have heard from You through Your word and through Your Holy Spirit and practice them wholeheartedly, in the name of Jesus.

6. Jehovah, by reason of my determination and my action to know more, to imitate Christ and to practice Your word, let me be perfect even as You are perfect, in the name of Jesus.

7. Thank You O God for answering my prayers, in Jesus' mighty name, amen.

If you have the need and the time, please feel free to add more prayers at this point.

Blessing: May you always imitate Christ and practice the word of the living God so that You can dwell within God's perfect will for your life, in the name of Jesus.

DAY 76

WHO IS MY NEIGHBOR?

"... A man was going down from Jerusalem to Jericho, and fell into the hands of robbers, who stripped him, beat him up, and went off, leaving him half dead. Now by chance a priest was going down that road, but when he saw the injured man he passed by on the other side. So too a Levite, when he came up to the place and saw him, passed by on the other side..." — Luke 10:30-32 (NET)

DAILY EXHORTATION

If you have been reading Command the Morning for a while, you would certainly have come across the phrase 'love your neighbor' a number of times. And you probably get the part about loving your neighbor but it is possible you are not sure who your neighbor is or should be? Is my neighbor the person who lives next to me or my co-worker OR is my neighbor a fellow Christian?

These persons are indeed your neighbors BUT according to Jesus, the scope of 'neighbor' is much more expansive than that.

One day, a man, an expert in religious law, approached Jesus wanting to know how he could inherit eternal life. After some back and forth, Jesus essentially told him that the way to do that was to love God with all his heart and to love his neighbor as himself. Then, the man asked Jesus to define the word 'neighbor'. It is at this point that we get to our opening scripture.

In the story Jesus used in answering the man's question, Jesus said a Jewish man was robbed, beaten and left for dead on the road. Again, this was a Jewish man. A priest, who was also Jewish, was passing along that road and from afar he saw this Jewish man lying on the road. He immediately crossed over to the other side. Another Jewish man also came down that road. He was a Levite. The Levite did better than the priest. He continued along the road until he got to where the battered man was, took a look at him and immediately crossed over to the other side.

These were country men of this man. By doing nothing, they showed that they did not care what happened to the man. It was none of their business. These holy men, whose job it was to care for people, saw a dying man and did nothing! If you haven't heard this story before, you might be curious to know how the battered man ended up — did he die? How quickly did he die after the priest and the levite passed him by? etc. Let's find out from scripture:

Luke 10:33-35 (NET) "*But a Samaritan who was traveling came to where the injured man was, **and when he saw him, he felt compassion for him.** He went up to him and bandaged his wounds, pouring oil and wine on them. Then he put him on his own animal, brought him to an inn, and took care of him. The next day he took out two silver coins and gave them to the innkeeper, saying, 'Take care of him, and whatever else you spend, I will repay you when I come back this way.'*"

The battered Jewish man did not die on that road. A Samaritan man saved him. *And that's a very unusual thing to say*. You see, for a number of historical reasons, Jewish people and Samaritans hated each other very profoundly. It's like the kind of hatred many Palestinians have for modern-day Jews or like the hatred many Iranians have for Israel. You would not, for instance, expect an Iranian or a Palestinian to help a Jew in trouble. That would be a miracle if it ever happened.

Yet, while the Jewish priest and the levite refused to help their own brother who was dying, their enemy—a Samaritan—helped him. The Samaritan had compassion on his enemy. He risked his own safety by staying on that road where a robbery had just happened whilst giving the Jew first aid. He then took him to some sort of hospital and paid for his healthcare. Amazing!

So, after Jesus told this story to the questioner, the answer to the question was apparent and clear:

Luke 10:36-37 (NET) "*Which of these three do you think became a neighbor to the man who fell into the hands of the robbers?' The expert in religious law said, 'The one who showed mercy to him.' So Jesus said to him, 'Go and do the same.'*"

To principles for making heaven are very different from the principles of the world. The world will tell you to hate those who hate you. They will tell you to give them hell! But Jesus is saying here that you should love your neighbor as yourself and that neighbor includes everyone including people you know and people you do not know.

Neighbor also includes people who hate you. This does not mean you should hang out with someone who is trying to kill you. No. However, it means that if you do find your enemy stuck in any kind of rut and he or she needs your help, just as the Samaritan did, have compassion for that person and help him or her out with wisdom. This could be on your street, at work, amongst your relatives or spouse's relatives, at your church, etc... wherever, have compassion and help them out.

If you do this, according to the words of Christ, eternal life in heaven is guaranteed. Do you want eternal life by being a good neighbor? If yes, get yourself ready!

TODAY'S PRAYERS

1. O Lord of hosts, I want to make heaven. Help me, in the name of Jesus.

2. Father, I love You with all of my heart and I want also to love my neighbor as myself so that I can inherit eternal life. Come to my aid, in the name of Jesus.

3. My God, this morning, invade my heart with Your precious Holy Spirit. Let Your Spirit bless me with the same kind of compassion that the Samaritan had, in the name of Jesus.

4. Eternal King, let the compassion in my heart drive my body, my mouth, my hands and my feet to carry out acts of mercy for anyone who needs it, in the name of Jesus.

5. Great and Mighty God, in the same manner the Samaritan was able to overlook history and bitterness in order to help the battered man, give me the wisdom to overlook negative history in order to help anyone including those who hate me, in the name of Jesus.

6. Now Lord, I ask: By reason of my determination and my action to be compassionate and to be kind to my neighbors, that is, all persons including those that hate me, according to Your word, let me inherit eternal life, in the name of Jesus.

7. Thank You El Shaddai for answering my prayers, in Jesus' mighty name, amen.

If you have the need and the time, please feel free to add more prayers at this point.

Blessing: May you receive grace to indeed love your neighbor as yourself so that you can inherit eternal life, in the name of Jesus.

DAY 77

YOUR NEED AND YOUR PERSISTENCE

"Then He (Jesus) said to them, 'Suppose one of you has a friend, and you go to him at midnight and say to him, 'Friend, lend me three loaves of bread, because a friend of mine has stopped here while on a journey, and I have nothing to set before him.' Then he will reply from inside, 'Do not bother me. The door is already shut, and my children and I are in bed. I cannot get up and give you anything.'"
— Luke 11:5-7 (NET)

DAILY EXHORTATION

The friend that suddenly came to visit the man in this story at midnight represents the vicissitudes of life. It means that the man did not know that he would be having a visitor. Therefore, he did not plan for the visit. Yet, the visitor still had to be entertained. Hence, the need for the man to visit his other friend, who had everything, at such an awkward time. This other friend's reaction would be the natural reaction of most people if they find themselves in the same position.

Once again, the sudden visitor represents the vicissitudes of life. It represents the needs that show up in the journey of life. This might include a need for healing, a need for deliverance, a need for money, a need for emotional stabilization, a need for marriage stability, a need for peace of mind, a need for character normalization in one's kids, a need for vindication in cases of false accusations, a need to develop a certain kind of trait or skill in order to take advantage of an opportunity, etc. Whatever it is, it could come and it would need to be solved.

But the other friend in our opening scripture said that he did not want to be bothered and he couldn't get up to meet his friend's need. How then did this man meet the need to entertain his visitor? Let's find out from scripture:

Luke 11:8 (NET) "*I tell you, even though the man inside will not get up and give him anything because he is his friend,* **yet because of the first man's sheer persistence he will get up and give him whatever he needs.**"

Jesus said that regardless of the reality on ground [that is, the friend was in bed, his door was shut, his children were all asleep, etc.], if that friend with a visitor waiting for him at home demonstrated sheer persistence and refused to go away, his friend who had the provisions will eventually get up and give him whatever he needs! Wow! This is also how it is in the spirit.

Sometimes, the spiritual reality may not permit that your prayer be answered immediately. God, who knows everything, may have an agenda in place already that He wants to follow. This agenda, to you, may translate to a delay in answering your prayers. What Jesus is saying this morning however is that if you refuse to quit and you demonstrate sheer persistence, just like the friend in this story, God will set aside protocol in order to give you whatever you need. This is why we say believers should P.U.S.H. That is, Pray Until Something Happens. If you want something done sooner rather than later, this is what you will need to do.

Do you have a need that has to be meet as soon as possible? Are you ready to P.U.S.H.? If yes, get yourself ready!

TODAY'S PRAYERS

1. O Lord, I recognize that any situation can arise at anytime that I will have to address. Therefore, I ask that you give ear to my

prayers this morning and answer me, in the name of Jesus.

2. Father, You are the only friend that has the answer to any need that may come my way in life. Therefore, I ask that You come to my aid, in the name of Jesus.

3. El Elyon, I know that You are omniscient and omnipresent. You know everything and You are everywhere meeting the needs of Your children all over the world and attending to matters of the universe that I can never comprehend. However, I also know that You are omnipotent and that there is nothing You cannot do. Let it be, O God, that when I come knocking on the doors of heaven, You shall hear me and answer me, in the name of Jesus.

4. Jehovah, whenever a need arises and I come to You, give me the fortitude to P.U.S.H. Help me to demonstrate sheer persistence through my prayers until You set aside protocol in order to answer me, in the name of Jesus.

5. Whenever I P.U.S.H., O God, have mercy on me and give me whatever I need, in the name of Jesus.

6. Messiah, by reason of the gift that You will place in my hands, let any need waiting for me be met completely. And let any problem that I have be solved totally, in the name of Jesus.

7. Thank You Mighty Father for answering my prayers, in Jesus' mighty name, amen.

If you have the need and the time, please feel free to add more prayers at this point.

Blessing: As you demonstrate sheer persistence before the Lord and you P.U.S.H, may your P.U.S.Hing be rewarded, in the name of Jesus.

DAY 78

CAN I BUY MY WAY INTO HEAVEN?

"And I tell you, make friends for yourselves by how you use worldly wealth, so that when it runs out you will be welcomed into the eternal homes."
— Luke 16:9 (NET)

DAILY EXHORTATION

During His earthly ministry, Jesus used many parables as well as stories in His ministrations. Recall that God is omnipresent and omniscient and so He has access to billions and trillions of records of human experiences from around the world and across the ages. Today's devotional focuses on an account of one of these human experiences.

One day, Jesus told His disciples an important story in order to illustrate a crucial mystery of God's kingdom. A very rich man received reports that his manager was wasting his assets. Specifically, many people who owed the

rich man were not paying back on time or at all.
And the manager was not really proactive in
collecting the debts. So, the rich man called in
this manager. He threatened to fire him but first
he required a complete record of the accounts.
Distressed, the manager's mind went into
overdrive. He knew he had to give a complete
account but after the sack, what would he do and
where would he go? He thought of digging
ditches to survive but decided against it because
he didn't have the strength to dig. Then, he
thought of begging but the shame would just kill
him. So, he began to think of a way to satisfy his
employer's need for accountability as well as his
own need for financial security after he got the
boot. This manager was trying to open two doors
with one key!

Finally, he hit upon an idea that could solve
his dilemma. Let's see what this was in scripture:

Luke 16:4-7 (NET) "*I know what to do so that when
I am put out of management, people will welcome me into
their homes.' So he contacted his master's debtors one by
one. He asked the first, 'How much do you owe my
master?' The man replied, 'A hundred measures of olive
oil.' The manager said to him, 'Take your bill, sit down
quickly, and write fifty.' Then he said to another, 'And
how much do you owe?' The second man replied, 'A
hundred measures of wheat.' The manager said to him,*

'Take your bill, and write eighty.'"

The manager's idea was to make sure he got back assets [not the whole of it] from all of his master's debtors. But at the same time, he wanted to win the favor of the debtors. His plan was that whenever he got fired, he would then cash in on the favors in order to secure himself financially. Perhaps one of these debtors would give him a job or food to eat or a place to stay.

He accomplished both aims by giving the debtors discounts on their debts as mentioned in the scripture above. These debtors were in distress as well. They were probably afraid that someday, the rich man would could come in and take away their property, their loves ones or themselves in lieu of the debt that they owed. Therefore, the partial debt forgiveness orchestrated by the manager was a great relief and a breath of fresh air. In other words, the manager, through his somewhat questionable tactics, had given them hope. He had reduced the weight of the burden that was on their lives. The manager's action probably encouraged many of these debtors to try to settle their discounted debts.

The rich man, on the other hand, saw the complete accounts rendered by the manager. Even though he probably knew that not all of His assets had been accounted for, he was nevertheless impressed by the industry and the results of his manager [we are not told whether he still sacked him].

Now, the important thing is this: How did Jesus feel about this story when He saw it unfold? And why did He decide to tell it to His disciples? Let's find out from the Bible:

Luke 16:8-9 (NET) "*The master commended the dishonest manager because he acted shrewdly. For the people of this world are more shrewd in dealing with their contemporaries than the people of light. **And I tell you, make friends for yourselves by how you use worldly wealth, so that when it runs out you will be welcomed into the eternal homes**.*"

This is a very powerful and mysterious statement from Jesus. Jesus is telling you this morning that in the same manner the manager became friends with his master's distressed debtors by doing them the favor of discounting their debts, you too should find people who are financially distressed [poor people], **help them out financially with your own wealth** and win them as friends! In addition, Jesus offers you a promise — if you do this, when your money runs out or better put, when you die, you will be welcomed into the eternal homes [a.k.a heaven].

So, take another look at the title of today's devotional. From what you've learned this morning, what do you think is the answer to that question? It is clear from Christ's statement that you can. All other things being equal [you are born again, you live a holy life, etc.], if you use your financial resources to help people who are in financial distress or who are poor, when you die, you will make heaven.

Do you want to benefit from this mystery of our faith? If yes, get yourself ready!

TODAY'S PRAYERS

1. Answer me O Lord and make me shrewd, in the name of Jesus.

2. Answer me O Lord and make me wiser than my contemporaries in this generation, in the name of Jesus.

3. Lord, let my shrewdness and my wisdom bring me a harvest of worldly wealth, in the name of Jesus.

4. Lord, let my shrewdness and my wisdom cause my worldly wealth to expand beyond my wildest imagination, in the name of Jesus.

5. Father, according to Your word, from today, let the consciousness be in me that **I Must use my worldly wealth to help holy people who are in financial distress** and by so doing make them into my friends, in the name of Jesus.

6. O Lord God, when my time on this earth is over, by reason of the shrewdness and wisdom with which I have utilized the wealth You have blessed me with, according to Your word, let me be welcomed into the eternal homes — let me be welcomed into heaven, in the name of Jesus.

7. Thank You Father God for answering my prayers, in Jesus' mighty name, amen.

If you have the need and the time, please feel free to add more prayers at this point.

Blessing: May God bless you with the shrewdness you need for your eternal security, in the name of Jesus.

DAY 79

THE GREAT, FIXED CHASM

"Besides all this, a great chasm has been fixed between us, so that those who want to cross over from here to you cannot do so, and no one can cross from there to us.'" — Luke 16:26 (NET)

DAILY EXHORTATION

One day, Jesus told another story. This was not a parable but an actual record of real events because Jesus provided names [including Abraham]. There was a rich man and there was a poor man. The poor man was called Lazarus. The name of the rich man was not given.

The rich man spent his days living in luxury whereas Lazarus was so poor that he had to depend on the crumbs that fell off the rich man's table for survival. Nevertheless, with the passage of time, both men died. Then, the story takes a radically different turn.

Perhaps for the first time, people got a

somewhat detailed glimpse into what happens in the hereafter. Jesus used this story to reveal to the people He was speaking to at the time [as well as us] about what happens on the other side of life. We will now spend the rest of today's devotional highlighting the characteristics of life after death based on Christ's story.

1. When a righteous person dies, the angels of God will appear in order to carry his or her spirit into heaven. (Luke 16:22)

2. Conversely, it is safe to say that when an unrighteous person dies, demons will appear to carry his or her spirit into hell.

3. Hell is down whereas heaven is up. (Luke 16:23)

4. Heaven and hell are very far apart. (Luke 16:23)

5. People in hell can see heaven and vice versa. (Luke 16:23)

6. There is thirst in hell and agony because of the fire that burns there. (Luke 16:24)

7. Heaven is a place of eternal comfort while hell is a place of eternal anguish and torment. (Luke 16:25)

8. There is a great chasm or gulf that has been fixed in place between heaven and hell. Therefore, the human spirits in heaven cannot cross into hell and those in hell can never cross into heaven. (Luke 16:26)

9. People in hell are concerned that their loved ones [spouse, children, friends, relatives, etc.] may be living in a manner that is guaranteed to land them in hell. They do not want anyone they love to come there because of the indescribable torment. (Luke 16:27-28)

10. Rich people can and do go to heaven. This is probably one of the reasons why Jesus emphasized "the rich man" and also emphasized that Lazarus went to "Abraham's bosom". Recall that Abraham is our spiritual ancestor. You are a Christian today because of the friendship that existed between God and Abraham and the generational blessing that resulted from that. And Abraham was remarkably wealthy as were his descendants. However, if you want to be wealthy and enter into heaven, you have to be as much a friend to God as Abraham was, at least. Keep this in mind.

11. Whether or not anyone goes to heaven or to hell is an individual matter. Listening to the

word of God (and doing it) is the only way to go to heaven and avoid hell. (Luke 16:27-31)

Our work this morning is very simple. No matter how hard anyone is on the outside, all human beings are concerned about eternal life. Jesus has given you a glimpse into how life is on the other side this morning. What would it be, heaven or hell? If you choose heaven, get yourself ready for prayers!

TODAY'S PRAYERS

1. Everlasting Father, I believe in heaven and I believe in hell. I believe that heaven is the place where You reside and where You are preparing for Your saints so they can be with You. I believe that hell is a place that is reserved for satan, his demons and unrepentant sinners.

2. Eternal King, when my time on the earth is done, I want to come to heaven and I do not want to go to hell. Help me, in the name of Jesus.

3. My God, through the Blood of Your Son, Jesus Christ, You have gracefully made provision for anyone on earth to be rescued from the torment of hell. You have assured

that anyone who believes in Your son will not perish BUT have everlasting life. Therefore, I declare this morning: Father, I believe in Jesus and in the Blood that He shed for me on the Cross of Calvary. Let everlasting life be assured for me, in the name of Jesus.

4. O God, this morning, I release myself to Your Holy Spirit. if there is any negative trait, bad habit or character flaw that is in my life, let Your Holy Spirit go to work and remove them from my life, in the name of Jesus.

5. Again Lord, I ask that if there is anyone out there that has been pushed into iniquity because of my negative actions in the past, I ask that You forgive me and also have mercy on him or her, in the name of Jesus.

6. Father, everyday of my life, as I listen to Your word, read it or watch it being preached, let it sink down into the core of my being and cause the kind of changes You desire to see in my life. By reason of this, when my time on this earth is done, let the angels carry me into heaven, a place of eternal comfort and reward, in the name of Jesus.

7. Thank You Mighty God for answering my prayers, in Jesus' mighty name, amen.

If you have the need and the time, please feel free to add more prayers at this point.

Blessing: May you never end up in hell but in the Kingdom of heaven, in the name of Jesus.

DAY 80

YOUR PAST
IS NOT THE REST
OF YOUR LIFE

**"'Which of the two did his father's will?'
They said, 'The first.' Jesus said to them,
'I tell you the truth, tax collectors and
prostitutes will go ahead of you into the
kingdom of God!'"
— Matthew 21:31 (NET)**

DAILY EXHORTATION

Remember the day Jesus cleared the temple?
That day, He got into the temple and found
people in there buying and selling. There were
also money changers there and persons who
traded in doves. He overturned the tables and
chairs of the traders and drove them all out.
When many people recount this episode, they do
not include what Jesus then did after He drove
these people out. So, let's find out from scripture:

Matthew 21:12-14 (NET) "*Then Jesus entered the temple area and drove out all those who were selling and buying in the temple courts, and turned over the tables of the money changers and the chairs of those selling doves. And he said to them, 'It is written, 'My house will be called a house of prayer,' but you are turning it into a den of robbers!'* **The blind and lame came to him in the temple courts, and he healed them.**"

Not only did Jesus say that the temple should be a house of prayer, by His acts, He also practically demonstrated that the temple of God should be a place of healing.

But if you think about this event for a minute, you would realize that Jesus' actions must have been offensive to the powers that were in place. For example, do you think that those traders, money changers and dove sellers didn't have some sort of arrangement with the priests? It couldn't have been possible that someone would, of his own accord, carry a table and chair and begin selling at a temple. Therefore, it was entirely possible that these traders were making some payments to the priests for space to trade in the temple. So, it shouldn't be out of place to assume that when Jesus drove these persons out, they went to complain to those they were paying for the use of temple space. How do we know all of this? Because of what happened the next day:

Matthew 21:23 (NET) "*Now after Jesus entered the temple courts, the chief priests and elders of the people came up to him as he was teaching and said,* **'By what authority are you doing these things, and who gave you this authority?'**"

If you are a corrupt chief priest or an elder and you are receiving regular payments from traders renting temple space, you will try to come up with a 'spiritual' way to discredit anyone trying to bring change. They couldn't have asked Him '*why did you drive out those people from the temple yesterday?*' That would have been too amateurish. Rather, they wanted to discredit him. After some back and forth between them, Jesus told them a parable which goes as follows:

Matthew 21:28-31 (NET) "*What do you think? A man had two sons. He went to the first and said, 'Son, go and work in the vineyard today.' The boy answered, 'I will not.' But later he had a change of heart and went. The father went to the other son and said the same thing. This boy answered, 'I will, sir,' but did not go. Which of the two did his father's will?' They said, 'The first.'*"

What did this parable actually mean? Who was Jesus referring to as the first son or as the second son? Let's find out from scripture:

Matthew 21:31-32 (NET) "...*Jesus said to them, "I tell you the truth, tax collectors and prostitutes will go ahead of you into the kingdom of God!* For John came to you in the way of righteousness, and you did not believe him. But the tax collectors and prostitutes did believe. Although you saw this, you did not later change your minds and believe him.*"

These were hard sayings. It's like being a manager in an office where everybody respects you because of your position. But unbeknownst to you, there's one colleague in that office who knows that you steal company money. Therefore, at whatever time he likes, he challenges you or confronts you because of the evil that he knows that you do. This is exactly how it was with the chief priests and elders. To the regular people, they were important personalities BUT in the eyes of Jesus, who is omniscient, they were essentially worthless people! This is why Jesus said that even tax collectors and prostitutes will go ahead of them into heaven!

In those days, tax collectors and prostitutes were considered as the lowest of the low amongst the people. So, for Jesus to make this statement, what the priests and elders were doing must have been really abysmal. But how come tax collectors and prostitutes could make it into heaven but priests and elders couldn't? Because, according to the scripture above, when they heard about the way of righteousness that John the Baptist was preaching as well as that which Jesus Himself spoke of, the tax collectors and the prostitutes believed. The priests and elders did not. The tax collectors and prostitutes repented of their sins and forsook them. [An example of this is Zacchaeus, a chief tax collector who repented of sins when Jesus visited his home]. By reason of this, the gates of the Kingdom of heaven opened itself to them — to people who they themselves thought were going to hell.

The lesson in today's devotional is that no matter what you may have done in the past, insofar as you have heard the word and you have been shown the way of righteousness and you believe, God will overlook your past sins, mistakes and errors. If you forsake your sins and from here onward decide to live a holy life, no matter what you have done in the past, heaven is guaranteed for you. And if you know that just as the elders and priests were hypocrites, you are one but you wish to come clean and change your ways so that you can also become a candidate of heaven, this is your day. Get yourself ready!

TODAY'S PRAYERS

1.   O God, if the same spirit of hypocrisy that

was in the priests and elders of Christ's day is in me, have mercy and cast it out of my life, in the name of Jesus.

2.   Father, if like the priests and elders I have heard certain aspects of Your word and yet I did not believe them, have mercy on me and forgive me, in the name of Jesus.

3.   O God, Your word says tax collectors and prostitutes will go into heaven ahead of priests and elders. That which they did in order to qualify for heaven, let me also begin to do, in the name of Jesus.

4.   Jehovah, in the same manner these tax collectors and prostitutes wholeheartedly believed in the way of righteousness when they heard about it, let any iota of doubt in my heart about the way of righteousness be removed from my heart. I declare that I totally believe in the way of righteousness that I have read about and heard of in Your word, in the name of Jesus.

5.   Messiah, in the same manner these prostitutes and tax collectors like Zacchaeus repented and forsook their evil ways, I repent and permanently forsake anything evil that I am doing. Do not let my negative past determine the rest of my life, in the name of

Jesus.

6. Finally Lord, I ask You for grace to be clean without and to be clean within. Save me from hypocrisy. Make me a real person. Make me someone that You can count on. Make me holy and make me rapturable, in the name of Jesus.

7. Thank You heavenly Father for answering my prayers, in Jesus' mighty name, amen.

If you have the need and the time, please feel free to add more prayers at this point.

Blessing: May you be real before God and may your reality be pleasing unto Him, in the name of Jesus.

DAY 81

MY BOOKS AND MY PARCHMENTS

"The cloke that I left at Troas with Carpus, when thou comest, bring with thee, and the books, but especially the parchments." — 2 Timothy 4:13 (KJV)

DAILY EXHORTATION

Paul wrote a letter to Timothy inviting him to come over to where he was. In that letter, he wrote about the fact that he was near the end of his assignment on earth. Yet, despite his nearness to death, Paul had some requests for Timothy. He told Timothy that when he was coming, he should bring along his books as well as his parchments. This little detail is quite profound. This man was about to die and here he was, still pining for books and parchments!

Herein lies one of the secrets of Paul's success as a great minister of God. Of the 27 books of the new testament, Paul the Apostle wrote 14 of them. These books are as follows: Romans, 1

Corinthians, 2 Corinthians, Galatians, Ephesians, Philippians, Colossians, 1 Thessalonians, 2 Thessalonians, 1 Timothy, 2 Timothy, Titus, Philemon and Hebrews. These books provide billions of Christians around the world with direction on how to live their lives for Christ. So when Paul said "*I have fought a good fight, I have finished my course, I have kept the faith*" (2 Timothy 4:7, KJV), he was confident enough to say that because he knew the quantity and quality of work he had done. He had done a great work and was leaving behind generational treasures by way of his writings.

Paul needed the books he was asking for, for many reasons. For example, it was important for him to study Jewish history in relation to the words the Holy Spirit was pouring into his heart. When examined in the light of Jewish history, his writings make a lot of sense. This would not have been possible if he wasn't a reader.

In addition, as we've seen, Paul was also a writer. He needed the parchments to write down his inspired thoughts. All the books written above by Paul were probably once written on parchments such as the ones he asked Timothy to come with. By reason of his openness to the voice of the Holy Spirit as well as his determination to get the truth out to others on parchments, the whole of Christendom is the better for it. Paul's life made impact and we know this because we have the evidence in his writings and in the lives that God has transformed through them. He died many hundreds of years ago but the words God used him to write still inspire people today and guide them on their Christian journey of destiny.

So, what will it be for you? Have you likewise opened yourself up to the voice of the Holy Spirit? Do you sense that God wants to use you to make impact in this generation? If the answer is yes, then, you too will need books and parchments [or notes or some kind of computing device for taking down notes]. You will need to get as much knowledge as possible from God's word and write them down. These words may be to benefit people in your own family. Or it could be to benefit people in your local church group. Or it may be to benefit people from around the world. If the Spirit of God is speaking to you and telling you to make yourself available in this regard and if you are willing to pick up your own books, parchments and pen, today is your day. Get yourself ready!

One more thing: This doesn't apply to your faith alone. In order to make impact in your professional field and to be recognized as an authority, you also have to be a reader of books and a user of parchments. If you need divine help in this area as well, get yourself ready!

TODAY'S PRAYERS

1. Elohim, I want to make inter-generational impact in Christendom and I also want to make inter-generational impact in my professional field. Come to my aid, in the name of Jesus.

2. Just as it was with Paul who pined for his books and his parchments, from today, O God, let me also pine for books and parchments, in the name of Jesus.

3. My God, anytime I have a book in front of me, open my understanding so that I can comprehend what is before me, in the name of Jesus.

4. Lord, in addition to my understanding, cause Your precious Holy Spirit to always fill my mind with fresh insight so that I can receive uncommon information that can change lives and / or move me ahead in my field, in the name of Jesus.

5. As I record my insights on my parchments, Father, coat my writings with sweetness so that anyone who reads them will be transformed by them, in the name of Jesus.

6. Great and Mighty God, let the knowledge I shall put down in my parchments outlive me. Let them become inter-generational so that from generation to generation, they will help to turn people to You, in the name of Jesus.

7. Thank You Everlasting Father for answering my prayers, in Jesus' mighty name, amen.

If you have the need and the time, please feel free to add more prayers at this point.

Blessing: May your love for books and parchments be magnified so that you can become an instrument of the Lord in your generation, in the name of Jesus.

DAY 82

THREE KINDS
OF LOVE

**"And Isaac loved Esau, because he did eat
of his venison: but Rebekah loved Jacob."
— Genesis 25:28 (KJV)**

DAILY EXHORTATION

In addition to our opening scripture, let's add one
more Bible verse:

Genesis 37:3 (KJV) "*Now Israel loved Joseph more
than all his children, because he was the son of his old age:
and he made him a coat of many colours.*"

Isaac loved Esau because Esau was a hunter
and Isaac loved eating meat. Israel [or Jacob]
loved Joseph more than all his children because
he was born to him in his old age. And Rebekah
loved Jacob for no stated reason.

When you put all these together, they reveal
that a person can be loved because of a
functionality or service that they provide, a

person can also be loved because of circumstances surrounding their arrival into another person's life and a person can be loved for no specific reason.

Being loved is not a trivial matter because it can spell the difference between a life of misery and a life of great breakthroughs. For instance, because of Isaac's love for Esau, he fully intended to give him his blessing when it was time for him to die. And because of Rebekah's love for Jacob, she was willing to do everything she could to get Isaac to give that blessing to Jacob rather than Esau. This blessing was so packed that anyone who received it would be set for life. To see how serious this issue of love is, let's take a look at the blessing of Isaac:

Genesis 27:27-29 (KJV) "*And he came near, and kissed him: and he smelled the smell of his raiment, and blessed him, and said, See, the smell of my son is as the smell of a field which the Lord hath blessed: Therefore God give thee of the dew of heaven, and the fatness of the earth, and plenty of corn and wine: Let people serve thee, and nations bow down to thee: be lord over thy brethren, and let thy mother's sons bow down to thee: cursed be every one that curseth thee, and blessed be he that blesseth thee.*"

These were not mere words spoken by Isaac. These were words backed by spiritual power and they had to manifest. Put yourself in the position of the son who would receive this blessing. How would you feel if someone told you that people will serve you and that nations will bow to you and you knew that whatever that person said had to come to pass? How would you feel about that? And to think that Isaac wanted to give this blessing to Esau simply because Isaac loved eating meat and Esau knew how to hunt and prepare meat! There is power in love!

Love can do anything for you. Whatever the brand of love [agape, philia or any other kind of clean, holy love], it can bring blessings into your life that will go beyond your biggest expectation.

So, our task this morning is simple: You will have to pray that God should cause people to love you with the three kinds of love we have seen in today's devotional. You will ask God to cause people to love you because of a honorable functionality or service that you offer, because of the circumstances in which you came into their lives and also for no stated reason. Then, you will also ask God to command that any blessing attached to these three kinds of love should be released into your life. If you want these three kinds of love to operate in your life, today is your day. Get yourself ready!

TODAY'S PRAYERS

1. Great Redeemer, let people love me for no stated reason. Let Your grace make this happen in my life, in the name of Jesus.

2. Jehovah, let people love me because of a trait in my life or a honorable service that I provide, in the name of Jesus.

3. Messiah, create pleasant circumstances in the lives of people. Then, cause me to enter into their lives at this time. Let them associate me with these pleasant seasons and love me by reason of this, in the name of Jesus.

4. O God, let the blessings associated with being loved for no stated reason enter into my life now, in the name of Jesus.

5. O God, load me with traits or abilities that people love. Let the blessings associated with being loved for a positive trait or a service that I provide enter into my life now, in the name of Jesus.

6. O God, let the blessings associated with people linking me with the pleasant times and seasons of their lives enter into my life now, in the name of Jesus.

7. Thank You O God for answering my prayers, in Jesus' mighty name, amen.

If you have the need and the time, please feel free to add more prayers at this point.

Blessing: May you have everything that you have declared this morning, in the name of Jesus.

DAY 83

PEOPLE SKILLS

"Before God and Christ Jesus and the elect angels, I solemnly charge you to carry out these commands without prejudice or favoritism of any kind."
— 1 Timothy 5:21 (NET)

DAILY EXHORTATION

Except one lives in a cave, human interaction is inevitable. If you want to be all you can be, you need to interact with people. That said, not knowing the proper way to interact with people can cause all kinds of problems.

There is no day that goes by these days that there isn't one report or another of someone being accused of inappropriate behavior toward coworkers, neighbors, etc. On the other hand, there isn't a day that goes by without reports of people being awarded for good conduct, excellent behavior, etc. The people accused of inappropriate behavior usually suffer damage to their reputation, shame, loss of position or opportunity, etc. But people who are commended for good behavior gain a good reputation, favor with people and all kinds of relevant open doors.

Now, in our opening scripture, Paul writes that the commands he had given be carried out without prejudices or favoritism of any kind. But what are these commands? These commands can be found in the whole of 1 Timothy 5 BUT this morning, we will only focus on those found in verses 1 and 2 of that chapter. Here's what they say:

1 Timothy 5:1-2 (NET) "*Do not address an older man harshly but appeal to him as a father. Speak to younger men as brothers, older women as mothers, and younger women as sisters—with complete purity.*"

So, there you have it. In these two short verses, Paul provides us with a template for clean and appropriate human interactions. He said that in our dealings with any older man, we should treat him as our father. In our dealings with a younger man, we should treat him as our brother. In our dealings with an older woman, we should treat her as our mother and finally, in our dealings with a younger woman, we should treat her as our sister.

Of course [and especially these days] not everyone grew up in a home having a father, mother, brother or sister. And even if a person had all these members in their family, their experiences with them may or may not have been ideal. Yet, all of us know that in many homes around the world, a person normally gives total respect to one's father and mother and one has pure love for one's siblings. When Paul talks about these interactions, he is focusing on the normal and this is what you should focus on as well.

You see, if you can take every older man or woman as a parent, you will notice a transformation of the atmosphere around your own life. Ditto if you can take younger men and women as siblings, all kinds of pressure that you may currently be enduring will ease away. This new mindset will help you to be a better person to get along with. It will remove all the mental inhibitions that may be affecting your relationships or work. It will help you become more effective and it will make your work of preaching Christ to others much easier. People will always want to be around you and through this, God will open all sorts of doors for you.

Perhaps, by reason of implementing this change in mindset commanded by Paul, one day soon, you will also appear on the evening news, receiving a reward for good conduct!

If you desire all of these pleasant benefits in

your life, get yourself ready!

TODAY'S PRAYERS

1. From today, according to the command of Paul, **I will treat every older man as my father**, in the name of Jesus.

2. From today, according to the command of Paul, **I will treat every older woman as my mother**, in the name of Jesus.

3. From today, according to the command of Paul, **I will treat every younger man as my brother**, in the name of Jesus.

4. From today, according to the command of Paul, **I will treat every younger woman as my sister**, in the name of Jesus.

5. Lord, by reason of this change of mindset in my life, let there be a change of atmosphere around me for good. Use my positive behavior to give me favor before people and let great doors open themselves wide for me, in the name of Jesus.

6. My God, I will not be ignorant. If anyone plans to take advantage of my respect, positivity and purity toward them by using

my goodness against me for evil, I hand them over to You for divine judgment. Do to them what only You can do, in the name of Jesus.

7. Thank You Mighty God for answering my prayers, in Jesus' mighty name, amen.

If you have the need and the time, please feel free to add more prayers at this point.

Blessing: May God provide you with the mental strength to carry out these commands of Paul so that you can reap all the associated benefits, in the name of Jesus.

DAY 84

WILLING AND DOING

**"For it is God which worketh in you both
to will and to do of his good pleasure."
— Philippians 2:13 (KJV)**

DAILY EXHORTATION

In the world of the spirit, God is the author and
human beings are actors of the script written by
Him, howbeit actors with freedom in acting out
the written script.

Today's opening scripture is directed at a
number of categories of believers. First, if you are
a child of God but you do not know in what area
to serve Him, this verse means that you can ask
God and He will reveal it you. Second, if you
already know in what area to serve God but you
lack the spiritual and physical fortitude to actually
do it, you too can ask God for fortitude and He
will supply it. Third, if you have the will and you
are actually carrying out the purpose of God for
your life BUT you noticed that you have become
pompous or arrogant by reason of this, this

scripture is also for you. It is reminding you that the desire in your heart as well as your ability to execute it are both from God. Therefore, you will do well to humble yourself so that you can leave room for God to elevate you.

So, our prayers for today will address all of these categories. If you want to perfectly will and do God's pleasure so as to fulfill destiny, get yourself ready!

TODAY'S PRAYERS

1. Rock of Ages, it is clear to me now that You are the author of the universe and I am an actor in the script You have written. Help me to play my part successfully, in the name of Jesus.

2. O Lord, I do not know in what area to serve You. I am not sure what Your specific will for my life is. Be merciful unto me and reveal to me what Your specific will for my life is, in the name of Jesus.

3. Adonai, when I have received revelation on Your will for my life, give me the spiritual and physical fortitude to carry it out successfully, in the name of Jesus.

4. Jehovah, when You have blessed me with

Your will and the ability to do it, help me so that arrogance will not bring me down, in the name of Jesus.

5. Abba Father, teach me to humble myself so that I can leave room for You to elevate me, in the name of Jesus.

6. Alpha and Omega, as I do Your will everyday of my life, use me to touch lives for good so that I can bring glory to Your holy name, in the name of Jesus.

7. Thank You Almighty God for answering my prayers, in Jesus' mighty name, amen.

If you have the need and the time, please feel free to add more prayers at this point.

Blessing: May God inspire you to will and to do His good pleasure, in the name of Jesus.

DAY 85

HOW NOT TO GATHER WEALTH

"The person who gathers wealth by unjust means is like the partridge that broods over eggs but does not hatch them. Before his life is half over he will lose his ill-gotten gains. At the end of his life it will be clear he was a fool."
—Jeremiah 17:11 (NET)

DAILY EXHORTATION

There are two sides to this morning's opening scripture. One of them is clear and apparent while the other is implied but very real.

First, the clear and apparent. This scripture describes the financial path of a foolish person who thinks he or she is wise. The fool here refers to anyone who makes and saves and invests money gotten from illegal activities. As he is doing these things, he would think to himself that he is wise. As he / she gambles or as he / she forges someone else's signature or as he / she breaks into someone's house or office to steal money or precious possessions or as he / she makes himself into a gigolo or herself into a prostitute or as he / she kidnaps and collects a ransom or as he or she tricks a vulnerable man or woman into parting with his or her wealth or as he or she blackmails an important person or as he or she lies in order to get a job or sleeps with someone in order to get a promotion or as he or she cheats others out of an inheritance, he or she will think of himself or herself as being wise.

As the illegally gotten wealth accumulates, this person will start making plans... "I will buy or build this type of house", "I will travel to such and such a place", "I will buy this or that kind of car", "I will marry such and such a person", "I will send my kids to such and such a school", "I will invest in the stock market", "I will invest in precious metals", etc. As he is doing this, his colleagues and friends, who are making real, steady, gradual progress might even envy his 'meteoric rise' BUT the Bible says that it is all a mirage.

The Almighty says that such a person is like that unfortunate partridge that broods over her eggs but doesn't get the chance to hatch them. He says that by the middle of such a person's life, anything he or she has acquired by means of illegality will somehow disappear. Only God can make a statement like this because only He knows the full length of a person's days. If this person persists on the path of evil, when they reach the end of their lives, they will look back in regret and see that rather than being wise, they were fools all along. You know this because you are reading about it in scripture. However, when a foolish person loses all that he has acquired illegally, he will see it as a temporary setback and persist. But the same cycle will keep repeating itself until the end. At old age, when he or she has lost determination and the strength for physical enterprise and he or she can no longer work and yet has nothing, it will become clear that the journey has been a foolish one.

Like we saw earlier, there is a flip side to today's scripture which is implied and very real. The scripture is saying that if you gather wealth through just and legal means, you will be like a partridge that broods over its eggs and hatches them successfully.

By the time you get to the middle of your life on earth, you would have become irreversibly financially established. Then, when you get to the end of your life, it will be clear to you that by reason of the narrow, honest path you have taken in life and the blessings God has given to you, you made the right and wise decision.

Do you want to gather wealth the right way?

Do you want to take the right path to greatness? If yes, get yourself ready!

TODAY'S PRAYERS

1. Any desire in me to acquire or gather wealth through any kind of unjust means, I command you to die completely today, in the name of Jesus.

2. I have decided to follow the honest, narrow and righteous path in life. By the grace of God, I will never be removed from this path, in the name of Jesus.

3. My Father and my God, look upon me with Your grace and mercy and bless the work of my hand, in the name of Jesus.

4. O Lord my God, through the work of my hands, let me experience promotion upon promotion, material increase and financial explosion, in the name of Jesus.

5. O Righteous Father, let me be like a partridge that broods over its own eggs. Let my eggs of wealth hatch right before my eyes, in the name of Jesus.

6. Everlasting God, by the time I reach the

middle of my life on earth, let me have become financially established in every way. And in my old age, when my time on the earth is about to end, let me look back and thank You for keeping me on the straight and narrow path, for my wisdom in accepting Your direction and for all the tangible and intangible blessings You would have showered me with, in the name of Jesus.

7. Thank You Lord for answering my prayers, in Jesus' mighty name, amen.

If you have the need and the time, please feel free to add more prayers at this point.

Blessing: May you never make unjust gain but only just gain to the glory of God, in the name of Jesus.

DAY 86

RESOURCES FOR DESTINY SUCCESS

"I said to the king, 'If the king is so inclined, let him give me letters for the governors of Trans-Euphrates that will enable me to travel safely until I reach Judah, and a letter for Asaph the keeper of the king's nature preserve, so that he will give me timber for beams for the gates of the fortress adjacent to the temple and for the city wall and for the house to which I go.' So the king granted me these requests, for the good hand of my God was on me. Then I went to the governors of Trans-Euphrates, and I presented to them the letters from the king. The king had sent with me officers of the army and horsemen." — Nehemiah 2:7-9 (NET)

DAILY EXHORTATION

Nehemiah was a Jew who, in his day, lived in Persia. He served King Artaxerxes of Persia as cup-bearer [a very important role at the time]. One day, he received reports that Jerusalem was in ruins and its gates had been destroyed by fire. This news made him sad and he decided he had to do something about it. So, with a lot of fear, he asked the king for permission to go to his homeland to fix the situation. The king agreed to let him go and it is at this point that we arrive at our opening scripture.

This passage is very important in that it highlights the essentials which are needed in the fulfillment of one's purpose in life.

First, the mission of Nehemiah was properly defined. He was going to Jerusalem for repair work — specifically to rebuild its walls.

Second, Nehemiah asked for letters that will enable him travel safely. In addition, the king provided him with army officers as well as horsemen.

Third, he was given access to the king's nature preserve so that he could get as much materials as he needed for his project.

Finally, Nehemiah mentioned that because the hand of God was on him, the king granted all his requests.

If you take all these together, the most important things to Nehemiah for his project were: **the good hand of God, a defined purpose, raw materials and security**. In the same manner, these are the four most important things that you need if you want to fulfill the reason you were sent by God into the world.

You will need the good hand of God to make people favor you and grant your requests. You will need a well-defined purpose so that you can harness your whole being and understand where you are going and what you will need in order to get there. You will need materials of every kind — spiritual power, self-control over your thoughts, your emotions, your mouth, your behavior, money, human connections, etc. And you will need divine security. God will have to send you his own army officers and horsemen so that the enemy will not have the opportunity to terminate you before your time.

If you have all these in place, destiny fulfillment will be yours. Since these were the resources that Nehemiah had and he fulfilled his purpose of rebuilding the wall, when you have these resources, you too will fulfill your own divine agenda. If you want all these to manifest and begin to operate in your life, get yourself ready!

TODAY'S PRAYERS

1. My Father, You are the one that did it for

Nehemiah, come and do it for me as well, in the name of Jesus.

2. Abba Father, as it was on Nehemiah, let Your good hand be on me as well so that I can find favor before You and before the people who are relevant to my destiny and so that they can help me and grant my requests, in the name of Jesus.

3. Yahweh, just as Nehemiah was inspired with a purpose in his mind, transmit into my mind that which You want to be my major assignment on the earth. Let my purpose in life become crystal clear to me so that I can harness the whole of my being to pursue after it, in the name of Jesus.

4. Elohim, just as Nehemiah received, let me also have access to the raw materials of destiny. Give me the spiritual, physical, psychological, emotional, human, financial and every other kind of resource that I need to go about and complete my own work of destiny, in the name of Jesus.

5. O Lord of hosts, as it was for Nehemiah, let me benefit from divine security on my journey of destiny. Release unto me the army officers and horsemen of heaven so that I can travel safely through life and concentrate on

my work of destiny, in the name of Jesus.

6. Now Lord, I ask for Your mercy: In the same manner Nehemiah had access to all these resources I have prayed for and he fulfilled his purpose with them, let me also use the resources I have prayed for to fulfill my own purpose to the letter, in the name of Jesus.

7. Thank You Father God for answering my prayers, in Jesus' mighty name, amen.

If you have the need and the time, please feel free to add more prayers at this point.

Blessing: May God give you all that you need to complete your divine assignment, in the name of Jesus.

DAY 87

HOW TO REALLY LOVE SOMEONE

"If I speak in the tongues of men and of angels, but I do not have love, I am a noisy gong or a clanging cymbal. And if I have prophecy, and know all mysteries and all knowledge, and if I have all faith so that I can remove mountains, but do not have love, I am nothing. If I give away everything I own, and if I give over my body in order to boast, but do not have love, I receive no benefit."
— 1 Corinthians 13:1-3 (NET)

DAILY EXHORTATION

According to our opening scripture, if you do not love, you are a noisy gong or a clanging cymbal, you are nothing and you cannot receive divine rewards for your good deeds.

Harsh words from the Bible... but they show how important love is. So what do I do to overturn these consequences of not having love in my life? In other words, what does it really mean to love someone? The answer is provided by the following passage:

1 Corinthians 13:4-6 (NET) "*Love is patient, love is kind, it is not envious. Love does not brag, it is not puffed up. It is not rude, it is not self-serving, it is not easily angered or resentful. It is not glad about injustice, but rejoices in the truth.*"

Whenever someone is being slow and you genuinely tolerate them and wait for them, you are loving that person. Whenever someone is in need and you freely give your time or your money to meet that person's need, you are loving that person. Whenever someone close to you achieves something, buys something or goes somewhere great and you are genuinely happy for that person, you are showing love.

Whenever you achieve something, buy something or go somewhere great but you refuse to let it get into your head or even boast about it to others, you are showing love. If despite the great blessings God has given to you thus far, someone annoys you or insults you but you refuse to talk back and instead speak to them with words of humility, you are showing love. If an opportunity opens up and you think about how you and someone else [and not just yourself] can secure the opportunity, you are showing love. If people do their best to upset you and yet you refuse to be angry or bitter, you are showing love.

Finally, if someone else is being maltreated and you can't take it or if you are asked to maltreat someone or lie against someone and you refuse to do it, you are showing love.

All of the foregoing is what it really means to love someone. If you can love someone in the manner that you have just read about, the Bible says that you are better than a person who only speaks in the tongues of men and of angels. It says you are better than someone who only prophesies or knows mysteries and spiritual knowledge. If you can really show love, you are better than someone who only has faith that can move mountains. With this kind of love, you are better than a person who dies for another but lacks love.

Do you want to meet heaven's standard for love this morning? If yes, get yourself ready!

TODAY'S PRAYERS

1. O Father, Lord of heaven and earth, I do not want to be a noisy gong, a clanging cymbal and a spiritual nothing. Neither do I want my good deeds to go unrewarded. Therefore, I ask You this morning to help me become a loving person in spirit, in truth and indeed, in

the name of Jesus.

2.   Everlasting King, I know that without Your Holy Spirit, it is impossible for me to meet heaven's standard for love. Therefore, I ask: Let Your Holy Spirit empower me to become a loving person, in the name of Jesus.

3.   Spirit of the living God, give me the ability to tolerate people that may be slow and to wait for them. When people are in need, make me automatically willing to give of my time and of my resources so that I can help them, in the name of Jesus.

4.   Spirit of the living God, when people close to me achieve anything or acquire something valuable or go to some wonderful place, make me into a person that is genuinely happy for them. And when the tables are turned, when it is I who achieves something or whenever I buy something valuable or go to some exotic place, enable me to refuse to let it get into my head and prevent me from boasting about it, in the name of Jesus.

5.   Spirit of the living God, let it be that regardless of the height that I get to in life through Your grace, if someone annoys me or insults me, I will refuse to talk back at them except with words of humility. Also,

when an opportunity that can benefit someone I know shows up, let me naturally think of how it can benefit them and let me make them know about it, in the name of Jesus.

6. Spirit of the living God, remove anger, resentment and bitterness from my life completely. Cause me to hate injustice and prevent me from becoming an agent of wickedness to anyone, in the name of Jesus.

7. Thank You Great and Mighty God for answering my prayers and for beginning a great and mighty work in my life, in the name of Jesus.

If you have the need and the time, please feel free to add more prayers at this point.

Blessing: May God make you into a person of love and turn your life around for good, in the name of Jesus.

DAY 88

BACKGROUND DELIVERANCE

"By faith Moses, when he was come to years, refused to be called the son of Pharaoh's daughter; Choosing rather to suffer affliction with the people of God, than to enjoy the pleasures of sin for a season; Esteeming the reproach of Christ greater riches than the treasures in Egypt: for he had respect unto the recompence of the reward. By faith he forsook Egypt, not fearing the wrath of the king: for he endured, as seeing him who is invisible."
— Hebrews 11:24-27 (KJV)

DAILY EXHORTATION

Many people are born into families that are far from the will of God for their lives. This was the situation Moses found himself in. As you know, he was born a Jew but during the time of his birth, there was an order by the slave masters of the Israelites [the Egyptians] that as soon as a

Jewish baby was born and was found to be male, he had to be killed in order to control the population of the Jews.

To save her newborn son, Moses' birth mother, Jochebed, orchestrated a move which resulted in him being adopted by Pharaoh's daughter. However, the home he was adopted into, that is, the Egyptian royal family, was an altar unto evil, idolatry and a throne room of wickedness! They believed in magicians, sorcerers and worshiped all kinds of gods and idols. At the time, they were also the largest operators of slavery in the world having millions of Israelites under their control. Plus, they weren't just slave owners for commerce, they yoked, tortured, tormented and killed the Jews everyday throughout the period of slavery. Imagine being an Israelite, seeing all of this evil and injustice and being called a Prince of Egypt. No! Something had to change!

Our opening scripture is careful to give us some very important details. It says that "*By faith Moses, **when he was come to years**, refused to be called the son of Pharaoh's daughter*". It is understandable to remain in an evil environment when one is a kid, without skills and without education or common-sense. However, if you live in an evil environment, after you have come of age, you must not continue to accept evil as good or as the truth. You must deny the evil and refuse to be associated with it any longer.

Further, even though he lived in a palace and enjoyed all of its pleasures, when he came of age, Moses preferred to suffer affliction with the people of God rather than continue enjoying the pleasures purchased by evil, idolatry and wickedness. With his eyes fixed on a reward he hoped to receive from God, he left Egypt behind and took a leap of faith as though he could physically see God.

Think what would have happened if Moses did not do all of the above. It would have been ridiculous. You a Jew supervising the torment of your own people? Absurd. Also, he would have become a hardened idol worshiper on the expressway to hell. Most importantly, Moses would have missed a golden opportunity to fight for the independence and oversee the administration of a new, special nation. God would have raised someone else and it is possible that Moses would have been destroyed by the plagues God raised against the Egyptians.

In the same manner, if you were born into a strange kind of home where there are all kinds of problems or vices — poverty, adultery, alcoholism, drug abuse, the practice of evil spirituality, atheism, sexual perversion, etc. — as a child, you may not have known what to do or how to escape. However, when you have come of age and you have been educated and developed, you need to forsake your negative background and move toward God. In essence, you need **background deliverance**.

You need the precious Blood of Jesus to flow into your life and deliver you from the harmful effects of the problems of your background, both those that you know about and those that you do not.

When you have done this, like Moses, you need to focus on the reward that only God can provide and that will far outweigh whatever you thought you were enjoying in an evil background.

Apart from fighting for the independence of Israel, Moses got the opportunity to be used mightily by God. Moses got to see an ordinary wooden staff become a symbol of divine power. He got to see a staff become a real snake which swallowed up the serpents of Egypt's magicians and sorcerers. He got to see instant healing of skin disease right before his eyes. He was used to bring ten powerful plagues upon Egypt which ultimately forced Pharaoh to end the over 400 year slavery of the Jews.

God used Moses to institute the Passover which shows God's power to protect His children and strike their enemies. God used Moses to separate a sea into two and caused dry land to appear in the middle so that over 2 million of His children could cross over safely and be saved from their pursuers. God transmitted the 10 commandments to the Israelites through Moses. The 10 commandments are the foundation of the laws of most countries of the world till today! God used Moses to make water sweet so that His people could drink good water. God used Moses to provide water when there was none in the desert. God used Moses to provide food [Manna] for His children as well as abundant meat [quail] in the desert. God used Moses to heal his children from bites of dangerous reptiles. That symbol of a serpent around a pole which Moses created for this purpose is still the symbol for most hospitals around the world today. God used Moses to lead his people to the edge of the promised land. God used Moses to write the first five books of the Bible so we can all understand how the world began and the story of the glorious blessing God bestowed on Abraham which is now ours through Jesus Christ! Wow!

If you are from a negative background and you have come of age, please do as Moses did. Take your time to plan your exit from your own Egypt and fix your eyes on the reward of the Lord.

Just as Moses got a great opportunity to be used in performing diverse wonders, who knows what God will do through you in your own time. Now, if your people also abandon their evil ways and genuinely decide to follow Christ, please open your arms of fellowship to them and embrace them.

So, do you need background deliverance? If yes, get yourself ready!

TODAY'S PRAYERS

1. Most High God, I thank You for preserving my life till this day, in the name of Jesus.

2. Father, I have come of age and henceforth, I refuse to be associated with any evil that is in my background, in the name of Jesus.

3. My God, as it was with Moses, I am fully ready to face anything for Your sake instead of continuing to enjoy the pleasures of sin. Help me, in the name of Jesus.

4. This morning, O Lord, I decree and declare that I forsake my own Egypt in order to focus on You and Your plan for my life, in the name of Jesus.

5. Any hook of the negativity or evil of my background that is already in me, I pull out now and I set you ablaze until you burn to

ashes, in the name of Jesus.

6. In the same manner, Moses gave himself entirely to the will of God, from today, I give myself completely to the will of the Father. Father, you used Moses to do exploits in his own time, use me to do exploits in my own time as well, in the name of Jesus.

7. Thank You Father God for answering my prayers, in Jesus' mighty name, amen.

If you have the need and the time, please feel free to add more prayers at this point.

Blessing: May God deliver you from the negative hold of your background, if any, so that you can be free to do His will, in the name of Jesus.

DAY 89

MEET THE
TRAMPLERS

**"Do not give what is holy to dogs or throw
your pearls before pigs; otherwise they
will trample them under their feet and
turn around and tear you to pieces."
— Matthew 7:6 (NET)**

DAILY EXHORTATION

In Matthew 13:45-46 (NET), the Bible says
*"Again, the kingdom of heaven is like a merchant searching
for fine pearls. When he found a pearl of great value, he
went out and sold everything he had and bought it."* Now,
if the merchant in the scripture we have just read
takes this precious pearl [that he sold everything
he had to get] and gives it to dogs and pigs, what
do you think will happen?

Our opening scripture makes it clear that
regardless of the price the merchant paid to get
his pearl, once he puts it before dogs and pigs,
they would trample it under their feet. Not only
that, these tramplers—the dogs and the pigs—

would also turn around and tear the merchant to pieces! Cruel! You might think "who'd be stupid enough to that anyway?" But it shouldn't surprise you that people do this every single day across the world.

This illustration given by Jesus has many applications. As a believer, you have to understand that your salvation is your key to victory and breakthroughs on the earth as well as your key into heaven. It is your pearl of great value.

If you cast this pearl before sheep or lamb, that is, people who may be sinners but who are willing to listen and repent, you are doing the right thing. Hopefully, when they listen to your message of salvation, repentance, victory and eternity, they will have a change of heart and like you, give their lives to Jesus.

Then, you have the tramplers. These are the dogs and pigs Jesus was referring to. No matter how much you try, they can never understand what you are telling them. Therefore, if you cast your pearl before them, not only will they trample it under their feet, they could also decide to harm you in one way or another.

Another application of this illustration of Jesus is in the area of human relationships. As a single person and a believer, when it comes to romantic relationships, only cast your pearl before people who are the same as you, that is, believers who truly believe in the things that you believe. Once you notice that a person you are interested in is a spiritual dog or pig, run away! Otherwise, they will trample upon your pearl [in this case, your salvation and your reputation] and then turn around to tear you to pieces. If against scriptural reasoning, you marry a spiritual dog or pig, that marriage will end up in divorce. But before getting to that point, the trampler may have converted you into an emotional wreck or something else.

If before the marriage, you were Mr. Gentle, by the time the trampler is done with you, you would've become Mr. Domestic Violence with a criminal record. As we've seen many times on the news, such a criminal record could cause you to lose friends, your reputation or even your source of income. If you were Ms. Sunshine before you married a trampler, weeks and months of neglect and verbal or physical abuse suffered in the home of a trampler would make you into Ms. Gloom or Ms. Regret. And even though Jesus forbids divorce, it is either that or death. This is why if you are reading this and you are not yet married, make sure that the person before whom you want to cast your pearl is not a trampler — a spiritual dog or a pig. This is the only way you can have a life of bliss and fulfillment in your marriage.

Finally, if you are a successful public personality such as a business person or politician, your reputation is your pearl. No matter the temptation, do not cast it before the tramplers. One night with a prostitute or with a drug dealer can ruin a professional, business or political career that you have been building for ages. A prostitute who sells herself or himself for money doesn't care about anything. He or she has no reputation in the first place. He or she will be willing to blackmail you or to sell the story of your experience with them to the highest bidder. They do not mind been interviewed in order to talk about lewd and offensive things in front of the whole world. Apart from the payment they'll receive, they'll also see it as an opportunity to advertise their services to the world. These are tramplers. If your customers hear of your experiences with such people, they may stop buying from you. If your political followers hear the grim details of your escapades with dogs and pigs, they may leave you and move over to someone else and it will be the end.

Mr. or Mrs. Business Person, please learn to love and to be contented with your spouse. Mr. and Mrs. Politician, let your life be for your spouse only. If you do not cast your pearls before dogs and pigs, they will NEVER be able to trample upon them neither will they be able to tear you into pieces.

If you want your pearls of great value safe from the reach of the tramplers, safe from the reach of the spiritual dogs and pigs of this world, get yourself ready!

TODAY'S PRAYERS

1. Holy One of Israel, I thank You for the pearl of great value that You have placed in my hands. Help me to keep it safe, in the name of Jesus.

2. I Am that I Am, give me the spirit of discernment so that whenever I see a person with whom I want to share the message of salvation, I will be able to tell whether or not he or she is a dog or a pig or a lamb or a sheep, in the name of Jesus.

3. If there be any foul spirit in my life magnetizing me to tramplers, magnetizing me to dogs and pigs, I bind you this morning with fetters of fire that can never break. Now, I command you: Get out of my life and depart forever, in the name of Jesus.

4. Have mercy on me O Lord and do not let me ever cast my pearls before dogs and pigs. Have mercy on me Lord so that dogs and

pigs will not tear me to pieces, in the name of Jesus.

5. Lord, make me contented with what and whom I already have in my life so that there can NEVER be a chance of me exposing myself to the dogs and pigs of this world, in the name of Jesus.

6. Jehovah, be merciful unto me. I commit everything I have worked for all of my life into Your holy hands. I commit who I have become and will become into Your holy hands. Keep me, protect me, guide me, be with me and cause me to always do Your will throughout the days of my life, in the name of Jesus.

7. Thank You Father for answering my prayers, in Jesus' mighty name, amen.

If you have the need and the time, please feel free to add more prayers at this point.

Blessing: May you never cast your pearls before dogs and pigs and by so doing may your pearls never be trampled upon and may you never be torn to pieces, in the name of Jesus.

DAY 90

YOUR GOALS AND YOUR BEHAVIOR

**"So Jesus said to them, 'The kings of the
Gentiles lord it over them, and those in
authority over them are called
'benefactors.' Not so with you; instead the
one who is greatest among you must
become like the youngest, and the leader
like the one who serves."
— Luke 22:25-26 (NET)**

DAILY EXHORTATION

Jesus always said that anyone who wants to be the
greatest among a group of people must be the
servant of the group. If you are not a Christian,
this might sound silly but this is actually how real
life works. And it is the ONLY WAY for a real
Christian to get to the top. If you consider sports,
for instance, the person who works the hardest
and scores the highest number of goals or points
for the team, isn't he or she usually considered as
the greatest player on the team? Isn't he or she

the one that gets the biggest salary? All other things being equal, the teacher who spends the most time with his or her students, isn't he or she the one most loved by them? And isn't he or she the one who wins all the awards? The church counselor who sees his counseling sessions as more than a hobby but engages himself or herself in in-depth study of the Bible [and other valuable books that can help individuals and families] in order to give them quality advice and prayer, won't he or she be the person everyone would want to see for their issues?

You can go on and on but you can see where this is going. Your goals of greatness are tied to your behavior.

If you want to be the greatest of all wherever you are, you must be the greatest servant of all. This applies to your role in your family (nuclear or extended), work, business, community, politics, government, etc.

Now, before we wrap up, let's take a quick look at one person from the Bible for whom becoming the greatest servant was a wise decision:

Esther 10:3 (NLT) "*Mordecai the Jew became the prime minister, with authority next to that of King Xerxes himself. He was very great among the Jews, who held him in high esteem, because he continued to work for the good of* *his people and to speak up for the welfare of all their descendants."*

Without Mordecai, Esther would never have been successful. Once when Haman was trying to destroy the Jews and Esther wasn't really applying herself to the task of rescuing her people, it was Mordecai's warning to her that woke her up and got her inspired to take steps that saved the Jews. All through Esther's life, it was Mordecai's hand that guided her aright.

After Haman received the king's judgment for his wicked activities against the people of his queen, the book of Esther became the 'Mordecai show'. Mordecai worked tirelessly for the welfare of his people. The scripture above says that he worked for the good of his people and he spoke up for the welfare of all their descendants. It was for this reason that God promoted him in a foreign land as prime minister to the king of Persia. Also, God used his heartfelt service to see to it that he became very great among the Jews. He also found favor with them and they held him in the highest regard. As long as he continued to serve his people, all was well with him.

This is how it should be for you as well. If you want to be the greatest sportsperson, lawyer, doctor, teacher, engineer, preacher, evangelist, missionary, professor, writer, etc., you must be the one who is most willing to serve and who actually serves the people.

Do you want to be the greatest in what you do? Are you willing to behave in ways that will cause your dream to manifest? If yes, get yourself ready!

TODAY'S PRAYERS

1. O God, I want to be the greatest in everything that I do. Come to my aid and make this possible, in the name of Jesus.

2. Most High God, this morning, fill me with the anointing of service, in the name of Jesus.

3. O Lord, I pray, by reason of this anointing in my life, let me seek for opportunities to serve and let me make myself available to serve others, in the name of Jesus.

4. My God, whenever and wherever I am serving, let the spirit of excellence fall on me. Let me give the highest quality of service possible. Let my work bring good to people as well as to their descendants, in the name of Jesus.

5. My Lord and my God, as it was for Mordecai, use my excellent service to enable

me enjoy favor with people. By reason of my excellent service, let me enter into an endless season of massive promotions and greatness, in the name of Jesus.

6. Again Lord, as it was for Mordecai, no matter the height that I get to in life, let the spirit of humble, true and pure service never ever depart from me, in the name of Jesus.

7. Thank You Almighty God for answering my prayers, in Jesus' mighty name, amen.

If you have the need and the time, please feel free to add more prayers at this point.

Blessing: May you know greatness through the spirit of service and may you never ever go down, in the name of Jesus.